U.S. RELIGIOUS
INTEREST GROUPS

**Greenwood Reference Volumes on
American Public Policy Formation**

These reference books deal with the development of U.S. policy in various "single-issue" areas. Most policy areas are to be represented by three types of sourcebooks: (1) Institutional Profiles of Leading Organizations, (2) Collection of Documents and Policy Proposals, and (3) Bibliography.

Public Interest Law Groups: Institutional Profiles
Karen O'Connor and Lee Epstein

U.S. National Security Policy and Strategy: Documents and Policy Proposals
Sam C. Sarkesian with Robert A. Vitas

U.S. National Security Policy Groups: Institutional Profiles
Cynthia Watson

U.S. Agricultural Groups: Institutional Profiles
William P. Browne and Allan J. Cigler, editors

Military and Strategic Policy: An Annotated Bibliography
Benjamin R. Beede, compiler

U.S. Energy and Environmental Interest Groups: Institutional Profiles
Lettie McSpadden Wenner

Contemporary U.S. Foreign Policy: Documents and Commentary
Elmer Plischke

U.S. Aging Policy Interest Groups: Institutional Profiles
David D. Van Tassel and Jimmy Meyer, editors

U.S. Criminal Justice Interest Groups: Institutional Profiles
Michael A. Hallett and Dennis J. Palumbo

U.S. Educational Policy Interest Groups: Institutional Profiles
Gregory S. Butler and James D. Slack

U.S. RELIGIOUS INTEREST GROUPS

///

Institutional
Profiles

Paul J. Weber
and
W. Landis Jones

GREENWOOD PRESS
WESTPORT, CONNECTICUT • LONDON

Library of Congress Cataloging-in-Publication Data

Weber, Paul J.
    U.S. religious interest groups : institutional profiles / Paul J.
Weber and W. Landis Jones.
        p.   cm.
    Includes bibliographical references and index.
    ISBN 0–313–26695–6 (alk. paper)
    1. Church and state—United States.   2. United States—
Religion—1960– .   3. Pressure groups—United States—Directories.
I. Jones, William Landis.   II. Title.   III. Title: US
religious interest groups.   IV. Title: United States religious
interest groups.
    BL2525.W413   1994
    200'.973—dc20   93–37502

British Library Cataloguing in Publication Data is available.

Library of Congress Catalog Card Number: 93–37502
ISBN: 0–313–26695–6

First published in 1994

Greenwood Press, 88 Post Road West, Westport, CT 06881
An imprint of Greenwood Publishing Group, Inc.

Printed in the United States of America

The paper used in this book complies with the
Permanent Paper Standard issued by the National
Information Standards Organization (Z39.48–1984).

10 9 8 7 6 5 4 3 2 1

CONTENTS

/

PREFACE

/

At first glance it seems quite simple, if a bit tedious, to sort out organizations that could be classified as religious interest groups and publish a modest encyclopedia volume describing them. We soon discovered ourselves to be in the realm of subjective, almost arbitrary, decision making. What is a *religious,* as opposed to a commercial, trade, ideological, or political, interest group? For that matter, what is an *interest group* as opposed to a lobby, a study club, or an educational association?

For purposes of this book we define *religious* very broadly to include (1) groups that directly and consciously represent religious denominations, such as the United States Catholic Conference and the Mennonite Central Committee—Washington Office; (2) independent associations that identify themselves as supporting religious values, such as the Traditional Values Coalition or Catholics for a Free Choice, even though they are independent of, and not endorsed (and may even be repudiated, for that matter) by, religious denominations; and (3) other groups that may not consider themselves religious but reflect directly or indirectly an ideology that approximates ''an ultimate meaning system'' and whose public policy interests are so clearly or so often in the area of concern to religion that they have to be considered players in the struggles of religious interest groups.

This third grouping is most controversial. Readers may be surprised to see the American Atheists, the American Ethical Union, and the American Civil Liberties Union included. None would identify themselves as religious, yet each reflects a point of view that is of great concern to religion and that often brings them into conflict with religious organizations, and each is politically active.[1]

This problem had at least one amusing side, as illustrated by a conversation Professor Jones had with a representative of the ACLU.

ACLU: "Really, you can't include us in your book; we're not at all religious."

Jones: "But surely you'll defend our right to call you religious under our definition?"

ACLU: "Well, ah . . . that's certainly a different point!"

Jewish groups pose a particular problem, since they reflect the Jewish community: some have a clearly religious focus, and others represent a more secular interest in Israel or in Judaism simply as an ethnic identity. We and often the Jewish groups themselves have never resolved this problem, so have tended to include more, rather than fewer, Jewish groups, possibly overstating their number and influence. We did avoid including the large number of political action committees that work to support candidates favorable to Israel.

Determining what is an "interest group" proved to be no less perplexing. We began with David Truman's classic political science definition: "any group that, on the basis of one or more shared attitudes, makes certain claims upon other groups in society for the establishment, maintenance, or enhancement of forms of behavior that are implied by the shared attitudes."[2] We then restricted ourselves to the more common understanding of interest groups—those that attempt to influence the establishment, maintenance, or enhancement of *public policy* by directing their claims to government officials or agencies, that is, politically active groups. This meant we excluded a number of groups, such as the Mormon Gay and Lesbian Alliance, that attempt solely to change internal church policy, but not government policy.

An even more difficult issue was trying to determine what "making certain claims" on government or "attempting to influence government" means and therefore which groups to include. We did find it easy to exclude prayer groups, of which there are a number, which indeed attempt to influence government, but indirectly through divine intervention. As political scientists we decided to stick to more clearly human and measurable influences! We did exclude those groups that are clearly and almost entirely (notice the hedge word) educational in their objectives, if that education is aimed at their own members or society at large, rather than specifically focused on government officials. Granted this was a judgment call, but for inclusion we looked for education *plus* a direct effort to influence.

Likewise, if an organization is almost entirely a service organization run by a religious organization, such as Catholic Charities, the Salvation Army, or Hadassah, we looked for more than social service. Do they, as a part of their mission, directly try to contact government officials to influence public policy in their areas of concern? So Hadassah and Catholic Charities are included; the Salvation Army is not.

Finally, in order to keep the book to a manageable size, we focused on national groups that intend to continue over time, even though a number of them strive to influence policy on both national and state levels. Thus we excluded groups active solely in a particular community or organized to work on a project only during a short time frame, for example, through one legislative session or in a pre-election campaign. We also did not include social, cultural, historical, or ethnic identity clubs and organizations on the same grounds that they do not attempt to influence government on more than a sporadic or incidental basis. This is not to diminish the importance of such associations, as they exist by the thousands and play a very critical role in American culture.

There are a number of organizations that we thought were at least candidates for inclusion in the encyclopedia but that for one of the above reasons did not seem to fit. Where possible we have simply included their names, addresses, and phone numbers so that readers can follow up more closely if they prefer.

Finally, a word about the format and content of the descriptions. For the most part we began with a perusal of the *Encyclopedia of Associations,* no mean task, since it includes some 84,000 entries. We then contacted likely groups, asking that information be sent to us. Not surprisingly, some cooperated better than others. We then scoured newspaper indexes, *The Readers' Guide to Periodic Literature,* and various magazines and newspapers. The format for describing each group is quite standardized, although where possible we took standard information from the brochures sent to us. In particular we made an effort to use the words of the organizations themselves when describing the "mission statement" for the group.

As is the case with any book, we owe thanks to far more people than we can possibly mention here. We wish to single out graduate students Paul Atterbury, Shannon Fitzgerald, and Jessica Jones for their research and organization of the data, plus the undergraduates in Paul Weber's 1992 Religion and Politics course. Of course we are most grateful to our editor Mildred Vasan for her patience.

NOTES

1. This problem can be even more complex. The Moral Majority, although now defunct, was clearly identified in the public mind with religion and Rev. Jerry Falwell, but it claimed very consistently and correctly that it was a political, not a religious, organization. Yet under our definition it would have been included in our study.

2. David B. Truman, *The Governmental Process: Political Interests and Public Opinion* (New York: Knopf, 1951), 33.

RELIGIOUS INTEREST GROUPS

/

1. African Faith and Justice Network — AFJN
2. AIDS National Interfaith Network — ANIN
3. American-Arab Anti-Discrimination Committee — ADC
4. American Association of Christian Schools — AACS
5. American Atheists — AA
6. American Baptist Church USA—Washington Office — ABCUSA
7. American Center for Law and Justice — ACLJ
8. American Civil Liberties Union — ACLU
9. American Coalition of Unregistered Churches — ACUC
10. American Ethical Union — AEU
11. American Family Association — AFA
12. American Freedom Coalition — AFC
13. American Friends Service Committee — AFSC
14. American Israel Public Affairs Committee — AIPAC
15. American Jewish Committee — AJC
16. American Jewish Congress — JEWCON
17. American Life League — ALL
18. Americans for Peace Now — AFPN
19. Americans for Religious Liberty — ARL
20. Americans United for Life — AUL
21. Americans United for Separation of Church and State — AU
22. Amnesty International — AI

HISTORY OF U.S. RELIGIOUS INTEREST GROUPS

———————— / ————————

If one were to write a history of religion in America, the first sentence might read, "Divided they came; divided they stayed." Religions in the United States have always been diverse, dynamic, and remarkably adaptable. They have also been heavily and continuously involved in politics, and many of the same themes and tensions have persisted through the years even as the political issues have changed.

One consistent element of American political culture has been a strong commitment to the ideal of "separation of church and state." The meaning of the term has never been agreed upon or, indeed, clear. What is clear is that even separation's most persistent advocates have appealed to, and depended upon, religious support and particularly church support to pursue their political objectives. James Madison, author of the critical and classic *Memorial and Remonstrance Against Religious Assessments,* scurried about Virginia collecting signatures, particularly among Baptists and Presbyterians, to defeat Patrick Henry's tax assessment bill and garner support for Jefferson's Bill Establishing Religious Liberty. The support of nonestablished churches was critical for passage of the bill.

Even Thomas Jefferson's famous "wall of separation" metaphor was written in a letter responding to a statement of support from a Danbury, Connecticut, Baptist church. Were Madison and Jefferson cynical manipulators of a popular ideal for political advantage? Not at all. They were politician-statesmen who understood that complete separation of religion and politics is not possible. This is because all great political issues—those that grip and divide large numbers of citizens who then seek solutions through the apparatus of government—are, at heart, moral issues. All great moral issues are, at heart, matters of religious belief and conviction. There is no escaping that reality.

Ideologues and the naive may argue that certain issues—civil rights, alcohol and drugs, wages, employment, abortion, the environment, and so on—are purely economic or social concerns or simply personal matters. But so long as enough citizens believe these or other issues are of public concern and petition the government to create laws, the issues become political. As long as some of those citizens act out of religious conviction or organize around and through churches or other religious organizations, religion is active in politics. In short, the overlap of political issues and religious issues is a persistent fact of life in the United States.

What does "separation of church and state" then mean? That question has been disputed in political and legal journals for at least half a century and will not be answered completely here.[1] At the very least it means that the government can grant no privileges or advantages, impose no disabilities, or exert no coercion based on religious belief or action. Separation does not mean that religious individuals or groups cannot petition the government, speak out on, or attempt to influence public opinion, or even litigate on issues of concern to them. This is a fundamental right, spelled out clearly in the Constitution.

Ordinarily when people speak of the legal basis for the interaction of religion and politics in the United States, they quote only the first clause of the First Amendment to the Constitution. But the whole amendment applies to religious individuals and groups just as much as it does to other individuals and groups. Indeed, when thinking of religious interest groups, it may be more profitable to focus on the last, rather than the first, clause. The First Amendment in its entirety reads: "Congress shall make no law respecting an establishment of religion or prohibiting the free exercise thereof; or abridging the freedom of speech, or of the press; *or the right of the people peaceably to assemble, and to petition the government for a redress of grievances* (emphasis added). Religious groups, in brief, have a right to organize and to petition the government.

We may summarize our first point by saying there has always been a dynamic relationship between religious advocates and government officials in American politics. It has been a mutually supported and constitutionally protected relationship, although certainly not without its tensions. While most attention has been paid to religious groups petitioning government, government officials have also looked to religion to support and legitimate their policies, as the example of Madison and Jefferson illustrate. This is nowhere better expressed than in a letter from President Abraham Lincoln. The 1865 General Conference of the Methodist Church had written an address to Lincoln, noting that thousands of its members had joined the Union army and pledging their continued support to bring the rebellion to an end. Lincoln responded as follows:

Gentlemen: In response to your address, allow me to attest to the accuracy of its historical statements, indorse the sentiment it expresses, and thank you in the nation's name for the sure promise it gives.

Nobly sustained as the Government has been by all the churches, I would utter nothing which might in the least appear invidious against any. Yet without this, it may fairly be said that the Methodist Episcopal Church, not less devoted than the best, is by its greater number the most important of all. It is no fault in others that the Methodist Episcopal Church sent more soldiers to the field, more nurses to the hospitals, and more prayers to heaven than any! God bless the Methodist Episcopal Church! Bless all the Churches! And blessed be God, who in this our trial giveth us the Churches![2]

Other presidents at other times might not wax so eloquently or view the matter in such a positive light, but all have realized that religious forces are indeed important players in the political arena.

A second consistent element of American political culture has been that religious groups have actively addressed the major political issues of their day. Often the churches and religious groups shoved particular interests onto the political agenda. A brief survey of these major issues shows some of the continuities and changes in religious activism.

THE REVOLUTION

The churches played a critical, indeed, indispensable, part in the fight for freedom from England. John Adams, one of the founders of the nation and its second president, keenly observed that the real revolution in America—in the minds and hearts of the people—had been taking place long before 1776. At a time when "the divine right of kings" was still a dominant political value, the developing ideals of individualism, voluntarism, dissension, and separation from the Church of England laid the intellectual framework for separation from the "duly constituted legitimate government of the colonies." But just as important, during the revolutionary years religious groups actively participated in the debate over revolt, the war itself, and then the reconstruction of the nation. They did not, however, speak with one voice—establishing a tradition that has continued unabated. As the late historian Sydney Ahlstrom wrote, "The years of mounting crisis found the churches implicated on both sides of every issue under debate, but in general they became increasingly identified with the Patriot tide of opinion and contributed powerfully to its rise."[3]

The impact of religious participation on both colonial and the new state governments was immense. More than anything else such participation gave legitimacy to the cause of revolution. "That the 'Black Regiment' of colonial clergy addressing large, regular audiences from positions of great prestige was a major force arousing the spirit of independence after 1761, was asserted at the time by both Tory and Patriot interpreters."[4]

In the development of justifying rationales for revolution, the churches served as mediating structures or transmission belts for the great Enlightenment ideals of freedom, equality, human rights, natural law, and social contract from such thinkers as John Locke to ordinary citizens. It is hard to overstate the importance and success of this transmission task. For example, when the revolution was won, every single colony set up a republican form of government, even though none existed upon which it could model itself at the time.

One final dimension of religious involvement in revolutionary politics merits attention: the various denominations and, within them, various congregations were divided among themselves on the question of rebellion, and when war came, there were winners and losers. The Anglican church in particular was devastated. Most Anglican clergy and many prominent lay leaders were loyalists who fled with the British troops. But curiously, there was a gap between the views of such leaders and the average person in the pews. A substantial number of political and social leaders as well as ordinary members inclined toward the patriot cause. In fact, two-thirds of those who signed the Declaration of Independence were at least nominally Anglican. Such differences between church leaders and laity have remained a consistent reality.

SLAVERY AND THE CIVIL WAR

Slavery and the Civil War reflect all that is best and worst in the political activism of religion. No other groups pushed for abolition as persistently and passionately over so many years or over so broad a spectrum of citizens as did the churches and the antislavery associations they founded. Not only did they provide the audiences, but from them came the literature, the songs, the leaders, and the motivation. No one else treated slavery so fully as a ''moral'' problem or suffered so much persecution on behalf of freedom for the slaves; no one else was so principled or uncompromising or willing to draw blood without regard for personal or social cost.

How important were the churches for the abolitionist movement? They were the heart and soul of it; they provided the institutional context for an idea political parties were ill-equipped and most reluctant to embrace. As Seymour Martin Lipset observes:

The leadership of the abolitionist organizations begun in the 1830s was drawn from substantial upper middle class and distinguished Federalist families, predominantly Congregational, Presbyterian, and Quaker, even though they included many Methodists, and were supported, of course, by Transcendentalist-Unitarian intellectuals. However, a number of studies have associated the subsequent mass growth of the anti-slavery movement in the North with the emergent evangelical denominations. *Abolition had particular strength in areas where there had been successful revivalist campaigns* [emphasis added].[5]

From a more sobering perspective, by their strident self-righteousness, casting the problem in absolutist terms of right and wrong, virtue and sin, and making the issue one of eternal salvation and damnation, church leaders made political solutions or gradualism impossible. The problem is best characterized by a description of William Lloyd Garrison, who, incidentally, had been editor of a Baptist temperance journal when he became converted to the abolitionist cause:

Never a colonizationist and no longer a gradualist urging emancipation sometime "between now and never," Garrison demanded abolition immediately. Yet he drastically reduced the useful effect of his zeal by his absolutism, his astounding lack of charity, his incapacity to understand the thought or predicament of others, his unyielding demand for women's rights within the movement, his fierce anti-clericalism and increasingly radical religious views, his almost anarchistic pacifism, his repudiation of political action and, after 1843, his demand for Northern secession on grounds that the Constitution was a diabolical compact. The extent of his influence on abolitionism will probably always be disputed; but there is little doubt that he did far more than any other man to heighten Southern opposition to emancipation.[6]

Perhaps war was inevitable in any event; the experience of other nations indicates that it was not. But the zeal of religious activists closed all other political options, and the nation witnessed a slaughter of as-yet unparalleled scope. As in the revolutionary war religious leaders supported both sides with great fervor. Impassioned denouncements of slavery on biblical grounds were met with impassioned defenses of slavery on biblical grounds. Moral righteousness and absolute truth followed the flags.

Religious activism was a crucial component in a struggle against a monumental evil, slavery. In that sense it was involvement in politics at its most noble. But the fact that such activists could be equally righteous, strident, and intransigent on both sides and steel the will to fight of both antagonists by making the issue a moral crusade must give pause.

THE SOCIAL GOSPEL

More than any other movement, the Social Gospel was the womb of modern religious group activism. After the Civil War the nation increasingly turned its energies to industrialization, with its attendant challenges and problems. The more liberal and progressive churches turned their attention to these issues as well, especially between 1880 and 1910. The driving passion of these liberal church people was to overcome human suffering and degradation caused by industrialization, urbanization, and immigration. Profoundly influenced by Charles Darwin and Karl Marx, Social Gospel advocates were Christians who took an optimistic view of human nature. They accepted evolution as a basis for hope in the possibility of bettering the human condition while flatly rejecting the laissez-faire passivity of social Darwinism and the determinism of Marxism. The organized selfishness of capitalism could be countered by organized altruism; the "iron law of wages" could be bent to the Great Commandment by the power of Christian activism.

The Social Gospel, despite its limited political success, pushed American re-

ligious interests even further from simple concern for personal salvation to an
abiding sense of social responsibility. Even those who rejected this "liberal"
idea could not ignore it. The impact of the Social Gospel on religious interest
groups can be seen in three areas: raising of social and moral consciousness
around the issues of economic exploitation and social responsibility, developing
social welfare agencies within various denominations, and creating interchurch
agencies for cooperation in providing social services. The foundation was laid
for such agencies to gradually add political advocacy to their services.

For example, during this time period the Episcopal and Congregational
churches formed social commissions (1901), the Northern Presbyterian church
organized its Department of Church and Labor (1903), the Methodists developed
a Federation for Social Services (1908), and the Northern Baptists and a dozen
smaller denominations made similar efforts to institutionalize their social mission. Also during this time the Federal Council of Churches, precursor to the
National Council of Churches, was formed to further the aims of its Social
Gospel advocates.

PROHIBITION

The temperance crusade represented a monumental shift in religious group political tactics, resulting first in a stunning success, then in an almost equally stunning reversal. It is still one movement most referenced by those who seek to limit
or guide the political activism of churches, and it has many lessons to teach.

Several temperance societies were formed well before the Civil War, and a
Prohibitionist third party was formed in 1869. The movement began to make
inroads on mainstream consciousness with the formation of the Woman's Christian Temperance Union in 1874. This was a remarkable group, much maligned
and misunderstood in later years, but with a vision and energy that gave it
influence far beyond its numbers. Assuming the presidency in 1881, Frances
Willard envisioned a broad-based, balanced, and principled movement. Willard
pushed for outlawing alcoholic beverages, of course, but also for women's
rights, protection of the poor, and urban reform. Influenced by the Social Gospel,
she dreamed of a long-term reform party rooted in local evangelical, especially
Methodist, churches. It was not to be. Perhaps the movement's efforts were
spread too thinly over too many issues; perhaps its insistence on women's rights
threatened too many potential male supporters; or perhaps it was because some
of Willard's views were too radical. She held, for instance, that poverty led to
alcoholism as well as the other way around, a view totally anathema to most
major business leaders—who at that time were vigorously fighting union or-
ganizers, minimum wages, and health and safety regulations—and their clerical
counterparts. In any event, in 1893 a rival group, the Anti-Saloon League, was
formed and quickly took over leadership of the temperance movement.

The Anti-Saloon League was the strongest interest group ever formed by the
churches. It was rigorously and narrowly focused on a single goal, a thoroughly

dry United States, and practiced pressure politics to a degree never before seen. The league attempted to organize in every congressional district in every state, utilizing local Protestant churches as recruiting, meeting, and funding sources. It was the largest cooperative effort ever among Methodists, Baptists, Presbyterians, and a host of smaller churches. It was also highly political. League members demanded a pledge to vote dry of every political candidate and officeholder at every level, placing every other issue or qualification on a distinctly lower level of concern. Members attempted to keep track of officials' votes and threatened swift retribution to those who wavered. In 1919, emboldened by its successes in the states, the league settled upon a national strategy of pushing for a constitutional amendment as a way to solve the problem of alcohol consumption once and for all. Aided by World War I—when many drinkers of voting age were overseas, widespread anti-German feeling was easily symbolized by stout brewers, and they could make a persuasive, if inaccurate, argument that grain was needed for fuel and bread rather than alcohol—the amendment was swiftly passed.

The results, of course, were far from what prohibitionists envisioned or could even have imagined in their worst nightmares. What happened? Undoubtedly the most important factor was the postwar mood that found expression in "the roaring twenties." Prohibition provided an ideal target for the revulsion against militarism, authority, and duty. Whole classes of people despised and flouted the law. Prohibition had a profoundly negative impact on American culture; not only did it provide an opportunity for mobs and Mafia to become firmly entrenched in both fact and folklore, but it added a streak of approval for breaking laws—the legitimation of illegality—that has never left the culture.

On the religious side, several other things happened as well. Grass-roots activists, having achieved victory with the approval of the Eighteenth Amendment, lost interest. Many leaders became caught up in other emerging issues such as the peace movement, communism, and immigration. Those who stayed focused on prohibition found themselves overwhelmed. Prohibition was finally repealed in 1933, and the Anti-Saloon League sank into oblivion.

The impact on political activism by the churches was devastating. "Morality" itself became a suspect political goal; the authority of clergy in political matters was immeasurably weakened in the eyes of citizens and politicians alike, and latent strains in the cooperative venture of mainline Protestantism ripped into open conflict. Never again would there be such a consensus among religious leaders on any great religiopolitical issue. Yet, for all of that, there was the haunting memory of a powerful crusade, the lingering taste of triumph, a subtle siren call to future possibilities.

WORLD WARS AND THE PEACE MOVEMENT

No issues are so totally moral and fully political as war and peace, and religious groups were to be found in both the militarist and pacifist camps in this critical period of American history. The militarism that flowered so fully in

World War I had its roots in the Spanish-American War a generation earlier in 1898. Mainline Protestants fervently backed Presidents William McKinley and Theodore Roosevelt. Methodists in particular seemed enamored of the idea of spreading democracy and attacking Spanish Catholicism in one blow. An editor of *The Nation* observed that ''the fervent Methodists at the beginning of the war resolved that it was going to be a righteous and holy war because it would destroy 'Romish superstition' in the Spanish West Indies.''[7] The Spanish-American War was short, however, and since American Catholics also supported the policy of liberating colonies from a corrupt and decrepit Spanish empire with which they had little in common, there was little critical reflection or debate afterward.

The militarist attitude continued unabated; during World War I mainline churches, Protestant and Catholic alike, were ardent patriots, and massive efforts were made by churches to support the war from the pulpit.[8] At this time also numerous groups were formed to strengthen and encourage the war effort. Among already existing groups, the Federal Council of Churches led the way, creating a General Wartime Commission to organize the efforts of such member groups as the Young Men's Christian Association (YMCA), American Bible Society, and the Home Mission Council. This commission then established a Committee of One Hundred to carry out day-to-day operations. This committee, in turn, created subcommittees for specific areas of concern such as chaplaincies, bible distribution, and recreation. Jews and Catholics likewise mobilized for the war effort. The former organized the Jewish Welfare Board and the Young Men's Hebrew Association. The latter established a straightforwardly named National Catholic War Council, which later became the National Catholic Welfare Council.

Several points about this enormous prowar activity are worthy of note. First, the mainline churches jumped quickly, enthusiastically, and without much reflection into a war effort that they rapidly turned into a moral crusade. The voices of traditional peace churches were overwhelmed, then ignored in the rush to judgment. The mainline religious community's self-righteousness was matched only by the simplicity of their understanding of world politics. From the perspective of religious interest group history, the one positive that came out of this effort was a new ecumenism: a lessening of distrust between Catholic and Protestant churches and a willingness to cooperate.

After World War I, when the enormous suffering and dislocation it caused became more generally known, and the differentiation between forces of good and evil became less clear, there was widespread revulsion at things military. Among mainline churches a belated period of reflection and some remorse began. As self-criticism mounted, there was a remarkable turn toward pacifism. Pacifism itself had its own deep roots in American religious tradition, of course, beginning with Quakers in prerevolutionary days. Modern variants had gotten an enormous boost in pre–World War I days when Andrew Carnegie endowed the Church Peace Union in New York. As war clouds gathered over Europe, the Peace Union helped found a group called World Alliance, the first truly international ecumenical pacifist movement. Although it barely stayed alive during the war, the postwar era, with its wide revulsion against violence, brought an abrupt change of tactics and fortune.

While before the war, leaders of the World Alliance tended to address their appeals directly to the consciences of political leaders, after the war they took a much more pragmatic attack. The new strategy had two thrusts: "to inform Christian public opinion with a broader sense of social responsibility, and to mobilize this opinion to form a pressure group on their governments for the constructive shaping of national and foreign policies."[9] How much of this they had learned from the prohibitionists is unclear, but the strategy was an immediate, overwhelming success. So many individuals were led to sign pledges of nonviolence and pacifism that a new organization, the Peace Pledge Union, was formed in 1936. Even the Federal Council of Churches had reversed itself completely and worked energetically in the pacifist cause. Liberal theologians were beginning to argue that perhaps Christianity was pacifist in its very essence. But this was different from the traditional absolute pacifism of other groups like the Fellowship of Reconciliation, formed in 1915. It was what William Marty has called "engaged pacifism."[10] It very much intended to have an immediate, direct influence on the formation of public policy.

How much these "activist pacifists" aided the cause of disarmament and isolationism in the United States between the wars is unclear, but they appear to have had considerable short-term impact. With German rearmament and Nazi belligerence on the rise, however, much of the hard-won support for pacifism evaporated as fast as it had risen. By 1939 lay membership left by the thousands, followed by their leadership. The traditional peace churches once more had the field to themselves. In retrospect, one commentator sums up the views many have of the Christian pacifist effort between the wars:

In the eyes of many of its critics, the Christian peace movement in the twentieth century has been the refuge of idealists and utopians, whose theology was weak, whose politics were naive and unrealistic and whose public advocacy was inadequate. These pacifists failed to recognize that the social function of the mainline churches, and of the educated bourgeois which upheld them, was largely if unconsciously preservative of the existing social order, and with an attendant attachment to the nation state and its apparatus of military defense forces, whose use could be justified in times of crisis.[11]

When World War II began, the cycle of enthusiastic support began again.

CIVIL RIGHTS

By the end of World War II most major denominations had permanent offices and staff in Washington, D.C., to monitor government activities and make certain their church's position on issues was well known to legislators. Most had begun to move from single-issue advocacy such as the abolition, prohibition, and pacifism battles, to a fuller range of political concerns. Initially, however, Catholics focused on making certain their educational and social institutions were included in government-funded programs such as the G.I. Bill, hospital construction grants, and their ultimate hope, aid for parochial schools. As the horrors of the Holocaust slowly became known, Jewish groups focused on immigration and gaining financial support for the new state of Israel. Several Protestant groups became so alarmed at the prospect of public funding for parochial schools that Protestants and Other Americans United for Separation of Church and State was formed to fight all funding schemes through litigation. But the issue that marked a turning point in religious interest group activism was civil rights.

Among African Americans the struggle to end slavery and the vestiges of slavery had not ended with the Civil War, but for most Americans, including in large measure the churches, race relations were a matter of not very benign neglect. African-American strategy for achieving equality and due process was to work through the court system to gain one small victory at a time. Progress was excruciatingly slow, but *Brown v. Board of Education* in 1954, declaring segregated schools to be unconstitutional, and the refusal of Rosa Parks to give up her seat to a white passenger in a 1955 Montgomery, Alabama, incident electrified the nation and reinvigorated the movement. The fact that African-American leadership came predominantly from black churches and used the language of Christian justice made the issue all the more salient for white church leaders. Slowly the religious interest groups got involved. In late 1958 the Catholic bishops, speaking through the National Catholic Welfare Conference, condemned racial discrimination and called for "equal rights and equal dignity."[12]

Liberal Protestant groups followed in short order with their own statements, the United Church of Christ, the Methodist Church, the United Presbyterian Church U.S.A., the National Council of Churches, the Episcopal Church, and then dozens of others. By 1962 interest was such that the National Catholic Welfare Conference called for an interfaith conference on religion and race that drew some 700 delegates from 67 major religious bodies—Protestant, Roman Catholic, and Jewish. They determined to forge an interfaith grass-roots alliance to end discrimination.

While church efforts were extraordinarily broad, ranging from sermons to teach-ins, from requiring their suppliers to sign nondiscrimination pledges to local marches, from letter writing to national rallies, the major focus of national leadership groups quickly became the 1964 Civil Rights Act. The specific task they undertook was to exert enough pressure on the Senate to overcome a southern filibuster, something that had never been done before.

The details of that struggle have been well described by Professor James Adams in *The Growing Church Lobby*. What is important for our purposes is to note that this effort marked a major step in the acceptance and maturity of religious interest groups. First, this was truly an ecumenical effort in which

Protestants, Catholics, Jews, and eventually Orthodox worked together and supported each other on a single project. While differences on other issues were not forgotten or resolved, opposing one another on some issues no longer precluded cooperation on others. This was a major step toward professionalization. There was another side to this, however, that was not recognized at the time. These were liberal churches cooperating with each other; conservatives were conspicuous in their absence. A few isolated ministers were vocal in their opposition to civil rights (they called it forced integration or even more pejorative terms), but they were unorganized and without a tradition of political activism. We shall return to that issue, but what is of significance is that the split between religious liberals and conservatives was rapidly becoming far more important than the split among Protestants, Catholics, and Jews.

Second, religious groups cooperated with, and became part of a much larger coalition of civil rights groups such as the National Association for the Advancement of Colored People (NAACP), the American Civil Liberties Union (ACLU), the Leadership Conference on Civil Rights (an umbrella group founded in 1949), and labor groups such as the American Federation of Labor and Congress of Industrial Organizations (AFL-CIO) and the United Auto Workers. In this process religious leaders became more sophisticated in the tactics of lobbying, but they also brought something the other groups lacked, an ability to emotionally engage large numbers of citizens in what can only be called a crusade, through rituals such as candlelight vigils and appeals to eternal values. For example, in August 1963, following a call through the churches, 200,000 people turned out for a march on Washington. Congress could not help but notice. A lesser-known task as part of the coalition was for religious groups to counter and defuse as much as possible a growing white backlash.

Finally, religious groups worked openly and over an extended period of time with the White House and congressional leaders, plotting strategy, dividing up tasks, and using their unique strengths in developing a supportive public opinion and keeping up constituent pressure on Congress. In fact, in one session President Lyndon Johnson spelled it out: "It is your job—as men of God—to reawaken the consciences of America, to direct the immense power of religion in shaping the conduct and thought of men toward their brothers in a manner consistent with compassion and love."[13]

It was an exhilarating feeling, and leaders of religious groups now felt and acted like truly established players on the national political scene.

VIETNAM

Following immediately on the heels of the civil rights movement, indeed, overlapping it in large measure, came an even more unsettling occurrence, the Vietnam War and the protests it engendered. Protests began in the streets and on college campuses, among students, potential draftees, and the younger clergy, not among church leaders or their interest groups. When opposition to the war began to be expressed by church leaders, the grand liberal coalition, so recently forged, began to crack. The Methodist church and United Church of Christ came out strongly antiwar and offered specific policy recommendations for President Johnson. Said a Methodist spokesman, "I believe this is the first time a church has sought to directly influence foreign policy."[14] Catholic leaders refused to go along for several years, apparently believing there was no moral clarity in this issue, although among protest leaders receiving the most publicity were the Berrigan brothers, both Catholic priests. Rabbi Arthur Hertzberg warned against claims to speak out as holding a mandate from God to pursue specific foreign policies. Even the National Council of Churches issued only balanced, cautious statements until national public opinion had moved more fully into opposition to the war effort.

The antiwar movement not only showed that the liberal coalition was fragile and limited to civil rights for blacks but exacerbated another split as well, between religious leaders and laity. As slow as many leaders were to oppose the war, they were way ahead of most of their church members. Laity supported the war effort far longer and more strongly than did their leaders, and many deeply resented the visible role played by clergy at all levels of the antiwar movement. The war finally came to an end, of course, but the moral authority so persuasively and powerfully wielded by mainstream religious leaders was severely wounded. Other leaders, appalled by liberal successes and excesses, restlessly strove to be heard.

CONSERVATIVE RESURRECTION

Evangelical Protestants—people who believe in biblical inerrancy, the primacy of faith over good works as the basis for salvation, redemption based on personal conversion, a mandate to spread the Gospel and the duty of government to enforce morality—had been mainstream Protestantism throughout the nineteenth century. Methodists and, to a slightly lesser extent, Presbyterians had been among the Evangelical ranks when they provided leadership for the abolition and prohibition movements, although many of the foot soldiers had been evangelical Baptists and members of independent Christian churches. A gradual split occurred somewhat along educational and socioeconomic lines, but primarily driven by attitudes toward evolution. More liberal folk accepted evolution as a scientific truth and rethought their belief in the literal truth of the Bible. Evangelicals rejected evolution and fiercely committed themselves to biblical inerrancy. Widely ridiculed and badly bruised in the media during and after the Scopes trial and the battle to repeal Prohibition, Evangelicals largely withdrew from political activism to focus on personal evangelism, which they continued to pursue with vigor and imagination. Except in local areas where they were strongly represented and could pursue efforts to prohibit alcoholic beverages, Evangelicals politically disappeared. They were, however, building churches, gaining converts, and vigorously spreading their values among rural and small-town people. Just as they had been among the first to recognize and use radio, they were among the first and most sophisticated in developing televangelism.

The 1960s and 1970s brought increasing frustration with the direction of American culture in general and politics in particular—a frustration made vivid and personal by radio and television coverage. Suddenly Evangelicals confronted in their own living rooms dramatic civil rights demonstrations, antiwar protests, and abortion rights movements, not to mention announcements of Supreme Court decisions that seemed to be against traditional Christian values— prohibition of prayer and Bible reading in the public schools, greater rights for criminal defendants, easy divorce, protection of pornography, and so on. It was becoming increasingly clear to Evangelical leaders that if they did not fight in the political arena for their own values, they would live under far more liberal values, the constellation of which they called "secular humanism."

The Supreme Court's *Roe v. Wade* decision in 1973 was a major catalyst, but by no means the only cause for Evangelical return to politics, and this time many of the elements of power and organization were in place. Several Evangelical ministers had pioneered and mastered the art of televangelism and had large, if politically latent, followings. Since they consciously complemented and supported local churches rather than supplanting them, televangelists had a potential network of local pastors who only needed to be persuaded that involvement in politics was a furtherance of, rather than a distraction from, their primary focus on personal salvation. (Not all were convinced, and this was but one of several splits among the Evangelicals.)

Political conservatives such as Paul Weyrich of the National Committee for the Survival of a Free Congress, Howard Phillips of the Conservative Caucus, and Terry Dolan of the National Conservative Political Action Committee seized the opportunity to forge links with religiously conservative figures and provided funding, fund-raising techniques (Weyrich had pioneered in low-cost mass mailing appeals), and political tactics. The New Christian Right was born. Religious interest groups quickly formed, beginning with Christian Voice, the Religious Roundtable, and Moral Majority. Although all have since disbanded or been supplanted, they led the way. When Ronald Reagan won the White House in 1980, they quickly received access, status, and legitimacy.[15]

With the awakening of the conservative religious giant in the 1970s, the hegemony of liberal groups was ended; conservative groups gradually became more experienced, and the balance of power between liberals and conservatives definitely tilted to the latter. Many of the policy initiatives now began with conservative groups, and liberals found themselves on the defensive. That did not last.

LOOKING INTO THE FUTURE

With the advent of the Bill Clinton presidency it is likely that liberal groups will rebound and conservative groups find themselves with less political access and influence. If they follow the liberal pattern of the 1980s, a number of groups will flounder. Others will focus their efforts on litigation in the courts, long the tactic of groups lacking influence in the congressional and executive branches. The only certainty is that both liberal and conservative religious interest groups will survive and remain active players in the drama of American politics. Not only will old issues refuse to leave the political agenda, but new issues will continually arise, including gay rights, the right to die at a time of one's own choosing, the content of textbooks in public schools, the right to educate one's children at home or in private schools, and others only dimly on the horizon. We can count on religious interest groups to remain diverse, dynamic, and remarkably adaptable.

NOTES

1. For a variety of viewpoints on the meaning of separation, see Paul J. Weber (ed.), *Equal Separation: Understanding the Religious Clauses of the First Amendment* (Westport, CT: Greenwood Press, 1990).

2. I am indebted to Luke Eugene Ebersole, *Church Lobbying in the Nation's Capitol* (New York: Macmillan, 1951), 7, for this quotation.

3. Sydney E. Ahlstrom, *A Religious History of the American People,* vol. 1 (Garden City, NY: Doubleday-Image Books, 1975), 438.

4. *Ibid.*

5. Seymour Martin Lipset (ed.), *Party Coalitions in the 1890s* (San Francisco: Institute for Contemporary Studies, 1981), 67.

6. Ahlstrom, vol. 2, 95–96.

7. *The Nation,* 11 August 1898, 105; quoted in Kenneth M. MacKenzie, *The Robe and the Sword: The Methodist Church and the Rise of American Imperialism* (Washington, DC: Public Affairs Press, 1961), 66.

8. See particularly Ray Abrams, *Preachers Present Arms* (New York: Roundtable Press, 1933).

9. John S. Conway, "The Struggle for Peace Between the Wars," *The Ecumenical Review* 15, no. 1 (January 1983): 29.

10. William Marty, "The Role of Religious Organizations in the Peace Movement Between the Wars," unpublished paper, no date.

11. Conway, 30.

12. For a fascinating, blow-by-blow, and somewhat critical discussion of religious activism in civil rights, see James L. Adams, *The Growing Church Lobby in Washington* (Grand Rapids, MI: William B. Eerdmans, 1970).

13. Adams, 30.

14. Rodney Shaw, quoted in A. James Reichley, *Religion in American Public Life* (Washington, DC: The Brookings Institution, 1985).

15. For a discussion of this problem, see James Davison Hunter, *Culture Wars: The Struggle to Define America* (New York: Basic Books, 1992).

U.S. RELIGIOUS
INTEREST GROUPS

A

/

AFRICAN FAITH AND JUSTICE NETWORK (AFJN)

401 Michigan Avenue, NE
Washington, DC 20017
Phone: (202) 832-3412
Fax: (202) 832-9051
Executive Director: Sr. Maura Browne, SND

ORIGINS AND DEVELOPMENT

AFJN started in 1983, when three Catholic religious congregations that were working in Africa came together to develop a common voice in Washington, D.C., to inform lawmakers and influence decisions affecting Africa. By 1992 the membership had grown to sixty religious orders, which have over 1,000 Americans working in Africa. In 1989 an affiliated office was established for the European Catholic religious congregations.

MISSION STATEMENT

"AFJN is concerned with issues affecting all of Africa or large parts of that continent. It focuses on the role America, Europe and the countries of the North have in causing injustices in Africa. AFJN seeks to challenge the policies of the Northern countries when it is determined that these policies are detrimental to the interests of African peoples."

ORGANIZATION AND FUNDING

With a budget of under $100,000, AFJN functions primarily through its member orders and their contacts throughout the world. All of the funding comes from membership donations. Member organizations include Dominican Sisters;

Sisters of Mercy; Franciscans; Holy Cross Missionaries; Jesuit Missions; Marianists; Marists; Maryknoll Fathers, Brothers and Sisters; Sacred Heart Fathers and Sisters; Sisters of St. Joseph; School Sisters of Notre Dame; Medical Mission Sisters; and several other groups.

POLICY CONCERNS AND TACTICS

"The network gathers information on issues and policies which unjustly affect Africa. This data is analyzed and sent to participating groups with recommendations for advocacy or action. Since many of the participating groups are European or international in character, documents are produced in French and English. . . . Trading and other economic policies are often unfavorable toward Africa. Often political unrest, refugee problems, military arms sales and other problems which affect the people of Africa have their origin in the policies of First World governments."

AFFILIATION

Roman Catholic.

PUBLICATIONS

None.

AIDS NATIONAL INTERFAITH NETWORK (ANIN)

110 Maryland Avenue, NE
Suite 504
Washington, DC 20002
Phone: (202) 546-0807
Fax: (202) 546-5103
Executive Director: Rev. Kenneth South

ORIGINS AND DEVELOPMENT

Conceived by representatives of Protestant, Catholic, and Jewish groups in the fall of 1987, ANIN was founded on 13 April 1988 in Rye, New York. It was first housed at 475 Riverside Drive before moving to Washington. The founding board had eighteen directors chaired by a retired Methodist bishop and included Christian, Jewish, and Unitarian faith groups and agencies.

MISSION STATEMENT

"ANIN's work is both faith centered and AIDS [acquired immunodeficiency syndrome] specific. The agency's mission is to, first, assist the rapidly growing number of AIDS ministries in America to become a true working network, helping them to better share information and resources and, second, to represent them in Washington through a public policy presence, of national import, on behalf of those they serve." They speak out on Capitol Hill on AIDS-related issues and "support responsible public policy initiatives."

ORGANIZATION AND FUNDING

ANIN now has a staff of three and has held national conferences, including one at the Carter Presidential Center in 1989. An active member of the Consortium for Citizens with Disabilities, ANIN saw early success with the Americans with Disabilities Act. ANIN also backed the Ryan White AIDS Care bill and the AIDS Housing Opportunity Act. It is a 501(c)(3) organization with individual memberships and receives assistance from religious organizations ($43,816 in 1992) and various foundations and corporations and had a total 1992 income of $290,946. Their programs budget of $125,000 included funds for the National Interfaith Directory, Housing Advocates, AIDS in the Black Church, and the National Skills Building Conference.

POLICY CONCERNS AND TACTICS

ANIN is active in coordinating meetings of the six national AIDS organizations with headquarters in Washington and in the whole network of fourteen national AIDS groups across the country. Working with the Interreligious Health Care Access Campaign* for universal health care legislation, they coordinate the WISC (Washington Interreligious Staff Council*) working group to coordinate strategies for action about specific AIDS-related legislation in the Congress. Using action alerts to their members to get support from Congress, ANIN contacts both executive agencies, such as the Department of Housing and Urban Development (HUD) and the Department of Health and Human Services (HHS), as well as Congress. It is especially concerned about housing programs for people infected with human immunodeficiency virus (HIV). ANIN is currently very active with African-American churches (54 percent of all children with AIDS in the United States are African-American, as are 54 percent of all women with AIDS and 32 percent of all men with AIDS). ANIN cooperates with, and has observer status with, the National Council of the Churches of Christ in the U.S.A.* and works with other religious interest groups in Washington.

AFFILIATION

Nondenominational—Ecumenical.

PUBLICATIONS

The newsletter is *Interaction. The HIV/AIDS Housing Handbook* published by ANIN outlines twenty-one different federal programs that can be used by nonprofit groups to house people with AIDS.

AMERICAN-ARAB ANTI-DISCRIMINATION COMMITTEE (ADC)

4201 Connecticut Avenue, NW
Suite 500
Washington, DC 20008
Phone: (202) 244-2990

Fax: (202) 244-3196

Executive Director: Albert Mokhiber

ORIGINS AND DEVELOPMENT

The American-Arab Anti-Discrimination Committee was organized in 1980 to defend the rights of people of Arab descent and to promote their heritage. It has served as a parallel to the Jewish antidefamation activity and at times as a balance to the pro-Israeli stance of the Jewish community.

MISSION STATEMENT

"ADC, as a grassroots organization based in Washington, D.C., serves a national membership of Arab Americans, joined by Americans of all ethnic origins, who are committed to challenging defamation, discrimination and disenfranchisement wherever they occur."

ORGANIZATION AND FUNDING

The ADC has 25,000 individual members, with four regional offices and seventy-five chapters in North America. While budget figures were not available, membership dues provide the primary funding for a staff of twenty-two, plus a number of intern volunteers. Its Board of Directors includes Muhammad Ali and former Senator James Abourezk as chairman.

POLICY CONCERNS AND TACTICS

Stereotyping and defamation of Arab Americans remain the central focus of the ADC, although the group will investigate claims of employment discrimination, work on immigration policy, and promote human rights among the Lebanese and Palestinians in Israeli-occupied areas.

ADC has joined numerous coalitions to promote human rights; it provides information to Congress, government agencies, and the media and testifies before Congress when the opportunity arises.

AFFILIATION

Secular, nonsectarian. Primarily Muslim but includes some Christian Arabs.

PUBLICATIONS

ADC Times (ten months a year), plus numerous books and pamphlets, including *American Public Opinion and the Palestinian Uprising; Children of the Stones; Harassment in the Holy Land; Through Different Eyes; Social and Political Attitudes of Arab-Americans; The TV Arab; Victims Speak Out;* and *Wrapping the Grapeleaves.*

AMERICAN ASSOCIATION OF CHRISTIAN SCHOOLS (AACS)

4500 Selsa Road	139 C Street, SE
Blue Springs, MO 64015	Washington, DC 20003
Phone: (816) 795-7709	(703) 818-7150

Fax: (816) 795-7709   (703) 818-7281
President: Dr. Carl Herbster

ORIGINS AND DEVELOPMENT

The American Association of Christian Schools was founded in 1972 to promote quality in Christian education and provide a voice in Washington to protect Christian schools from government interference.

MISSION STATEMENT

''We seek to maintain and improve the moral, spiritual, and academic standards of the Christian schools. A well-balanced education includes all areas of student lives—spiritual, academic, social, and physical. Our purpose is to help protect parents' rights to do this without government encroachment.''

ORGANIZATION AND FUNDING

The AACS has a membership of 1,250 Christian schools and a 1993 budget of $300,000, which supports a staff of seven. Funds are provided by membership dues.

POLICY CONCERNS AND TACTICS

The bulk of AACS's time and resources are devoted to enhancing the quality of Christian schools. It provides a certification program and teacher placement program and is a resource and clearinghouse for teaching materials and ideas. In addition AACS staff monitor government activity in the area of education, provide information on Christian schools to government agencies, and lobby against regulations they deem intrusive. Most recently it has supported a voucher system for support of nonpublic schools.

AFFILIATION

Independent Protestant (prefers to be called independent fundamentalist).

PUBLICATIONS

AACS Newsletter (monthly); *AACS Directory* (annual); and *The Builder* (periodic).

COMMENTS

The AACS is a primary force in defending and promoting independent non-Catholic Christian schools before both state and national governments.

AMERICAN ATHEISTS (AA)

P.O. Box 140195
Austin, TX 78714
Phone: (512) 458-1244
Fax: (512) 467-9525
President: Jon Murray

ORIGINS AND DEVELOPMENT

American Atheists was founded in 1959 by Madalyn Murray O'Hair. First conducted out of the Murray home in Maryland, the organization moved with the Murrays to Austin, Texas, in the mid-1960s as a result of continuous harassment in Maryland. In 1977 the $250,000 American Atheists Center opened in Austin and continues to house the national headquarters.

MISSION STATEMENT

"Atheists are people who think, who reason, who unshackle themselves from the myths and hostilities of organized religion." The goals of American Atheists are to "support atheism, separation of church and state, taxation of the church on real estate, income, business and other profits." "American Atheists wish to unite the 10% of Americans who subscribe to no religious faith in the fight to create a total separation between church and state."

ORGANIZATION AND FUNDING

American Atheists is an individual membership organization that has a 1993 budget of $500,000. The national headquarters has a staff of fifteen. Funding sources are membership dues from about 100,000 members and revenues from the sale of books.

POLICY CONCERNS AND TACTICS

American Atheists has been active in a variety of attempts to remove religion from public schools and other tax-supported endeavors and organizations, including prayer in public schools, aid to parochial schools, the inscription "In God We Trust" on U.S. currency, and "one nation under God" in the Pledge of Allegiance. It has advocated legislation to tax church property and income on an equal basis with other business property and income.

American Atheists focuses its efforts on educating the public and providing support for atheists around the nation, through publications, debates, letter-writing campaigns, and so on, including a "Dial-an-Atheist" phone service in forty-five cities to counter "Dial-a-Prayer." When appropriate, American Atheists has engaged in litigation to stop activity it believes violates the establishment clause of the U.S. Constitution.

AFFILIATION

Independent, secular.

PUBLICATIONS

American Atheist (monthly newsletter), *Media Handbook* (annual). In addition, American Atheists has published or reprinted some eighty books.

AMERICAN BAPTIST CHURCH USA/ÆWASHINGTON OFFICE (ABCUSA)

110 Maryland Avenue, NE
Washington, DC 20002-5693

Phone: (202) 544-3400
Fax: (202) 544-0277
Director: Robert Tiller

ORIGINS AND DEVELOPMENT

The national offices of the American Baptist Churches in the United States are in Valley Forge, Pennsylvania. The Washington office was established about 1970 and has had just two directors since its inception.

MISSION STATEMENT

"Out of our understanding of God's purposes and priorities we have extended our mission by opening a door for witness in Washington, D.C. The Office of Governmental Relations is staffed by two commissioned missionaries of the Board of National Ministries and one support person. The group exists to express God's creative, redemptive love and justice in the area of government."

ORGANIZATION AND FUNDING

The Office of Government Relations of the American Baptist Church, as the Washington office is called, has an annual budget of about $150,000 to support its three-person staff and all operations. As a denominational entity, the Washington staff reports directly to the national office in Valley Forge, Pennsylvania.

POLICY CONCERNS AND TACTICS

The ABC Washington office currently focuses on food stamps, unemployment legislation, and economic justice issues in general. While a substantial amount of staff time is devoted to grass-roots education, ABC joins coalitions that support its policy positions and lobbies before congressional committees whenever appropriate.

AFFILIATION

American Baptist Church USA.

PUBLICATIONS

American Baptist (monthly) and *ABC Newsletter* (monthly).

COMMENTS

The American Baptist Church USA is by far the most liberal of the Baptist conventions and so often finds its policy positions at odds with other Baptist conventions and conservative Christians in general.

AMERICAN CENTER FOR LAW AND JUSTICE (ACLJ)

1000 Centerville Turnpike   1000 Thomas Jefferson Street, NW
P.O. Box 64429   Suite 520
Virginia Beach, VA 23467   Washington, DC 20007
Phone: (804) 523-7570   (202) 337-2273

Fax: (804) 523-7546   (202) 337-3167
Executive Director: Keith A. Fournier

ORIGINS AND DEVELOPMENT

The American Center for Law and Justice was founded by Reverend Pat Robertson in late 1990 as a not-for-profit public interest law firm and educational organization dedicated to defending traditional values. The center is working to develop a national network of attorneys and, in addition to the Virginia Beach and Washington offices, has regional offices in Atlanta, Mobile, and New Hope, Kentucky.

MISSION STATEMENT

"The American Center for Law and Justice . . . is dedicated to the promotion of pro-liberty, pro-life and pro-family causes. . . . As a not-for-profit organization that does not charge for its legal services, the American Center for Law and Justice is dependent upon God and the resources He provides through the time, talent and gifts of people who share our concerns over the erosion of our religious and civil liberties."

ORGANIZATION AND FUNDING

The ACLJ functions out of its national headquarters but has affiliate offices in several locations. It appears that these are offices of other groups pursuing the same agenda. For example, Jay Sekulow of Christian Advocates Serving Evangelism* and Thomas P. Monaghan of Free Speech Advocates serve as counsel for the center. Since the center does not charge for its services, all funding comes from individual contributors. The 1993 budget is projected to be approximately $6 million.

POLICY CONCERNS AND TACTICS

"The Center engages in litigation, provides legal services, renders advice and counsel to clients, and supports attorneys who are involved in defending the religious and civil liberties of Americans."

AFFILIATION

Independent Evangelical.

PUBLICATIONS

Law & Justice (quarterly journal).

AMERICAN CIVIL LIBERTIES UNION (ACLU)

132 West 43rd Street   122 Maryland Avenue, NE
New York, NY 10036   Washington, DC 20002
Phone: (212) 944-9800   (202) 544-1681
Fax: (212) 354-5290   (202) 546-0738
Executive Director: Ira Glasser

ORIGINS AND DEVELOPMENT

The ACLU was founded in 1920 by Roger Baldwin, who fought to free prisoners jailed by the United States for holding antiwar views. The organization he founded has played important roles in critical cases before the courts involving civil liberties, including the right of John Scopes to teach evolution. It has taken stands that build a high barrier between church and state, including religious displays on public property. The ACLU has taken strong stands on the teaching of religion in public schools and school prayer. Schools "may teach about religion as a force in human events, but they may not promote religion." Their position has been consistently opposed to subsidy of parochial education. "The constitutional right to seek a parochial eduation is not a right to have that education subsidized."

MISSION STATEMENT

"To defend and preserve individual rights and liberties guaranteed by the U.S. Constitution, including the Bill of Rights, as well as state constitutions and state and federal statutes designed to implement those rights and liberties."

ORGANIZATION AND FUNDING

The 1991 budget of the ACLU was $20 million, of which 60 percent was raised from membership dues and contributions, 25 percent from foundation grants, 11 percent from court-awarded attorneys' fees, and 4 percent from other sources. The ACLU has 280,000 members, with affiliates in all fifty states, and 218 local chapters. The national staff totals 162—119 professionals and forty-three support. By far the majority of the local work of the ACLU is done by lawyers on a volunteer basis.

POLICY CONCERNS AND TACTICS

As a general principle, the ACLU defends the legal rights of individuals against both government and private institutional encroachment. Within this context its current areas of concern are AIDS, particularly privacy issues; censorship; constitutional rights of those in state custody; rights of defendants in criminal proceedings; discrimination in housing, employment, and education based on race, religion, gender, disability, or sexual orientation; freedom of speech, press, and assembly; privacy; religious liberty; reproductive freedom; rights of aliens, immigrants, and refugees; rights of the poor. While the ACLU engages in all the traditional interest group tactics, such as congressional testimony, coalition formation, lobbying at all levels of government, and media outreach, it specializes in litigation to protect individual liberties. In 1992 Ira Glasser suggested exploring constitutional amendments to protect the right of privacy and gender equality. They fear that the religious right has as an ultimate goal "the creation of a Christian theocracy in America."

AFFILIATION

Independent.

PUBLICATIONS

Civil Liberties (quarterly); *Civil Liberties Alert* (quarterly); *First Principles* (bimonthly); *Prison Project Journal* (quarterly); *Reproductive Rights Update* (biweekly); as well as a large number of pamphlets, informational books, and briefing papers, such as *Bill of Rights Bicentennial Briefing Papers, Epidemic of Fear: Survey of AIDS-Discrimination in the 1980s, Immigration Reform Act: Employer Sanctions and Discrimination Prohibitions, Your Right to Privacy, With Liberty and Justice for Women, Lie Detector Testing, The Rights of Older Persons, The Rights of Patients, The Rights of Prisoners, The Rights of Students, Church and State,* and *Crime and Civil Liberties.*

COMMENTS

The *New York Times* has called the ACLU "the nation's oldest mainstream civil liberties group" (January 14, 1990). It is certainly preeminent among groups defending individual liberties against government and large institutions. The ACLU has become controversial as conservatives have struggled to give liberalism a bad image. Indeed, its strong stands for individual rights have led it to defend a wide variety of unsavory people and causes in the pursuit of consistent application of its principles.

AMERICAN COALITION OF UNREGISTERED CHURCHES (ACUC)

P.O. Box 11
2711 South East Street
Indianapolis, IN 46206
Phone: (317) 787-0830
Fax: (317) 781-2775
National Chairman: Greg Dixon

ORIGINS AND DEVELOPMENT

The American Coalition of Unregistered Churches grew out of a symposium on Christian Resistance held by 100 fundamentalist pastors in Chicago during the summer of 1983. Symposium members determined to form a group to encourage fundamentalist churches not to incorporate under state laws (or to disincorporate) and not to pay property taxes, Federal Insurance Contributions Act (FICA) taxes, and so on for church property or employees. The coalition remains a ministry of the Indianapolis Baptist Temple, with expenses picked up by the temple.

MISSION STATEMENT

"The ACUC is a voluntary coalition of Bible-believing pastors and churches who hold fast the historic, fundamental Christian faith. These pastors and churches have united to speak out against government interference with and encroachment upon the God-given rights of churches, pastors, evangelists, and

Christians in America. There is no membership. Participation and support are voluntary. Free-will gifts for the work of the ACUC are gratefully received.

"The ACUC believes that Churches must be unregistered and free as the embassies of God on earth. The pulpit must be free to cry out against public servants whenever necessary. Unless we do so now, it will not be long before the voice of the preachers and churches will be silenced forever through registration, licensure, regulation and taxation."

ORGANIZATION AND FUNDING

The American Coalition of Unregistered Churches has no formal members; it is maintained by voluntary contributions from regular participants. It holds annual information conferences and annual prayer and fasting conferences.

POLICY CONCERNS AND TACTICS

ACUC provides an interesting perspective on religious group activism. Those in fellowship believe in as total a separation of church and state as possible and that any cooperation on the part of the churches with government must be totally voluntary, for example, participation in fire prevention measures. Specifically, the group holds that churches should not be incorporated; collect or pay Social Security taxes; use zip codes (use judicial districts instead); apply for zoning permits, building permits, or licensure of any kind; obey court orders concerning garnisheed wages; sign state marriage licenses; file or sign any state forms of any kind; allowing building code or fire inspection, and so on.

In addition to its educational mission, explaining biblical principles and constitutional issues, ACUC will provide encouragement and assistance to churches and pastors that come under government attack. Such assistance may be legal or financial, as each situation dictates.

AFFILIATION

Independent fundamentalist (most participants are Baptist).

PUBLICATIONS

The Trumpet (occasional) and a monthly newsletter. "Sound of the Trumpet," a radio broadcast, is available upon request.

AMERICAN ETHICAL UNION (AEU)

2 West 64th Street   6214 Crathie Lane
New York, NY 10023   Bethesda, MD 20816
Phone: (212) 873-6500   (301) 229-3759
Fax: (212) 595-7258
Executive Secretaries: Margaret E. Jones (New York office), Herb Blinder (Bethesda office)

ORIGINS AND DEVELOPMENT

The American Ethical Union was founded in 1887 and now is a federation of some twenty local ethical societies in the United States. It is affiliated with the International Humanist and Ethical Union. It once shared Washington offices with the Unitarian Universalist Association* and the American Humanist Association but created a separate volunteer-staffed office of its own in the early 1960s.

MISSION STATEMENT

''Ethical culture is a humanistic religious and educational movement inspired by the ideal that the supreme aim of human life is working to create a more humane society. Our faith is in the capacity and responsibility of human beings to act in their personal relationships and in the larger community to help create a better world. Our commitment is to the worth and dignity of the individual, and to treating each human being so as to bring out the best in him or her. Members join together in ethical societies to assist each other in developing ethical ideas and ideals . . . to celebrate life's joys and support each other through life's crises . . . to work together to improve our world and the world of our children.''

ORGANIZATION AND FUNDING

The AEU has a membership of 4,500 divided among the local societies. The Washington Office has a volunteer executive secretary and a 1993 budget of less than $10,000.

POLICY CONCERNS AND TACTICS

The AEU's interests include human rights, humanistic ethics, world peace, and especially education. While it is primarily a service organization, it does monitor legislation, make the organization's positions known to Congress and federal regulatory agencies, and maintain a speakers' bureau. Through the *Washington Report,* the office alerts members to issues related to their interests in promoting gun control, strengthening families and children, advocating separation of church and state, and civil rights and liberties in general. Members are urged to contact their own members of Congress. The office participates in the Religious Coalition for Abortion Rights* and works with other faith groups on issues held in common.

AFFILIATION

Humanistic, secular.

PUBLICATIONS

Dialogue (quarterly); *Religious Education Newsletter* (monthly); *Washington Report* (ten per year).

AMERICAN FAMILY ASSOCIATION (AFA)

P.O. Box 2440
Tupelo, MS 38803
Phone: (601) 844-5036

Fax: (601) 844-9176
Executive Director: Donald E. Wildmon

ORIGINS AND DEVELOPMENT

The American Family Association began as the National Federation for Decency begun by Rev. Wildmon in 1977. The name was changed in 1988. As a result of being sued for its boycott activities, the AFA created a legal branch, the American Family Association Law Center, in 1990. The Law Center both defends the AFA and its activities and also trains lawyers and prosecutors in the effective use of obscenity laws.

MISSION STATEMENT

"To promote the Biblical ethic of decency in American Society with a primary emphasis on television and other media." AFA encourages a positive emphasis in the media on "clean, constructive, wholesome and family oriented" programs.

ORGANIZATION AND FUNDING

The AFA has some 425,000 members divided into some 560 local branches and chapters. The budget for 1992 was estimated to be about $5,000,000, of which $750,000 went to the Law Center. Money is raised primarily from individual donations.

POLICY CONCERNS AND TACTICS

AFA focuses its attention on mass media portrayal of sex and violence that it sees as deviant, anti-family, and violating basic norms of decency. AFA drew a great deal of attention for its efforts to halt National Endowment for the Arts's funding of controversial sexual/artistic projects. It uses a wide variety of tactics from simple publicity to boycotts. A most effective means has been placement of advertisements in national newspapers and magazines soliciting signatures of people who support its efforts.

AFFILIATION

Independent Protestant.

PUBLICATIONS

AFA Journal (eleven per year); *Anti-Christian Bias in America; The Case Against Pornography; Christianity and Humanism: A Study in Contrasts; Executive Summary: Images of Children; Crime and Violence in Playboy, Penthouse, and Hustler; A Guide to What One Person Can Do About Pornography; The Home Invaders; The Man the Networks Love to Hate; Pornography: A Report; Public Schools Sex Education: A Report* (pamphlets and reports). In addition, the AFA Legal Center publishes *The Christian Lawyer* (monthly).

COMMENTS

The following comments were reported in *Public Interest Profiles, 1992–93* (Washington, DC: Foundation for Public Affairs, 1993): "Rev. Donald Wildmon . . . is one of the most powerful, effective and least-understood leaders of the religious right. To oppose him is to need to know him. He has been called the 'Ayatollah of the Airwaves,' 'nutcase,' and 'Puritan prude'—and worse. To the electronic media and the publishing industry, the 50 year old reverend is the foremost advocate of censorship in America.

"Don Wildmon is hardly a household name, but almost everyone has heard about the controversies to which he is party. In the past few years the Mississippi-based United Methodist minister has spearheaded efforts to stop federal funding of 'obscene' or 'anti-Christian' art. It was Wildmon who brought Andre Serrano's . . . photograph of a plastic statue of Jesus in a bottle of the artist's urine—to the attention of Congress and the media. . . . He has forced such major advertisers as Ralston Purina, General Mills, Domino's pizza, Clorox and Noxell to not sponsor the 'offensive' TV shows on his hit list. Pepsi dropped a $5 million ad campaign featuring Madonna under pressure from Wildmon. In 1989 he cost NBC $1 million by leaning on would-be-sponsors for *Roe vs Wade,* a docudrama about the Supreme Court decision guaranteeing a woman's right to abortion. His successful advertiser boycotts—and threats of boycotts—have fundamentally altered the television industry. And Wildmon hasn't peaked yet. . . .

"Though Wildmon is often pigeonholed as an obscure moralist, he is in fact a top religious-right leader who has been on the boards of such groups as the Council for National Policy, Christian Voice,[*] the American Coalition for Traditional Values and the Coalition for Religious Freedom" (*In These Times,* July 4–17, 1990).

"Boycotts by conservative outfits like the American Family Association have made advertisers more sensitive to consumers and less tolerant of the networks" (*U.S. News & World Report,* Sept. 21, 1992).

AMERICAN FREEDOM COALITION (AFC)

7777 Leesburg Pike
Suite 314 N
Falls Church, VA 22043
Phone: (703) 790-8700
Fax: (703) 790-8711
President: Robert Grant

ORIGINS AND DEVELOPMENT

The American Freedom Coalition was formed in 1986 as a grass-roots organization, but with financial support from the Unification church.

MISSION STATEMENT

It is the task of the AFC to represent common religious values in the political process, based on the conviction that such common values underlie the differences among Republicans and Democrats, African Americans and whites, men and women, and Catholics, Protestants, Mormons, and Jews but are often lost in public debate.

ORGANIZATION AND FUNDING

The AFC is a grass-roots network of 300,000 individual members organized into ten regions encompassing all fifty states. There are eight national staff members and an annual budget of over $1 million. AFC is supported primarily by direct mail solicitation but also receives some major donations, including support from the Unification church.

POLICY CONCERNS AND TACTICS

The AFC is a conservative group that is attempting to solve social problems and family-related problems by applying conservative principles. At one time it focused on support for the contras in Nicaragua. Most recently it has supported a "Unite to Serve America" campaign to strengthen community-building activists in inner-city neighborhoods.

AFFILIATION

Independent Ecumenical.

PUBLICATIONS

American Freedom Journal (currently suspended publication).

COMMENTS

According to Reverend Robert Grant, AFC takes no positions on religious doctrinal questions, and while it has publicly acknowledged its business connection with the Unification church, it currently has no Unification members on its national board.

AMERICAN FRIENDS SERVICE COMMITTEE (AFSC)

1501 Cherry Street
Philadelphia, PA 19102-1403
Phone: (215) 241-7000
Fax: (215) 864-0104
Executive Secretary: Kara Newell

1822 R Street, NW
Washington, DC 20009
(202) 483-3341
(202) 232-3197

ORIGINS AND DEVELOPMENT

The American Friends Service Committee was founded in 1917 to allow conscientious objectors to aid European civilians injured in World War I. The AFSC was established by the Religious Society of Friends but is supported and staffed by individuals sharing basic values of the committee, regardless of religious affiliation. It attempts to relieve human suffering and find new approaches to world peace and social justice through nonviolence. In 1955 the AFSC published *Speak Power to Truth,* which presented a strong, if controversial, argument for pacifism. More recently the AFSC established an affiliate called the National Action/Research on the Military Industrial Complex, which works to provide educational resources and action tools on human rights and disarmament issues to interested social change groups. It has nine regional groups, and thirty members sit on its board. It has been a co-recipient of the Nobel Peace Prize.

MISSION STATEMENT

The American Friends Service Committee claims to be ''an expression of Quaker faith in action.'' ''We hold a vision of a world where justice and peace prevail, where conflicts are resolved nonviolently, and where each person and group is assured the opportunity to live in dignity and participate in the decisions affecting their lives. We work to bring about a nonviolent society free from all forms of oppression.'' The purpose of the Washington Office is two-part: ''to bring AFSC's experience and perspective to bear on policy makers in Washington, D.C. and to listen for policy developments of concern to AFSC. The Washington office remains open to opportunities for mediation and reconciliation as well as for effective advocacy.''

ORGANIZATION AND FUNDING

The AFSC is divided into three divisions: community relations, peace education, and international relief. AFSC's work in twenty-two countries and forty-three program sites in the United States includes economic development, refugee relief, peace education, and community organizing. The AFSC staff totals 385 nationally and overseas and has a 1993 budget of approximately $25 million, most of which is raised by donations from members, Society of Friends gatherings, and a mass mailing solicitation. In addition AFSC has nine regional offices within the United States and is affiliated with Quaker organizations around the world. While no exact membership figures are available, its newsletter has a circulation of 80,000.

POLICY CONCERNS AND TACTICS

All of AFSC's policy objectives seek to eliminate human suffering and find nonviolent solutions to achieve world peace and social justice. While the great majority of the Service Committee's efforts go directly to service among the poor, suffering, and dispossessed around the world, a significant effort is made to educate citizens about nonviolent alternatives to problem solving. The Washington Office in particular focuses on making the AFSC's views known to Congress and appropriate federal agencies. While AFSC staffers do some lobbying, they also utilize coalitions to press for their goals.

AFFILIATION

Society of Friends (Quakers).

PUBLICATIONS

Annual Report; Quaker Service Bulletin (semiannual newsletter); the *Literature Resources Catalog, 1991–1992,* which lists forty or so titles available from AFSC.

AMERICAN ISRAEL PUBLIC AFFAIRS COMMITTEE (AIPAC)

440 1st Street, NW
Suite 600
Washington, DC 20001
Phone: (202) 639-5200
Fax: (202) 347-4889
Executive Director: Neil Sher

ORIGINS AND DEVELOPMENT

AIPAC was founded in 1954 as an outgrowth of the American Zionist Council. It is a single-issue registered lobby in support of Israel that functions as an umbrella agency for other pro-Israeli organizations. Although a secular organization that believes support of Israel is important and positive for the United States, it works closely with many Jewish religious agencies in America. Many of the top leaders of the latter organizations serve on its board. Thomas A. Dine, former executive director, called his group "American as apple pie," and he explained it as a support system to policymakers who are concerned with Israel's security. It is not a political action committee (PAC) in terms of giving or bundling contributions to candidates for office.

MISSION STATEMENT

AIPAC strives to "secure economic assistance for Israel, obtain military aid for Israel, strengthen congressional support for Israel, reduce arms sales to Arab States, help Soviet Jews emigrate, secure aid for resettlement of immigrants in Israel, combat the Arab boycott, and counter Arab propaganda."

ORGANIZATION AND FUNDING

The Washington staff of approximately 150 persons works out of a tightly secured office with a budget of over $14 million, secured by after-tax donations from a membership of 55,000. Six of the staff members are registered lobbyists. They keep close watch on the Congress, following legislation, gathering information, doing research, preparing speeches, and issuing statements and analyses of pertinent issues. AIPAC also has offices in nine other American cities. It is well known for being able to mobilize grass-roots support very quickly through action alerts. The *New York Times* has called it "the most powerful, best-run and effective foreign policy interest group in Washington."

POLICY CONCERNS AND TACTICS

Its major concerns of the last few years have been foreign aid and the Middle East peace process. As an explicit lobby, AIPAC is able to concentrate fully on lobbying the Congress and the executive branch. Closely allied with AIPAC is Near East Research, Inc., a nonprofit, tax-exempt organization.

AFFILIATION

Jewish.

PUBLICATIONS

Near East Report (weekly newsletter).

COMMENTS

AIPAC's own evaluation of its acknowledged strength as a lobby stems not from organization skills alone but from the broad support of Israel by Jews and non-Jews alike.

AMERICAN JEWISH COMMITTEE (AJC)

165 East 56th Street	1156 15th Street, NW
New York, NY 10022	Washington, DC 20005
Phone: (212) 751-4000	(202) 785-4200
Fax: (212) 319-0975	(202) 785-4115

Executive Vice President: David A. Harris

ORIGINS AND DEVELOPMENT

The American Jewish Committee is one of the oldest human relations organizations in the United States. It was founded in 1906, following a series of pogroms in Russia that had killed thousands of Jews and had left other thousands homeless. It began with a membership of only fifty American Jews. Its membership includes Jews from all three traditions—Orthodox, Conservative, and reform—and it crosses lines of liberal-conservative or Democrat-Republican. After World War II, it expanded in size and scope and supported the rights of non-Jews as well, particularly the civil rights of African Americans. It has successfully impacted many political and social issues. It is one of twelve national agencies that constitute the National Jewish Community Relations Advisory Council (NJCRAC).

MISSION STATEMENT

''Protects the rights and freedoms of Jews the world over; combats bigotry and anti-Semitism and promotes human rights for all; works for the security of Israel and deepened understanding between Americans and Israelis; advocates public policy positions rooted in American democratic values and the perspectives of the Jewish heritage; and enhances the creative vitality of the Jewish people.''

ORGANIZATION AND FUNDING

The American Jewish Committee had a 1991 budget of $15.7 million. Of this 80 percent was raised from contributions; 8 percent came from legacies and bequests, rent, interest, and dividends; 6 percent came from membership dues; and 6 percent from sale of publications. The AJC has a membership of 50,000 and thirty branch offices across the nation, as well as an office in Israel. In addition, the AJC has developed a number of affiliate institutes and programs organized and supported to pursue specific interest areas: the Institute for American Pluralism, the Skirball Institute on American Values; the Institute on American Jewish-Israeli Relations; The Nathan Appelman Institute for the Advancement of Christian-Jewish Understanding; the Hilda Katz Blaustein Leadership Development Program; the Jacob Blaustein Institute for the Advancement of Human Rights; the William Petschek National Jewish Family Center; the Ruth U. Samuels Institute for Interreligious Programs in International Relations; the Mirowitz Center for Central and Eastern European Affairs; and the Lawrence and Lee Romer Center for German-Jewish Relations.

POLICY CONCERNS AND TACTICS

AJC continues its primary concern with countering anti-Semitism and political extremism; it also promotes democratic pluralism and human rights around the world, with an emphasis on religious liberty; it is a strong supporter of Israeli security and the quality of Jewish life in the United States. AJC engages in coalition formation, congressional testimony, media outreach, and litigation to pursue its objectives.

AFFILIATION

Jewish.

PUBLICATIONS

Commentary (monthly); *AJC Journal* (quarterly); *American Jewish Yearbook* (annual); plus a large number of books, pamphlets, briefing papers, and videos, such as *Anti-Zionism: The Sophisticated Anti-Semitism; Crown Heights: A Case Study in Anti-Semitism and Community Relations; The Dimensions of American Jewish Liberalism; Israel in a Postcommunist World; Japanese Attitudes Toward Jews; The Jewish Dimension of the Yugoslav Crisis; The New Face of Anti-Semitism in Romania; The 1992 New York City Intergroup Relations Survey; The Quality of American Jewish Life; United Germany and Jewish Concerns; What Do Americans Think About Jews?; What Do We Know About Black Anti-Semitism?*

COMMENTS

The American Jewish Committee is one of the most influential interest groups in Washington. With a staff of 214 (120 professional and 94 support) and with a long tradition of working with politicians, the AJC has developed an expertise that is well respected.

AMERICAN JEWISH CONGRESS (JEWCON)

15 East 84th Street
New York, NY 10028
Phone: (212) 879-4500
Fax: (212) 249-3672
Executive Director: Henry Siegman

2027 Massachusetts Avenue, NW
Washington, DC 20036
(202) 332-4001
(202) 387-3434

ORIGINS AND DEVELOPMENT

In 1918 a meeting of leading American Jewish organizations was held in Philadelphia to formulate a program to assist European Jews after World War I and to name a delegation to the Versailles Peace Conference. When these goals were reached, according to a written agreement among the attending groups, the Congress was to disband. However, a number of Zionist members assembled the next day to lay the foundation for an ongoing group, which was finally fully operational in 1928. The American Jewish Congress became a leader of anti-Nazi efforts before World War II. In 1945 it shifted directions. Believing that the welfare of Jews depended on a broadly liberal, democratic political regime, it worked within American society to eliminate racial discrimination, support a vigorous separation of church and state, and in general support liberal causes. Internationally it supported a militarily strong, independent Israel, which it continues to do. It also supports efforts to secure civil rights for Jews in the former Soviet Union.

MISSION STATEMENT

"To secure political rights and equal status of Jews in America; to enlist the power and influence of America for the protection of Israel and of Jewish communities abroad; and to enlist American Jews in the struggle to safeguard and enlarge democratic pluralism and constitutional protections for all Americans."

ORGANIZATION AND FUNDING

The American Jewish Congress had a 1993 budget of approximately $6 million, of which 60 percent came from direct fund-raising efforts, 20 percent from membership dues, and 20 percent from publications, bequests, grants, convention income, and funds from local Jewish federations and other miscellaneous sources.

The congress has 50,000 members and 13 regional offices with 145 local chapters. It has a national staff of 100 (30 professional and 70 support).

POLICY CONCERNS AND TACTICS

Current concerns are passage of the Religious Liberty Restoration Act, prayer in public facilities, reproductive freedom, Black-Jewish relations, bioethics, Israeli security, the Arab boycott, Soviet Jewry, and European anti-Semitism.

The American Jewish Congress participates in coalition formation, boycotts, congressional testimony, litigation, and media outreach.

AFFILIATION

Jewish.

PUBLICATIONS

Judaism (quarterly); *Boycott Report* (nine times a year); *Congress Monthly* (seven times a year); as well as books, reports, and briefing papers, such as *A Bankrupt Palestinian Policy; Fetal Tissue Transplant Research; Israel's Search for Peace and American Jews; Less Suffering, Less Fear: Meeting the Human*

Needs of America in the 90's; Religion in the Public Schools: Questions and Answers; Religious Holidays in the Public Schools: Questions and Answers; Resolution on Middle East Peace; Return of the Hard Line: Arafat's 1989 Intifada Message to the Palestinians.

AMERICAN LIFE LEAGUE (ALL)

P.O. Box 1350
Stafford, VA 22554
Phone: (703) 659-4171, (202) 690-2049
Fax: (703) 659-2586
President: Judith Brown

ORIGINS AND DEVELOPMENT

Begun in 1979, it claims 300,000 individual and family members, with fifty-three chapters.

MISSION STATEMENT

''To educate the public on life issues and generate support for prolife, pro-family legislation, primarily the Paramount Human Life Amendment; and work on related issues such as stopping permissive sex education in the schools and taxpayer funding of abortion and abortion-promoting activities.''

ORGANIZATION AND FUNDING

With a budget of $6.8 million in 1993, ALL has a staff of forty-five, twenty professional and twenty-five support, plus five part-time workers and an intern. Sixty-five percent of the budget comes from contributions, 22 percent from magazine and newsletter subscriptions, and 13 percent from the sale of educational materials.

POLICY CONCERNS AND TACTICS

Current concerns are euthanasia, living will legislation, school-based birth control dispensaries, parental consent/notification laws, and, of course, abortion. ALL has been an active participant in pro-life coalitions; it has engaged in boycotts, demonstrations, and marches and provided pro-life advertising and educational literature. Members have testified before congressional committees on numerous occasions.

AFFILIATION

Independent Christian.

PUBLICATIONS

ALL About Issues (nine times a year) and *ALL News* (biweekly), as well as numerous pamphlets, broadsides, and books, such as *Aborting Planned Parenthood; Abortion: Choice or Chance?; Abortion-Free Zones; The Abortion Holocaust: An Introduction; American Life League's Position on Birth Control; Birth Control: Why Are They Lying to Women?; Choices in Matters of Life and*

Death; 50 Questions on Abortion, Euthanasia and Related Issues; The Fetus as Transplant Donor; and *A Matter of Conscience.*

COMMENTS

''The American Life League . . . in some respects, makes the National Right to Life Committee seem 'liberal' '' (Nat Hentoff review of *Abortion, Boston Globe,* 10 June 1990).

AMERICANS FOR PEACE NOW (AFPN)

27 W. 20th Street	2025 Pennsylvania Avenue, NW
Ninth Floor	Suite 716
New York, NY 10011	Washington, DC 20006
Phone: (212) 645-6262	(202) 728-1893
Fax: (212) 645-7355	(202) 728-1895
Executive Director: Gail Pressberg	

ORIGINS AND DEVELOPMENT

Founded in 1981 as a support group of American Jews representing the Peace Now Movement in Israel. Peace Now, also known as Shalom Achshav, is an Israeli peace movement that supports a negotiated settlement between the Israeli government and Palestinian leaders based on exchanging territory for peace and security guarantees.

MISSION STATEMENT

''Americans for Peace Now is a national organization of American Jews committed to a strong and secure Israel. We support the Israeli peace movement—PEACE NOW—because attempts to rule over the Palestinians or to annex the land in which they live jeopardize Israel's security and threaten Israel's democratic, Jewish character.''

ORGANIZATION AND FUNDING

APN is an individual membership organization of about 10,000 people and over two dozen chapters throughout the country. Its 1993 budget was around $1,300,000, raised through membership fees, programs, and special events. It has a staff of ten.

POLICY CONCERNS AND TACTICS

APN takes as its primary function to educate American Jews about the goals and history of Peace Now, to provide support for their viewpoint on how to achieve peace in Israel, and where possible to influence the American Congress and the non-Jewish population in a positive manner in order to provide continued support for Israel. APN's primary tactic is publicity through its newsletter, news releases, and grass-roots activism.

AFFILIATION

Jewish.

PUBLICATIONS

Peace Now: A Newsletter for Our Friends in North America (three per year), as well as educational pamphlets on the West Bank and Lebanon and a Platform Statement.

COMMENTS

The Forward, an American Jewish newspaper, writes that "Americans for Peace Now has emerged among the half-dozen or so Jewish groups focused on the Israeli-Palestinian problem as a dominant force, listened to on Capitol Hill, cited in the press, and no longer ignored by the Jewish establishment." *Ha'aretz,* a daily in Israel, says that Americans for Peace Now, once a marginal organization on the American Jewish scene, has significantly gained importance with Bill Clinton's presidential victory: "Some of its active members are both officials in the new Administration and personal friends of Clinton's and their position on the Middle East will influence the new Administration's decisions" (5 January 1993).

AMERICANS FOR RELIGIOUS LIBERTY (ARL)

P.O. Box 6656
Silver Spring, MD 20906
Phone: (301) 598-2447
Fax: (301) 598-1685
Executive Director: Edd Doerr

ORIGINS AND DEVELOPMENT

"In early 1981 The Voice of Reason was founded in the midwest and the Center for Moral Democracy was formed on the east coast. The principal founders of the two groups were, respectively, Sherwin T. Wine and Edward L. Ericson. In early 1982 the two groups merged under the Voice of Reason name. With the growth of membership, the organization's board voted in October 1983 to change the name to Americans for Religious Liberty."

MISSION STATEMENT

"We believe in the American tradition of religious and intellectual freedom within a secular democratic state. . . . A free and secular democratic state guarantees religious liberty. It guarantees equal freedom to the religious and the non-religious. It makes religious faith a private matter and gives no special privileges to any religious idea or practice. Both prayers sponsored by public schools and public aid to private schools are violations of its integrity. . . . In a world where many voices of extremism seek to subvert freedom, we need to be voices of reason and to rally to its support."

ORGANIZATION AND FUNDING

ARL had a 1992 budget of $196,480 and a membership of 9,400.

POLICY CONCERNS AND TACTICS

ARL was formed to counter attacks on church-state separation by sectarian special interests. ARL's principal foci, but not its only ones, include opposing efforts to provide tax support for nonpublic schools, to move public schools away from a position of religious neutrality, and to limit birth control and abortion rights. ARL is primarily an educational organization engaged in publishing, research, and consulting and operates a speakers' bureau.

AFFILIATION

Ecumenical secular.

PUBLICATIONS

Voice of Reason (quarterly) plus several books: *Abortion Rights and Fetal "Personhood,"* edited by Edd Doerr and James Prescott; *The Great Quotations on Religious Freedom,* edited by Albert Menendez and Edd Doerr; *Church Schools and Public Money: The Politics of Parochiaid,* by Edd Doerr and Albert Menendez; *Visions of Reality: What Fundamentalist Schools Teach,* by Albert Menendez.

AMERICANS UNITED FOR LIFE (AUL)

342 S. Dearborn Street
Suite 1804
Chicago, IL 60604
Phone: (312) 786-9494
Fax: (312) 786-2131

ORIGINS AND DEVELOPMENT

Founded in 1971, Americans United for Life claims to be the oldest national pro-life organization. It has 7,500 contributors, is directed by a twenty-six-member board, including some Protestant and Catholic clergy, and has a staff of twenty-three, of whom seven are lawyers. The Legal Defense Fund serves as the legal arm of the antiabortion movement. They have participated in more than twenty cases before the Supreme Court, including *Roe v. Wade.* It has been active in all fifty states. It has had a regional office in Raleigh, North Carolina, and plans are being made to open an office in Washington, D.C.

MISSION STATEMENT

"Americans United for Life (AUL) is working to re-establish societal conviction and public policies that reflect an unconditional valuation and protection of human life from conception to natural death." The first objective of AUL is to overthrow the Supreme Court's decision in *Roe v. Wade.* It is seeking to write, pass, and defend laws that give every conceived child a right to be born. They also seek to convince the public that every unborn child and mother need protection from abortion. They believe that they are providing "an intelligence" that is impacting the courts and the public toward this end.

ORGANIZATION AND FUNDING

Americans United for Life, Inc. had a 1993 total of revenues of $1.2 million and nearly the same amount of expenses. The twenty-five member governing board includes Congressmen Henry Hyde and Christopher Smith.

POLICY CONCERNS AND TACTICS

AUL concentrates on three or four areas of activity. The first of these is legal, and they are active in state legislatures as well as the Congress and in state and federal courts. In education, they sponsor periodic forums including annual conferences for seventy-five pro-life legislators from thirty-four states.

AFFILIATION

Nondenominational.

PUBLICATIONS

AUL has published thirty monographs and five books, including *Life Docket* (monthly pro-life news summary sent to over 3,500 reporters and decision makers); *AUL Insights* (periodic); *Lex Vitae* (quarterly report on pro-life litigation and legislation); and *AUL Briefing Memo* (periodic in-depth analysis of pro-life legal issues).

AMERICANS UNITED FOR SEPARATION OF CHURCH AND STATE (AU)

8120 Fenton Street
Silver Spring, MD 20910
Phone: (301) 589-3707
Fax: (301) 495-9173
Executive Director: Rev. Barry Lynn

ORIGINS AND DEVELOPMENT

Begun in 1947 by a group of conservative Protestant clergy and laymen concerned about the rising power and political activism of the Roman Catholic church, Americans United for Separation of Church and State was originally known as Protestants and Other Americans United for the Separation of Church and State. Widely perceived as "anti-Catholic" (not without some justification), the group changed its name to Americans United. Along with the name change came a far more professional, less strident, issue-oriented approach to promoting its values. While it still finds itself in opposition to many positions taken by the Catholic hierarchy, it also opposes certain initiatives taken by conservative Protestant groups. Perhaps because of its history, the group is somewhat unusual in that its membership currently comes from all across the political spectrum.

MISSION STATEMENT

"Since 1947 Americans United has worked to protect the constitutional principle of Church-State separation—a vital cornerstone of religious liberty. Americans of many faiths and political viewpoints, individuals from all walks of life, have come together to defend their freedoms."

ORGANIZATION AND FUNDING

Americans United has a membership of about 50,000, many of whom are organized into 115 state and local groups. Its budget for 1993 was $1,100,000. Funds come from membership dues plus donations from individual churches and associations such as Baptist State Conventions and the Seventh Day Adventist Church.

POLICY CONCERNS AND TACTICS

Traditionally AU has opposed all efforts, whether on a national, state, or local level, to provide public financial support for sectarian schools in whatever form such aid might take. While it continues that effort, more recently it has opposed efforts to bring religion into the public schools, whether through public prayers or religious activities. On a more positive note, it has joined with a number of groups to support the objective teaching about religion, its role in American history in public schools, and the rights of students to engage in truly voluntary and private religious exercises.

AU was one of the first religious interest groups to rely primarily on litigation to achieve its objectives, and filing cases in court continues to be a major tactic. AU members and staffers also provide information to national and state legislators and engage in lobbying and join coalitions when appropriate. Through press releases, publications, and participation in academic conferences, it also continues a broad citizen education program.

AFFILIATION

Independent Protestant.

PUBLICATIONS

Church and State (monthly), as well as occasional research studies and topical pamphlets.

AMNESTY INTERNATIONAL (AI)

322 8th Avenue   1118 22nd Street, NW
New York, NY 10001   Washington, DC 20037
Phone: (212) 807-8400   (202) 775-5161
Fax: (212) 627-1451   (202) 775-5992
Executive Director: John G. Healey   DC office: Carey Johnson

ORIGINS AND DEVELOPMENT

In 1960 Peter Benenson, a forty-year-old British lawyer, was deeply moved by an article describing how two Portuguese students in Lisbon had been sentenced to seven years in prison for raising their glasses in a public toast to freedom during the Salazar dictatorship. He decided to ''bombard governments with letters of protest at the imprisonment of prisoners of conscience.'' Benenson, Eric Baker, and Louis Blam-Cooper, along with several others, launched a trial one-year campaign called ''Appeal for Amnesty, 1961.'' This campaign received such an overwhelming response that out of it Amnesty International was formed. AI currently has more than 4,000 local groups around the world. At the end of 1990 the organization was working on more than 3,000 cases involving more than 4,300 individuals in eighty-three countries. An additional 1,296 cases had been closed during that year. To date AI has worked on behalf of 42,000 prisoners and has been able to close over 38,000 cases.

MISSION STATEMENT

Amnesty International works worldwide to secure the observance of the Universal Declaration of Human Rights. AI works for the release of men and women detained for their conscientiously held beliefs, color, ethnic origin, sex, religion, or language, provided they have neither used nor advocated violence. AI opposes torture of any kind and the death penalty without reservation and advocates fair and prompt trials for all prisoners.

ORGANIZATION AND FUNDING

AI operates under a mandate to remain independent, impartial, and voluntary. Therefore no money is accepted from governments. The international organization is run entirely on contributions from its members and supporters from around the world. Currently there are in excess of 100,000 members and 100 staff in Amnesty International USA. There are the national office and five regional offices, a Washington, D.C., office, and an Urgent Action Network Office. In addition there are 400 local adult groups and 2,700 groups on college, university, and high school campuses around the country.

POLICY CONCERNS AND TACTICS

AI focuses on the release of prisoners of conscience, fair and prompt trials for all political prisoners, an end to the death penalty, and an end to torture or any cruel, inhuman, and degrading treatment or punishment of any prisoner, without reservation. Amnesty applies pressure to governments through letter writing, public demonstrations, media outreach, and official-to-official contact.

AFFILIATION

Independent, nondenominational.

PUBLICATIONS

Amnesty Action (bimonthly) and *Amnesty International Report* (annual). AI also publishes country briefing papers, mission reports, and other special reports as needed.

COMMENTS

Amnesty International was not, strictly speaking, a religious organization in its origins, nor now. However, it is the major force for urging freedom of conscience, respectful treatment of prisoners, and due process of law around the world, all matters of great interest to religion. Therefore, we have included it for the information of our readers.

ANTI-DEFAMATION LEAGUE OF B'NAI B'RITH (ADL)

823 United Nations Plaza
New York, NY 10017

1100 Connecticut Avenue, NW
Suite 1020
Washington, DC 20036

Phone: (212) 490-2525
Fax: (212) 867-0779

(202) 452-8310
(202) 296-2371

Executive Director: Abraham H. Foxman

ORIGINS AND DEVELOPMENT

The Anti-Defamation League was founded by B'nai B'rith in Chicago in 1913 and is one of the nation's oldest and largest civil rights/human relations organizations.

MISSION STATEMENT

''To stop the defamation of the Jewish people and to secure justice and fair treatment for all citizens alike.''

ORGANIZATION AND FUNDING

B'nai B'rith ADL had an operating budget of $30 million in 1991, raised from private contributions. With that it supported a staff of 400, 200 professional and 200 support. B'nai B'rith has thirty U.S. regional offices, an office in Jerusalem, a consulate office for Vatican affairs in Rome, and affiliated offices in Latin America and Canada.

In addition there are several affiliates created and supported for specific areas of concern: Anti-Defamation League Foundation; Leon and Marilyn Klinghoffer Memorial Foundation; Braun Center for Holocaust Studies; Jewish Foundation for Christian Rescuers/ADL; Hidden Child Foundation/ADL.

POLICY CONCERNS AND TACTICS

The Anti-Defamation League is dedicated to combating anti-Semitism, prejudice, and bigotry of all kinds, defending democratic ideals, and safeguarding civil rights. Through its World of Difference Institute, ADL has evolved as a leader in the development of materials, programs, and services that build bridges of communications, understanding, and respect among diverse racial, religious, and ethnic groups. The league releases an annual Audit of Anti-Semitic Incidents, which receives widespread coverage in the United States and abroad. ADL monitors extremists and maintains the largest library/clearinghouse in the United States on this topic. The league pursues litigation in support of civil liberties, provides expert testimony before congressional committees, and presents a wide array of awards to those who support its causes in an outstanding manner. Current concerns include anti-Semitism, discrimination, hate crimes,

Arab-Israeli relations, interfaith relations, separation of church and state, and Holocaust education.

AFFILIATION

Jewish.

PUBLICATIONS

ADL on the Frontline (monthly except July and August); *Law Enforcement Bulletin;* and a series of books, pamphlets, and videotapes such as *Blacklisting Israel: A Current Perspective on the Arab Boycott; Combatting Bigotry on Campus: The Problems and the Strategies for Counteraction; Current Perspectives on the Middle East; Dimensions: A Journal of Holocaust Studies; Discrimination: What to Tell Your Children About Prejudice and Hate; Hate Crime Statutes: A Response to Anti-Semitism, Vandalism, and Violent Bigotry; Hate Groups in America: A Record of Bigotry and Violence;* and *Hate Crime,* a police training video.

COMMENTS

The Anti-Defamation League of B'nai B'rith was the earliest and most successful of antidiscrimination groups and a model for other such groups such as the Catholic League for Religious and Civil Rights.* The *Washington Times* called ADL "the nation's leading monitor of instances of anti-Semitism" (18 May 1989) as reported in *Public Interest Profiles 1992–93* (Washington, DC: Foundation of Public Affairs, 1993).

ASSOCIATION FOR PUBLIC JUSTICE (APJ)

1835 H Forest Drive
Annapolis, MD 21401
Phone: (410) 263-5989
Fax: (410) 263-3857
Executive Director: James W. Skillen

P.O. Box 48368
Washington, DC 20002
(202) 546-9781

ORIGINS AND DEVELOPMENT

The Association for Public Justice was founded in 1969. In 1973 the Center for Public Justice was formed as a tax-exempt education and research unit. Mr. Skillen is director of both organizations.

MISSION STATEMENT

"APJ seeks to provide a perspective on public policy and political service from a biblical standpoint. Members believe that justice is revealed through the work of Jesus Christ, and that biblical revelation can guide citizens in the fulfillment of their responsibility to live justly with all people."

ORGANIZATION AND FUNDING

The APJ has some 1,200 supporters, of whom roughly half are active financial contributors. The national staff consists of three full-time people plus visiting research scholars. Funding for 1992–93 was $100,000 for the Association for

Public Justice and $250,000 for the Center for Public Justice. Financing is provided primarily by supporting members with additional funding through church and foundation grants and corporate contributions.

POLICY CONCERNS AND TACTICS

The Association focuses its efforts on political education and promoting the idea of proportional representation for the United States. It also works to defend the rights of religious and ethnic groups in a pluralistic society. More recently it has worked on developing the idea of welfare responsibility. The association functions something like a think tank. The executive director often testifies before various congressional committees and provides information to legislators. The group also sponsors seminars and workshops for congresspeople and their aides, as well as maintaining a speakers' bureau and media outreach program.

AFFILIATION

Independent Christian.

PUBLICATIONS

Public Justice Report (bimonthly). Also publishes books and reports on specific policy issues.

ASSOCIATION OF JESUIT COLLEGES AND UNIVERSITIES (AJCU)

1424 16th Street, NW
Suite 300
Washington, DC 20036
Phone: (202) 862-9893
Fax: (202) 862-8523
Executive Director: Rev. Paul S. Tipton, S.J.

ORIGIN AND DEVELOPMENT

Founded in 1970 upon the dissolution of the Jesuit Educational Association. At that time it also absorbed the Jesuit Research Council of America.

MISSION STATEMENT

The purpose of the organization is to coordinate educational efforts of Jesuit higher education, collect and disseminate statistics about Jesuit institutions, coordinate and cooperate with other educational associations to promote the interest of private higher education before Congress, and work with government agencies to provide information and present policy positions.

ORGANIZATION AND FUNDING

The AJCU functions on a budget of $300,000 (1993) with a staff of four (one priest and three lay) and occasional volunteer help. Funding comes from the dues of the twenty-eight member institutions and a small number of grants and gifts. It is classified as a trade group.

POLICY CONCERNS AND TACTICS

AJCU monitors all legislation, litigation, and rule making that affect higher education. Its primary concerns at the present time are equal access to federal grants and contracts, funding of scholarships, and government regulation. The AJCU staff does no direct lobbying but joins larger coalitions to present policy positions before Congress and agencies in the executive branch. When issues of extraordinary urgency or importance arise, AJCU requests that board members directly contact their elected representatives.

AFFILIATION

Roman Catholic.

PUBLICATIONS

Annual Directory of Jesuit High Schools and Universities; AJCU Higher Education Report (a monthly newsletter); and the *Directory of Jesuit Degree Programs.*

B

—————————— / ——————————

BAPTIST JOINT COMMITTEE ON PUBLIC AFFAIRS (BJCPA)

200 Maryland Avenue, NE
Washington, DC 20002
Phone: (202) 544-4226
Fax: (202) 544-2094
Executive Director: James M. Dunn

ORIGINS AND DEVELOPMENT

The Baptist Joint Committee was founded in 1945, when four Baptist Conventions voted to maintain an office and staff in Washington, DC. Since that time BJCPA has grown to include eight national Baptist conventions and conferences: (1) American Baptist Churches in the U.S.A.; (2) National Baptist Churches in the U.S.A.; (3) Progressive National Baptist Convention; (4) Baptist Federation of Canada; (5) National Baptist Convention, U.S.A.; (6) Seventh-Day Baptist General Conference; (7) Baptist General Conference; and (8) North American Baptist Conference. The Southern Baptist Convention was a founding member and the chief source of funding. In 1990, however, as the convention became more conservative and less interested in strict separation of church and state, it withdrew funding for the Baptist Joint Committee and organized its own Christian Life Commission.*

MISSION STATEMENT

''To act in the field of public affairs whenever the rights of or Baptist principles of its members are jeopardized through government action; to serve as an information base to its members on policy concerning the group, and to communicate with the President of the United States, the federal and state courts and federal and state governments.'' Motto: ''Because you aren't there, you need a voice.''

ORGANIZATION AND FUNDING

The BJCPA approved a 1994 budget of about $790,000 and a staff of nine. Funding comes primarily from the membership conventions, apportioned according to their size, with about $45,000 coming from independent donations.

POLICY CONCERNS AND TACTICS

The Baptist Joint Committee focuses its efforts on issues of religious liberty and establishment, based on a long Baptist tradition of supporting separation of church and state. The committee has a strong research component, provides expert testimony before congressional committees and regulatory agencies, joins numerous coalitions that support its policy positions, and occasionally goes to court.

AFFILIATION

Independent Baptist.

PUBLICATIONS

Report from the Capitol (ten a year) and *Baptist News Service,* a daily news report to members about events of interest in Washington. BJCPA also publishes staff reports, conference papers, pamphlets, and briefs on religious issues.

COMMENTS

In recent years the Baptist Joint Committee has found itself in conflict with some of its more conservative backers within the Southern Baptist Convention. While the BJCPA opposes prayer in public schools, federal aid for religiously affiliated private schools, and a constitutional amendment banning abortion, more fundamentalist Baptists have begun to support these measures.

B'NAI B'RITH WOMEN (BBW)

1828 L Street, NW
Suite 250
Washington, DC 20036
Phone: (202) 857-1300
Fax: (202) 857-1380
Executive Director: Elaine K. Binder

ORIGINS AND DEVELOPMENT

B'nai B'rith Women was founded in 1897 as a Jewish service organization dedicated to meeting the needs of Jewish women and their families. It is affiliated with B'nai B'rith International but is independent and self-governing.

Membership includes about 100,000 Jewish women in the United States and Canada.

MISSION STATEMENT

"B'nai B'rith Women supports Jewish women in their families, in their communities, and in society. B'nai B'rith Women focuses its programming in three areas: to perpetuate Jewish values and secure world Jewry; to foster the emotional well-being of children and youth; to strengthen the influence and effectiveness of women in the Jewish community and in society."

ORGANIZATION AND FUNDING

B'nai B'rith is an individual membership organization divided into twelve regions and over 700 local groups often associated with local synagogues. Funding in 1992 was approximately $6,000,000, raised from membership dues, bequests, and grants for specific projects.

POLICY CONCERNS AND TACTICS

B'nai B'rith Women continues to be a service organization, funding such things as a home for emotionally disturbed boys in Jerusalem, caregiving for older adults, a "safe-house" system for victims of domestic violence in Canada, the Anti-Defamation League, and various youth programs such as Hillel.

The organization also advocates for women's rights with the U.S. government and before the United Nations, including access to abortion, affirmative action, child care, help for the homeless, health care, and campaign reform. In addition to taking positions it urges its followers to support, B'nai B'rith joins coalitions to strengthen its advocacy role.

AFFILIATION

Jewish.

PUBLICATIONS

Women's World (quarterly newsletter).

BREAD FOR THE WORLD (BFW)

802 Rhode Island Avenue, NE
Washington, DC 20018
Phone: (202) 269-0200
Fax: (202) 529-8546
President: David Beckman

ORIGINS AND DEVELOPMENT

In 1972 a group of Protestants and Catholics met to explore how persons of the Christian faith could be advocates for hungry people. In 1973 a "test group" was formed in New York City, and in 1974 a nationwide effort was begun. BFW has grown to a national movement of over 40,000 individuals organized in 355 local chapters with 2,500 volunteer leaders. In addition, it has received public endorsement from most major Christian denominations, and over 1,000 local congregations support and participate in its work.

MISSION STATEMENT

"Bread for the World is a nationwide Christian movement that seeks justice for the world's hungry people by lobbying our nation's decision makers." Bread for the World does not provide direct relief or development assistance.

ORGANIZATION AND FUNDING

BFW has an operating budget of over $3 million, raised from individual membership dues, contributions from individuals, churches, and religious communities, and grants from foundations. While BFW is essentially an individual membership organization, with members loosely and voluntarily organized into local chapters, it also has what it calls "Covenant Churches," which assist in fund-raising and contacting members of Congress when important issues arise. BFW is emphatically a lobby organization; therefore contributions made to it are not tax-exempt. However, in order to encourage contributions, it has also created the BFW Institute on Hunger and Development, which is tax-exempt and which supports research and educational efforts.

POLICY CONCERNS AND TACTICS

BFW focuses on issues closely related to hunger, ranging from emergency famine relief to immunization of children, to small-scale agricultural development in Third World countries, to domestic nutrition programs, to tax relief for poor families. BFW provides no relief itself but specializes in lobbying Congress and the executive branch. Most recently it has focused on using money cut from the defense budget to support food programs. Its tactics are to have members engage in letter-writing campaigns for specific legislation, meet with their congressional delegations, speak before church and other community groups to develop grass-roots support, and research and develop policy positions to present before legislative committees and other government agencies. It publicizes a scorecard of Congress members' votes on hunger relief issues.

AFFILIATION

Christian Ecumenical.

PUBLICATIONS

Bread for the World Newsletter (bimonthly) and *Action Alert* (monthly legislative bulletin on hunger).

COMMENTS

Bread for the World is one of the more remarkable success stories among religious interest groups. With a common, noncontroversial mission, very broad interdenominational and geographic base, avoidance of divisive policy issues or excessive publicity, and use of traditional mainline lobbying techniques, it has managed to build and sustain a remarkable coalition to support hunger relief legislation. Because it enjoys such broad-based grass-roots support and publicizes congressional voting records, BFW has a good deal of influence on national legislation.

C
/

CATHOLIC CHARITIES USA (CCUSA)

1731 King Street
Suite 200
Alexandria, VA 22314
Phone: (703) 549-1390
Fax: (703) 549-1656
President: Rev. Alfred Kammer, S.J.

ORIGINS

"In 1910 the National Conference of Catholic Charities was convened at Catholic University to bring about a sense of solidarity among more than 800 charitable institutions operating under Catholic auspices throughout the United States." The name was changed in 1990 to Catholic Charities USA. At the present time 633 local Catholic Charities agencies, organized along diocesan lines, make up the membership of the organization.

MISSION STATEMENT

"The national office of Catholic Charities USA shares with its member organizations a mission to provide quality services on the basis of need, to advocate for better conditions to empower individuals and families to live more freely, and to convene other people of good will to join in these endeavors. Ultimately the effectiveness of Catholic Charities USA must be measured by its capacity to do three things: strengthen family life, build communities, and reduce poverty." Basic services are provided by the member agencies; the national office coordinates public policy initiatives, provides liasion with numerous government agencies and legislative committees, and works on leadership and resource development.

ORGANIZATION AND FUNDING

Catholic Charities USA is the national organization representing groups in each diocese. It has a staff of twenty-five and a budget of over $3,300,000, not including money raised and spent by local agencies, a far larger sum. About 25 percent of the budget comes from member agency dues. Contributions account for 12 percent. The rest comes from sale of publications, workshop and training fees, interest income, and restricted funds for designated projects.

POLICY CONCERNS AND TACTICS

In addition to its traditional activities in providing social services on the local diocesan level, Catholic Charities USA has focused on AIDS education and service to those infected, immigration and refugee settlement, disaster relief, homelessness, international adoption, child day care, and elder care.

AFFILIATION

Roman Catholic.

PUBLICATIONS

Charities USA (quarterly); *Social Thought* (scholarly quarterly reporting and developing Catholic social philosophy); *Federal Grants Memo* (newsletter); and *Legislative Update* (tracks social policy activities in Washington and provides Catholic Charities's views and positions on national legislation both to its own agencies and to national decision makers).

COMMENTS

Catholic Charities USA does not receive the publicity of many other interest groups, but it is very active not only in coordinating local agencies but in advocating its positions before Congress and the executive branch. *The Non Profit Times* in its November 1991 issue listed Catholic Charities USA as the nation's largest nonprofit human service organization, and within its areas of interest it has considerable influence. It is also a conduit for numerous government grants for social service delivery. Since 1990 the agency has been a defendant in *Kendrick v. Sullivan,* in which the American Civil Liberties Union* challenged Catholic Charities USA and other religiously affiliated grantees under the Adolescent Family Life Act.

THE CATHOLIC LEAGUE FOR RELIGIOUS AND CIVIL RIGHTS (CLRCR)

1011 First Avenue
New York, NY 10022
Phone: (212) 371-3191
Fax: (212) 371-3394
President: William Donohue

ORIGINS AND DEVELOPMENT

Founded in 1973 by Reverend Virgil Blum, S.J., who served as its president for many years, the league is an individual membership organization with some 17,000 members. There are state chapters in ten states. Headquarters have moved from Milwaukee to Philadelphia to New York as the organization has sought to stabilize itself after the retirement, then death, of Father Blum.

MISSION STATEMENT

''The Catholic League dedicates itself to defending the Faith within the context of American society. . . . It struggles to protect the religious freedom rights and constitutional guarantees of the First Amendment. We insist upon the right of all religious people to worship as they choose, and on the right to believe without intrusion of public policy or ridicule. The Catholic League proclaims the rights of parents to maintain control over the values education of their children, and to maintain the right of parental freedom of choice in the type of education they choose for their children. The Catholic League works with other religious groups embracing the same concerns and professing the same goals and objectives, for the truth is obvious that where one religion is attacked, if that attack is not resisted, all religion is thereby weakened.''

POLICY CONCERNS AND TACTICS

The Catholic League maintains that most Catholics are not aware of the many attacks on the Catholic faith and particularly on its leaders, not only by religious bigots but by mainstream media as well. Therefore it has mounted an educational campaign to generate awareness. It has been very alert to attacks by prochoice advocates who go beyond policy advocacy into anti-Catholic rhetoric or action. More recently it has defended the church against attacks by gay rights groups, particularly ACT-UP. The league continues a traditional effort to collect and disseminate accurate information about Catholic schools in urban areas.

In addition to its newsletter, the league maintains a vigorous media outreach program, initiates and supports legal action to maintain religious liberty, and has an extensive award program to honor public officials who support its views, including the Virgil C. Blum Award, the Catholic League Award, the Equal Justice Under Law Award, and the Religious Freedom Award.

AFFILIATION

Independent Roman Catholic.

PUBLICATIONS

The league publishes *Catholic League Newsletter* (monthly). It also publishes books and pamphlets from time to time on specific subjects.

COMMENTS

The Catholic League is simply an antidefamation league for Catholics. It has engaged in numerous litigations against infringements on religious liberty. Often its simple intervention brings a halt to offensive activity. The league also intervenes on behalf of non-Catholics whom it believes have been injured because of religious belief or action.

CATHOLICS FOR A FREE CHOICE (CFFC)

1436 U Street, NW
Suite 301
Washington, DC 20009
Phone: (202) 986-6093
Fax: (202) 332-7995
Executive Director: Frances Kissling

ORIGINS AND DEVELOPMENT

CFFC was founded in 1973 to promote support for *Roe v. Wade* and education about abortion in the Catholic community and to provide a counterweight in the larger political community to official Catholic doctrine concerning birth control and abortion.

MISSION STATEMENT

"Catholics for a Free Choice is a national educational organization that supports the right to legal reproductive health care, especially to family planning and abortion. CFFC also works to reduce the incidence of abortion and to increase women's choices in childbearing and child-rearing through advocacy of social and economic programs for women, families, and children."

ORGANIZATION AND FUNDING

CFFC has no membership as such but mails its newsletter to about 12,000 "associates," who provide its donor base. The 1993 budget was $1,200,000. There are fourteen full-time staff in the Washington office who maintain contact with activists in twenty-eight states.

POLICY CONCERNS AND TACTICS

CFFC works specifically for women's right to choose abortion when they think it necessary; it also works on the more general area of women's health care needs and economic advancement. Tactics include publication of alternative views within the Catholic community, testimony before Congress, and joining various coalitions.

AFFILIATION

The membership of CFFC is predominantly made up of people who were raised as Catholics and who may or may not be currently active participants in their local parishes. There are some priest and nun members. Not surprisingly the group has no official connection with the Catholic church and is actively opposed by the hierarchy. Indeed, several bishops have stated that no one can be both pro-choice and a Catholic.

PUBLICATIONS

Conscience (monthly) and a series of pamphlets under the general title "Abortion in Good Faith." Pamphlets include *I Support You But I Can't Sign My Name; We Are the Mainstream; The Church in a Democracy: Who Governs?;* and *The History of Abortion in the Catholic Church.* Reports called "Bishop Watch" include *A Church Divided: Catholic Attitudes About Family Planning, Abortion and Teenage Sexuality; Civil Rights Held Hostage: The United States Catholic Conference and the Civil Rights Restoration Act;* and *All Work and No Say.*

COMMENTS

CFFC considers itself primarily an educational and internal advocacy group, but it is an active member of the Religious Coalition for Abortion Rights* and participated in that group's court challenge to the United States Catholic Conference* tax-exempt status. CFFC members conduct special briefing sessions for Catholic members of Congress and have been active participants in numerous demonstrations and marches. Its publications and public announcements have several major themes: there is no unanimity within the Catholic community on abortion, and the hierarchy does not speak for the whole community on this issue; within Catholic history and moral teaching there has been far more diversity than the hierarchy acknowledges; and a person can be both pro-choice and a good Catholic.

CENTER FOR NEW CREATION (CNC)

845 N. Lincoln Street
Arlington, VA 22201
Phone: (703) 528-1446
Fax: (703) 243-5779
Executive Director: CNC has no executive; its leadership functions as a participatory team, hoping to model what it sees as a desirable component of the new creation. All staff members serve on the Board of Directors and have an equal voice in decision making. One contact person is Joan Urbanczyk.

ORIGINS AND DEVELOPMENT

Begun in 1979 by a group of Catholic women working out of their homes, the Center for New Creation has a mailing list of 1,100 persons, of whom 600 are regular contributors. The group has very consciously made itself an ecumenical Christian group, rooted in religious values but not identified with any denomination. It first gained recognition for its role in organizing the 1985 International Peace Ribbon Ceremony—unveiling of a fifteen-mile ribbon put together from 30,000 individual pieces depicting what people would most hate to lose in a nuclear war.

MISSION STATEMENT

The center picks areas for developing public awareness and advocacy that it believes are critical for social justice. These are economic justice, alternatives to violence, Third World development, and women and peacemaking.

ORGANIZATION AND FUNDING

CNC is a small group totally dependent on contributions from individuals; while donations fluctuate, the 1993 budget is about $50,000.

POLICY CONCERNS AND TACTICS

Current areas of concern are homelessness, violence and injustice in the Middle East, and the North American Free Trade Agreement (NAFTA). The Center for New Creation works to inform and motivate its members concerning its core issues, then advocates for them with policymakers. CNC considers itself a grassroots center, focusing its efforts on a middle-class clientele.

AFFILIATION

Independent Ecumenical.

PUBLICATIONS

Center for New Creation Newsletter (four times a year).

CENTER OF CONCERN (COC)

3700 13th Street, NE
Washington, DC 20017
Phone: (202) 635-2757
Fax: (202) 832-9494
Executive Director: Rev. James E. Hug, S.J.

ORIGINS AND DEVELOPMENT

In 1971 three Jesuits, Bill Ryan, Peter Henriot, and Bill Callahan, launched the center with the idea of analyzing, developing, and spreading Catholic social teaching both within and beyond the Catholic community. While members do little direct lobbying, the center is an active participant in numerous coalitions and through its research provides information to legislators, coalition members, and interested citizens.

MISSION STATEMENT

''The Center of Concern is an independent, interdisciplinary team engaged in social analysis, theological reflection, policy advocacy, and public education on the issues of peace, justice and ecology. Center projects are rooted in a faith commitment and guided by a global vision. The faith commitment is articulated through Catholic social thought and the World Council of Churches theme: Justice, Peace, Integrity of Creation. Our vision is of a more just and peace-filled world characterized by a deep sense of the unity of the whole creation and of the human family. Our perspective is the view from the underside, looking through the lenses of race, poverty and gender" (*Annual Report,* 1990).

ORGANIZATION AND FUNDING

Current budgets are in the $500,000 range. The center has a staff of fifteen, a volunteer internship program, and a large mailing list from which it raises about half of center funding. Other sources include grants from foundations and religious orders, stipends for speaking engagements and workshops, and the sale of publications.

POLICY CONCERNS AND TACTICS

Center issues are chosen by the staff based on its mission statement. Current focus is on women's issues, Latin America and the debt, health care, ecology, and hunger in the Horn of Africa. The basic tactic of the Center of Concern is to provide basic research into the problem area and develop occasional papers that are shared with its various networks, culminating in policy recommendations.

AFFILIATION

Roman Catholic.

PUBLICATIONS

Center Focus, a bimonthly newsletter; "Continuing Dialogue on Debt"; "Comments on the Second Draft of the NCCB Pastoral Letter: Partners in the Mystery of Redemption [on Women]"; "The Struggle for Sudan's Soul" (occasional papers); "The Bigger Picture: Applying Social Analysis"; "The Options for the Poor" (videotapes); and numerous books, including *Catholic Social Teaching: Our Best Kept Secret; Opting for the Poor: A Challenge for North Americans; Transforming Feminism;* and *Wisdom Seeks Her Way: Liberating the Power of Women's Spirituality.*

COMMENTS

The Center of Concern is one of those organizations on the borderline between being an advocacy group and an educational one. Its research tends to focus on what it calls "structural analysis," by which it tries to show the interconnectedness of problems and solutions, for example, global and local problems, poverty, education and national debt, women, and export-led development in Third World countries.

CHRISTIAN ACTION COUNCIL (CAC)

101 West Broad Street
Suite 500
Falls Church, VA 22046-4200
Phone: (703) 237-2100
Fax: (703) 237-8276
President: Guy Condon

ORIGINS AND DEVELOPMENT

The Christian Action Council was founded in 1975 by a number of concerned Christians, including Dr. and Mrs. Harold Brown, Dr. C. Everett Koop, and Reverend H. Stanley Wood, with advice and encouragement from Reverend Billy Graham and Dr. Francis A. Schaeffer. Since its inception, CAC has focused exclusively on issues relating to endangered human life: abortion, fetal research, genetic engineering, assisted suicide, infanticide, and euthanasia.

In addition to its political activities, CAC began researching and developing a model for crisis pregnancy centers in 1978. The first center opened in Baltimore in 1980. By 1986 the Christian Action Council Education and Ministries Fund (CACEMF) was established to manage a growing ministry to women facing crisis pregnancies and postabortion syndrome. Some 420 crisis pregnancy centers now operate in the United States and Canada. Each center offers free pregnancy tests, counseling, housing, postabortion counseling, and parenting classes and helps with financial, medical, and physical needs. In 1991 CACEMF launched a national Post-Abortion Counseling and Education Institute to train interested counselors.

MISSION STATEMENT

''The Christian Action Council is a Christian prolife ministry development and education organization. Our primary goal is to proclaim the sanctity of human life within the church community and mobilize evangelicals to provide ministry and life-affirming alternatives to women facing pregnancy related issues.''

ORGANIZATION AND FUNDING

CAC has 450 state and local groups, with no total membership or budget figures being released. The national office has a staff of fifteen. The Christian Action Council Education and Ministries Fund is recognized as a charitable social welfare agency. A CAC spokesperson states that it is no longer involved in direct lobbying, boycotting, or protest activities, so the 501(c)(4) part of the organization is dormant.

POLICY CONCERNS AND TACTICS

Formerly, CAC members testified before national and state legislatures and directly lobbied for legislation that upholds the sanctity of human life. Recently they have stopped this and changed to ''education and ministry'' to reach the voter rather than the elected official. The group also works with local churches to educate Christians on issues related to the sanctity of human life, including a speakers' bureau, informational literature, and instructional videotapes. Through CACEMF it works to develop crisis pregnancy centers and postabortion counseling ministries.

AFFILIATION

Independent Protestant.

PUBLICATIONS

CAC publishes a full range of periodicals, books, audiovisual materials, training and educational manuals, and brochures, including the following. Books: *Abortion: Toward an Evangelical Consensus; Achieving an Abortion-Free America by 2001; Sex: It's Worth Waiting For; Pro-Life Answers to Pro-Life Arguments; School-Based Clinics: A Trojan Horse in Our Schools.* Periodicals: *Action-Line* (bimonthly); *Centers on Life* (quarterly); *Pro-Life Advocate* (quarterly).

CHRISTIAN ACTION NETWORK (CAN)

P.O. Box 606
Forest, VA 24551
Phone: (804) 385-5156
Fax: (804) 385-0115
President: Martin Mawyer

ORIGINS AND DEVELOPMENT

CAN was begun in 1990 as an organization of individuals. The founder, Reverend Martin Mawyer, was an official of Moral Majority and editor of Jerry Falwell's *Liberty Report.* When the Moral Majority was disbanded, the Christian Action Network was organized among a number of its supporters. CAN has a current list of active contributors numbering 75,000.

MISSION STATEMENT

"Will America survive the sex, greed and power of the 1990s? It will if Christians follow the three steps outlined: 1) support Christian activist groups and their efforts to erect God's pillar of truth in the nation's capitol and in the 50 states. 2) Understand and defend the truth on the complex social, moral and political issues tearing the nation apart. 3) Be the sinner's friend and demonstrate how God's hope is genuine, fulfilling and everlasting. Be there when false hope—sex, greed and power—comes to a shattering end."

ORGANIZATION AND FUNDING

The Christian Action Network remains a single-office operation with a largely volunteer staff. Funding comes from direct mail solicitation of potential contributors and in 1992 amounted to slightly under $1 million.

POLICY CONCERNS AND TACTICS

In addition to its pro-life activities the Christian Action Network has focused its efforts on prayer in the public schools, child pornography, and what it calls the gay rights agenda, most recently, gays in the military. It has also been active in changing the policies of the National Endowment for the Arts. Originally working for the abolishment of the NEA, it abandoned that effort when the endowment appeared willing to become more conservative in its policies.

CAN has utilized radio and television spots to get its message across, including a number of controversial ads prior to the 1992 presidential campaign highlighting Bill Clinton's promises to gay Americans. In the campaign to change the National Endowment for the Arts, CAN sent over 500,000 signatures to the White House.

AFFILIATION

Independent Christian.

PUBLICATIONS

Family Alert Newsletter (monthly) and *Silent Shame* (book).

COMMENTS

CAN was very active and visible during the Republican National Convention in 1992, gaining much of its notoriety at that time for its intense attack on gay rights and the Clinton social agenda.

CHRISTIAN ADVOCATES SERVING EVANGELISM (CASE)

P.O. Box 64429
Virginia Beach, VA 23457
Phone: (804) 523-7239
Fax: (804) 523-7546
Executive Director: Jay Sekulow

ORIGINS AND DEVELOPMENT

CASE is one of an emerging group of litigation teams. It developed out of attorney Jay Sekulow's law practice in 1990 and has four full-time staff attorneys, one in San Francisco near Jews for Jesus, one in Washington, D.C., one near Louisville, Kentucky, and Sekulow in Decatur, Georgia, with a small administrative staff.

MISSION STATEMENT

"CASE was started because I saw a gap. There were already aggressive, effective Christian organizations that specialized in litigating religious freedom issues . . . but I saw a growing need to challenge the state's infringement upon the right of Christians to proclaim the gospel" (Jay Sekulow, as quoted by Hubert Morken in "The Evangelical Legal Response to the ACLU").

ORGANIZATION AND FUNDING

CASE has a mailing list of 85,000 and had a 1992 income of $1,672,000. Attorneys remain separated, as noted above, and have no plans to expand at the present time.

POLICY CONCERNS AND TACTICS

CASE limits itself to defending Christians who believe their right to proclaim the Gospel free of government interference has been infringed. The sole tactic is litigation.

AFFILIATION

Independent Protestant.

PUBLICATIONS

Sekulow has a three-times-a-week television show aired on the Trinity Broadcasting cable network, and a free mailing on religious rights is sent upon request.

COMMENTS

Sekulow has already taken five cases to the Supreme Court, winning three. He was successful in *Board of Airport Commissioners of Los Angeles v. Jews for Jesus,* dealing with the distribution of free literature in public places; *Board of Education of the Westside Community Schools v. Mergens,* which allowed voluntary student Bible clubs; and *United States v. Kokinda,* which upheld free distribution of literature outside a post office. He was defeated in *Alexandria Women's Health Clinic,* in which he argued that the Ku Klux Klan Act of 1871, forbidding conspiracies against a class of people, can be applied to Operation Rescue's 1991 efforts to close down abortion facilities in Wichita, Kansas, and *Lee v. Weissmann,* in which the Court struck down as coercive and a violation of the establishment clause any religious invocations and benedictions at public high school graduation ceremonies.

CHRISTIAN CHURCH (DISCIPLES OF CHRIST) (CCDC)

P.O. Box 1986
Indianapolis, IN 46206
Phone: (317) 353-1491
Fax: 1 (800) 458-3318
Executive Director: Donald B. Manworren

ORIGINS AND DEVELOPMENT

This church with a double name arose on the frontier of America in the early 1800s. It was a product of a union of followers of Alexander Campbell and Barton W. Stone, both from Presbyterian backgrounds. Stone preferred the name "Christian" while Campbell preferred "Disciples of Christ." The more conservative Churches of Christ withdrew in 1906. There are 4,200 congregations in forty-six states and seven Canadian provinces. It has around 1.1 million members and is strongest in the Midwest and Southwest, particularly Texas and Missouri. About 50,000 of its members are African Americans. It has seven seminaries and links to eighteen colleges and universities, the largest being Texas Christian University.

MISSION STATEMENT

"Ever focusing on unity as their 'polar star,' Disciples have no creedal statement and no body of dogma, fearing those tend to divide Christians." The church is identified with the liberal mainstream of American Protestantism, and the General Assembly of the church speaks out regularly on moral and social issues.

ORGANIZATION AND FUNDING

The church is congregationally governed, but it has regional and a national or "general" office. The General Assembly meets biennially with 4,000–5,000 voting participants. A General Board of 180 members meets annually, and an Administrative Committee of 44 members meets twice a year. The top staff officer is the general minister and president. The Department of Church and Society and the Division of Homeland Ministries are most responsible for placing the church's influence behind social issues. Since they have no Washington office, they work through various coalitions in Washington, such as the National Council of the Churches of Christ in the U.S.A. (NCC).*

POLICY CONCERNS AND TACTICS

The Disciples do little direct lobbying but rely on their connections in the NCC in Washington and many ecumenical groups, such as Interfaith Impact* and Washington Interreligious Staff Council* to put forward their views to Congress and the executive agencies. They once had a cooperative office with the United Church of Christ* but now rely on distributing information to their constituency, join in action alerts with ecumenical groups, join in their letters and petitions, work through IMPACT Network on a selective basis, and ally on topics with the Catholic Conference and other groups such as Christic Institute.* They occasionally take amicus briefs or enter into dialogue with an agency, but the guide to all of their actions is the positions affirmed by the General Assembly. They started on conscientious objection in the 1920s, are prochoice, endorse Palestinian participation and a Palestinian homeland, and oppose capital punishment. They oppose prescribed prayers in public schools, favor the Equal Rights Amendment (ERA), favor civil liberties for homosexuals without endorsing their life-style, and favor a guaranteed annual wage to assist the poor.

AFFILIATION

Christian Church (Disciples of Christ).

PUBLICATIONS

None.

CHRISTIAN COALITION (CCOA)

1801-L Sara Drive   227 Massachusetts Avenue, NE
Chesapeake, VA 23320   Washington, DC 20002
Phone: (804) 424-2630   (202) 547-3600
Fax: (804) 424-9068   (202) 543-2978
Executive Director: Ralph Reed, Jr.

ORIGINS AND DEVELOPMENT

In 1989 the Christian Coalition was formed from the remnants of former presidential candidate Pat Robertson's 1988 election campaign. Building on Robertson's campaign mailing list of 1.8 million names, by January 1992, the coalition had a membership of 375,000 individuals with 859 local chapters in fifty states. The focus of the Christian Coalition has moved away from national politics to electing members to state and local political office, thereby building a grass-roots political base.

MISSION STATEMENT

"Christian Coalition was founded for the express purpose of giving Christians a voice in their government again. The Coalition is composed of evangelical Christians and pro-family Catholics working together to promote Biblical moral values in politics and public policy."

ORGANIZATION AND FUNDING

In 1993, the coalition's budget was $12 million. It was raised from membership dues and donations from such groups as the National Republican Senatorial Committee. The 1993 budget is $10 million. The coalition is a 501(c)(4) tax-exempt organization. Membership is in local chapters, and members work through these chapters, primarily on local issues and elections. Guidance and assistance are provided by national headquarters. Dr. Pat Robertson, Dr. Ralph E. Reed, Jr., Mr. Dick Weinhold, Dr. Billy McCormack, and Mr. Gordon Robertson constitute the Board of Directors.

POLICY CONCERNS AND TACTICS

The general theme of the coalition is "pro-family values." The coalition works "to give people of faith a voice in government." The issues they support are lower taxes, limited government, safe neighborhoods, quality education, and strong families. Specifically, they support a balanced budget amendment, term limits, tax relief for families, and "civil rights for all Americans born and unborn." The grass-roots partisan emphasis is unique among religious interest groups, and its struggles within the Republican party are part of an ongoing struggle between moderates and the right to control that organization.

AFFILIATION

Independent, conservative Christian.

PUBLICATIONS

The Christian American (bimonthly) and *Religious Rights Watch* (monthly).

COMMENTS

Many people consider the Christian Coalition to be the successor to the Moral Majority and the Freedom Council.

CHRISTIAN COLLEGE COALITION (CCC)

329 8th Street, NE
Washington, DC 20002
Phone: (202) 546-8713
Fax: (202) 546-8913
President: Dr. Myron Augsburger

ORIGINS AND DEVELOPMENT

In 1976 representatives of seventy-seven colleges representing twenty-eight different Christian denominations and a dozen interdenominational institutions determined to pool resources, ideas, and talent to promote Christian higher education, provide faculty and student development opportunities, provide a common voice with the federal government, and provide legal counsel for issues concerning government relations, religious liberty, and reporting regulations.

MISSION STATEMENT

"The Christian College Coalition, an association of approximately 85 colleges, was founded to serve and strengthen one vital sector of private education in North America: regionally accredited four year liberal arts colleges committed both to being excellent educational institutions and to keeping the Christian faith central to every facet of campus life."

ORGANIZATION AND FUNDING

As a professional organization CCC receives its funding directly from member schools. In 1993 it had a budget of $2.5 million and a national staff of twenty-four. An additional $1 million is raised from corporations, foundations, and individuals for designated projects.

POLICY CONCERNS AND TACTICS

The majority of CCC staff's time and energy is spent on faculty development, curricular development, internship programs, and promoting the Christian College option. It does involve itself in issues of government interference with religious institutions, monitor relevant legislation, inform Congress and federal agencies of Christian College concerns, and provide legal advice when needed. Through its internship programs in Costa Rica, Egypt, Russia, Hollywood, California, and Washington, DC, the CCC strives to stimulate interest in, and prepare young Christians for, leadership positions in American society.

AFFILIATION

Independent Christian.

PUBLICATIONS

Christian College News (monthly); *Directory of Administrative Personnel* (annual); *Choose a Christian College* (book); and other materials.

CHRISTIAN LAW ASSOCIATION (CLA)

c/o Gibbs and Craze Law Firm
P.O. Box 30
Conneaut, OH 44030
Phone: (216) 593-3933
Executive Director: Mr. David Gibbs

ORIGINS AND DEVELOPMENT

"The religious liberty law practice of Gibbs and Craze began in 1977 when David Gibbs came to the assistance of a couple in Ohio whose daughters had been seized by the state for the failure of the couple to enroll them in school. The children were being home-schooled by their mother, an experienced state certified school teacher. The parents had gone to jail rather than shut their religiously motivated home school. Following a victory in this case, Gibbs chose to redirect his law firm toward defense of religious rights" (taken from Hubert Morken, "The Evangelical Legal Response to the ACLU: Religion, Politics and the First Amendment," paper presented at the American Political Science Association 1992 Annual Meeting).

MISSION STATEMENT

The Gibbs and Craze firm handles litigation for the Christian Law Association, representing clients who range from local churches to individuals who believe their religious rights are being threatened or taken away.

ORGANIZATION AND FUNDING

The Christian Law Association appears to function much like an insurance company, collecting regular dues from its members (twenty-five dollars a month from churches and five dollars a month from individuals), who then become "minutemen" in the association. When members and some nonmembers become entangled in religious liberty claims, they are then represented at no extra cost. Most of the clients supported by the CLA come from modest financial circumstances, so this provides a method to afford legal representation. At any one time Gibbs and Craze have 300 cases pending, and the office handles 400 or more other inquiries or requests for help each month. The CLA also provides up-to-date legal information and mobilizes support through a monthly newsletter, *The Briefcase*.

POLICY CONCERNS AND TACTICS

The Christian Law Association focuses entirely on religious liberty claims and utilizes litigation or the threat of it to protect its members' interests.

AFFILIATION

Independent Christian.

PUBLICATIONS

The Briefcase (monthly).

COMMENTS

The Christian Law Association appears to be a unique type of organization tied to a single law firm. Whether it will grow into something larger remains to be seen.

CHRISTIAN LEGAL SOCIETY (CLS)

4208 Evergreen Lane
Suite 222
Annandale, VA 22003
Phone: (703) 642-1070
Fax: (703) 642-1075
Executive Director: Bradley P. Jacob

ORIGINS AND DEVELOPMENT

Founded in 1961, the CLS was modeled after the Christian Medical Society and required its members to subscribe to a statement of Christian faith. In 1970, after a Mormon lawyer applied for membership, the organization decided to add an associate membership category rather than change its statement of faith requirement. Nonlawyers can also become members under this category. In 1971 the CLS also dropped a requirement that members be Protestant. While continuing to serve as a fraternal support group for lawyers, judges, law students, and law professors, in 1975 CLS established the Center for Law and Religious Freedom to defend religious discrimination cases and to lobby Congress in a very limited manner in selected legislation. In the mid-1980s CLS moved its headquarters from Oak Park, Illinois, to the Washington, D.C., area to strengthen the center's Supreme Court and legislative efforts.

MISSION STATEMENT

"To nurture, challenge and equip lawyers and law students to serve Jesus Christ in and through the legal profession."

ORGANIZATION AND FUNDING

The CLS currently has 4,500 individual members, drawn primarily from the legal profession, as well as student chapters in 150 of the nation's 175 law schools. It has an annual budget of $1 million and a staff of eighteen. Funding comes in roughly equal amounts from dues, contributions, and grants.

POLICY CONCERNS AND TACTICS

A primary concern of the Christian Legal Society continues to be networking and support for Christian legal professionals and students in their professional lives. This support includes encouraging members to become involved in legal aid or pro bono service, to help resolve clients' disputes out of court through Christian conciliation, to support law students through mentoring, and to contribute time and effort toward the Center for Law and Religious Freedom's work.

Through the Center for Law and Religious Freedom, CLS has played an activist role in promoting and defending religious liberty. Its staff and volunteers were heavily and successfully involved in drafting, lobbying for, and defending Equal Access legislation in the Congress and in the courts. More recently the center has helped draft and lobby for the Religious Freedom Restoration Act. The center supports CLS member attorneys, other organizations, and individuals fighting religious discrimination by providing legal expertise and writing amicus briefs.

AFFILIATION

Independent Christian.

PUBLICATIONS

Christian Legal Society Quarterly (quarterly); *Briefly* (bimonthly membership newsletter); *The Intercessor* (monthly prayer newsletter); and *A Guide to the Equal Access Act* (pamphlet).

CHRISTIAN LIFE COMMISSION OF THE SOUTHERN BAPTIST CONVENTION (CLCSBC)

400 North Capitol Street, NW
Suite 594
Washington, DC 20001
Phone: (202) 638-3223
Fax: (202) 347-3658
Executive Director: Richard D. Land

ORIGINS AND DEVELOPMENT

The Washington office of the Christian Life Commission (CLC) was opened in 1987 by the Southern Baptist Convention. In 1990, the convention reallocated more than $340,000 in funding from the Baptist Joint Committee (BJC)* to the CLC. By 1992 all funding and ties to the Baptist Joint Committee were severed (half of all BJC funds had been from the Southern Baptists) because the convention believed that the BJC was incapable of fully and accurately conveying the views of Southern Baptists. The CLC works with the BJC as it does with other groups when their views overlap.

MISSION STATEMENT

''The Christian Life Commission (CLC) assists Southern Baptists in the propagation of the gospel by (1) helping them become more aware of the ethical implications of the Christian gospel in such aspects of daily living as family life, human relations, moral issues, economic life and work, citizenship, world peace and related fields, (2) helping them create, with God's leadership and by his grace, the kind of moral and social climate in which the Southern Baptist witness for Christ will be most effective. This emphasis on applied Christianity is pursued with full awareness that the chief concern of the CLC is Christian

Social Ethics, by which is meant the application of Christian principles to every-day living.'' The Washington office is to ''serve in a liaison capacity with non-Southern Baptists in the fields of social ethics and religious liberty'' and ''bring to bear Baptist statements, convictions, and insights in the field of Christian ethics and religious liberty upon important policy making groups.''

ORGANIZATION AND FUNDING

The Christian Life Commission is the ethics, public policy, and religious liberty agency of the Southern Baptist Convention. The Washington office has a staff of four and a 1993 budget of approximately $500,000.

POLICY CONCERNS AND TACTICS

The CLC has a broad range of interests, including pro-life policies, religious liberty (international as well as domestic), church-state issues, homosexual rights, alcohol advertising and tax policy, gambling, pornography (including abuses of the National Endowment for the Arts), family tax policy, AIDS policy, and sex education. The CLC provides congressional and agency testimony and communication with members of Congress and executive branch officials (including the president and White House staff). It works in coalitions with other groups and serves as information source and policy adviser for the convention, state CLCs, local Baptist pastors, and other interested Southern Baptists. It has a growing outreach to secular and religious media and conducts an annual seminar for local associations and churches.

AFFILIATION

Southern Baptist.

PUBLICATIONS

Light (bimonthly ethics, public policy, and religious magazine); *Salt* (bimonthly public policy newsletter); and a ''multitude'' of audio- and videotapes on various moral, ethical, and public policy issues.

COMMENTS

Despite having two Southern Baptists as the president and vice president of the United States, the Southern Baptist Convention and the CLC are controlled by a conservative majority that is unhappy with some of the stands of the president and vice president. See ''Clinton's Stand on Gays, Abortion Give Baptists Jitters,'' *The Washington Times,* 5 December 1992; ''Southern Baptists Show Political Clout,'' *Philadelphia Tribune,* 5 June 1992.

CHRISTIAN VOICE (CV)

208 Patrick Street
Alexandria, VA 22314
Phone: (703) 548-1421

Fax: (703) 548-1424
Executive Director: Jina Jarmen

ORIGINS AND DEVELOPMENT

Founded in 1978 by a group of conservative Christian ministers, Christian Voice rose to prominence in the early 1980s with its publication of "Report Cards," publicizing and evaluating the voting records of members of Congress according to CV's listing of key moral/family issues. It distributed 4 million such report cards in 1980, 8 million in 1984, and over 17 million in 1986. Along with a number of other groups it suffered some decline in support in the late 1980s. CV pioneered not only in the development of report cards but its methods of organizing and mobilizing voting blocs through the nation's churches.

MISSION STATEMENT

"Christian Voice is working to mobilize grass roots Christians into an effective conservative political voice. Its concerns include returning prayer to the schools and opposing homosexual rights legislation, tax funding of abortions, IRS [Internal Revenue Service] interference in church activities, sex and violence on television, and U.S. abandonment of traditional allies like Taiwan."

ORGANIZATION AND FUNDING

Christian Voice is primarily a professional lobbying organization with a mailing list of over 300,000 supporters, including many ministers from several dozen denominations. It has several state and regional coordinators, and its 1993 budget was about $500,000.

POLICY CONCERNS AND TACTICS

As the early mission statement indicates, CV has had a broad policy agenda. It currently focuses almost exclusively on opposing the homosexual agenda in general and gays in the military specifically. CV also opposes statehood for the District of Columbia. Christian Voice's most effective tool remains its congressional scorecard.

AFFILIATION

Independent Christian.

PUBLICATIONS

Congressional Report Card (annual), plus brochures and pamphlets.

CHRISTIC INSTITUTE (CI).

8773 Venice Boulevard
Los Angeles, CA 90034
Phone: (213) 287-1556
Fax: (213) 287-1559
Executive Director: Sara Nelson

ORIGINS AND DEVELOPMENT

Begun in 1980 by a Jesuit priest, William Davis, and a group of Harvard Law graduates as a public litigating group dedicated to pursuing and/or defending liberal causes in a conservative era, the Christic Institute has developed some powerful friends and enemies. Due to the financial difficulties noted later, it has moved its main office out of Washington, DC, and cut back its operations until its legal problems are resolved. The Christic Institute continues to be a small group of highly skilled Left-leaning lawyers who litigate ''in the public interest.''

MISSION STATEMENT

''Christic Institute is an interfaith center for law and national policy in the public interest. We commit our resources to legal investigations carefully selected for their potential to advance human rights, social justice, and personal freedom—at home and abroad.''

ORGANIZATION AND FUNDING

The 1991 budget of $1.9 million (latest figure available) was raised primarily from direct mail solicitation (53 percent), with another 35 percent raised from special projects and fund-raising events, 6 percent from grants, and 6 percent from sales of publications and other miscellaneous sources.

POLICY CONCERNS AND TACTICS

The Christic Institute engages in coalition formation, congressional testimony, some grass-roots organizing, and media outreach, but its main focus is on public interest litigation. Its current concerns are covert criminal operations by the U.S. government, preservation of democratic institutions, and the causes and cures of the U.S. narcotics epidemic. For a time the institute was heavily engaged in litigating to uncover illegal support of the Nicaraguan contras. It has tried to show a contra-cocaine connection between savings-and-loan institution loans and illegal aid to the contras.

AFFILIATION

Independent Christian.

PUBLICATIONS

(Publication is currently suspended, but back issues are in stock.) *Convergence* (quarterly magazine), plus a number of reports and briefing papers, such as *Contragate: A Moral Challenge to People of Faith; Drug Outreach and Organizing Packet; Inside the Shadow Government: A Declaration of Evidence; The Vice-President and the Contras; Drugs, Democracy and Dirty Wars; Covert Operations, the Persian Gulf, and the New World Order* (briefing paper, audiotape, and videotape).

COMMENTS

As reported in *Public Interest Profiles, 1992–93* (Washington, DC: Foundation for Public Affairs, 1993), the Christic Institute was called a ''maverick public interest law group'' by the *National Law Journal* (26 March 1990) and ''far left'' by Georgie Anne Geyer in the *Washington Times* (18 April 1989). The institute received a major blow in 1988 after it had filed suit against several supporters of the contras whom it suspected of illegal activities. A federal judge dismissed their suit and ordered the Christic Institute to pay court costs and defendants' legal fees, a total of $1.7 million. They had to post this amount before they could even appeal the judge's ruling.

CHURCHES FOR MIDDLE EAST PEACE (CMEP)

110 Maryland Avenue, NE
Suite 108
Washington, DC 20002
Phone: (202) 546-8425
Fax: (202) 543-7532
Executive Director: Corrine Whitlatch

ORIGINS AND DEVELOPMENT

Churches for Middle East Peace was started in 1984 by other religious interest groups ''out of the conviction that the policy perspectives and long Middle East experience of our member bodies can play a useful role in the public arena.''

MISSION STATEMENT

''The work of the churches for Middle East Peace focuses on Washington in the knowledge that sound U.S. policy is crucial to achieving and maintaining just and stable relationships throughout the area. In addition CMEP seeks to help the members of our various organizations advocate in a knowledgeable, timely and effective way their concerns about justice and peace for all people and countries in the region.''

ORGANIZATION AND FUNDING

CMEP is a working coalition of its member organizations, which include American Baptist Churches USA,* American Friends Service Committee,* Church of the Brethren,* Episcopal Church,* Evangelical Lutheran Church in America, Friends Committee on National Legislation,* Maryknoll Fathers and Brothers, Mennonite Central Committee,* National Council of the Churches of Christ in the U.S.A.,* Presbyterian Church USA,* Roman Catholic Conference of Major Superiors of Men, Unitarian Universalist Association—Washington Office for Social Justice,* United Church of Christ,* and the General Board of Church and Society of the United Methodist Church.* The annual budget is less than $100,000, funded by constituent groups.

POLICY CONCERNS AND TACTICS

CMEP advocates policies seeking to avoid or resolve armed conflicts, aid human rights, block arms sales, expand foreign aid, and affect the unique status of Jerusalem. It recognizes both Israel's right to exist peacefully with its neighbors within internationally recognized borders and the right of Palestinians to self-determination. CMEP encourages negotiations, demilitarization, creating a nuclear-free region in the Middle East, and development and humanitarian aid by the United States and other countries. CMEP recognizes the religious significance of the region to Christians, Jews, and Muslims and supports an active role for the United Nations in maintaining peace.

The coalition actively lobbies Congress and the diplomatic community as well as informing and stimulating their own members to communicate with Washington officials.

AFFILIATION

Independent Ecumenical.

PUBLICATIONS

Middle East Advocacy: A Handbook.

CHURCH OF CHRIST, SCIENTISTÆWASHINGTON OFFICE (CCS)

910 Sixteenth Street, NW
Washington, DC 20006
Phone: (202) 857-0427
Fax: (202) 331-0587
Federal Representative: Phil Davis

ORIGINS AND DEVELOPMENT

Christian Science is a Christian denomination founded in 1879 by Mary Baker Eddy, with this purpose: "to commemorate the word and works of our Master, which should reinstate primitive Christianity and its lost element of healing." The "Mother Church" was established in Boston in 1889 and continues to be the headquarters of the denomination. Since "faith healing" has always had a cool, if not suspicious, reception from government officials and health care regulators, the Christian Science Church found it expedient to establish a Washington, DC, office in 1906, the Committee on Publication, to monitor health regulations and provide information to Congress about the healing practices of Christian Scientists. The Christian Science Church has 3,300 branches scattered throughout sixty-five countries.

MISSION STATEMENT

"The Washington Office for the Committee on Publication has the same mission . . . to correct in a Christian manner impositions on the public in regard to Christian Science, injustices done Mrs. Eddy or members of this Church . . . (*Manual of the Mother Church,* Article XXXIII, Section 2). Since legislative bills may contain language restrictive to the practice of our religion this would fall under our mission of correcting 'in a Christian manner impositions on the public.' "

ORGANIZATION AND FUNDING

The manager of the Washington office reports directly to the manager of Committees on Publication in Boston. The position is filled by the Board of Directors and his or her salary is paid by the Mother Church, supplemented by volunteer funding of local churches. Presently the staff is three persons. Budgets are not divulged.

POLICY CONCERNS AND TACTICS

The Church of Christ, Scientist limits its direct lobbying in Washington to matters of religious liberty, particularly in regard to First Amendment rights and medical practices. When health care legislation is being proposed, it always works to include exceptions or provisions for its own healing practices. It has worked informally with other denominations through WISC* and other groups concerned with these same issues. The church does not use the word *lobbying* but views its action as "protecting the practice of our religion."

AFFILIATION

Church of Christ, Scientist.

PUBLICATIONS

The Christian Science Monitor (daily international newspaper); *Christian Science Sentinel* (weekly); *The Christian Science Journal* (monthly); *The Herald of Christian Science* (publication varies according to the language). The church also supports reading rooms around the world in which interested people can find out about the faith. They have several kinds of radio broadcasts as well as the World Service of *The Christian Science Monitor.*

COMMENTS

In recent years the church has found itself in the midst of litigation, primarily with former members, over whether its healing methods provide adequate "medical attention" for children. As medical science improves and government takes a more pervasive role, this type of controversy will very likely continue.

CHURCH OF THE BRETHREN/ÆWASHINGTON OFFICE (COB)

110 Maryland Avenue, NE
Washington, DC 20002
Phone: (202) 546-3202
Fax: (202) 544-5852
Executive Director: Timothy A. McElwee

ORIGINS AND DEVELOPMENT

The Church of the Brethren had its origins in the pietist movement in Germany in the early 1700s. Members migrated to the United States as early as 1719 and settled in Pennsylvania. The church currently has approximately

170,000 members in 1,064 churches in the United States, located primarily in Pennsylvania, Virginia, and Kansas. The Washington office calls itself ''Witness to Washington'' and opened in 1962.

MISSION STATEMENT

''We believe that Christians should be alert to situations in which government neglects or misuses its trust from the people or the purpose given it by God. In such situations the Christian is called to express convictions of a living faith. If the state demands what the Christian cannot in clear conscience do, what is deeply held to be forbidden by God, then the believer must obey God and act in good conscience.''

ORGANIZATION AND FUNDING

The Washington office is established by, and responsible to, the Church of the Brethren Annual Conference. It is essentially a two-person office supplemented by volunteers. The 1993 budget was less than $100,000.

POLICY CONCERNS AND TACTICS

Current concerns are U.S. policy in Central America, peace and justice in the Middle East, relations with former Soviet nations, arms control and disarmament, and civil and religious liberties. The duties of the Washington office are to monitor federal legislation, occasionally provide or facilitate testimony before Congress or federal agencies, explain the church's positions on various issues, and work together with other religious groups in an advocacy role. The Washington office also provides seminars for youth and adult groups and briefings for visitors, and staffers join various coalitions to pursue the church's policy agenda.

AFFILIATION

Protestant.

PUBLICATIONS

None.

COMMENTS

The Church of the Brethren—Washington office is an excellent example of how a small group expands its influence by joining and supporting numerous coalitions with other groups.

CHURCH WOMEN UNITED (CWU)

475 Riverside Drive
Room 812
New York, NY 10115
Phone: (212) 870-2347
Fax: (212) 870-2338
President: Ann Baker Garvin

110 Maryland Avenue, NE
Washington, DC 20002

(202) 544-8747
(202) 543-1297
Washington Director: Nancy S. Chupp

ORIGINS AND DEVELOPMENT

Begun in 1941 as a project of the National Council of the Churches of Christ in the U.S.A.,* CWU retains close ties with the council but functions independently. It is supported by a number of Christian groups, such as the African Methodist Episcopal Church, the Christian Church (Disciples of Christ),* Church of God, Church of the Brethren,* Episcopal Church,* Evangelical Lutheran Church in America, Reorganized Church of Jesus Christ of Latter Day Saints, Salvation Army, United Church of Christ,* and United Methodist Church. In addition a number of individual Roman Catholics belong.

MISSION STATEMENT

"Church Women United is a national ecumenical movement that brings Protestant, Roman Catholic, Orthodox and other Christian women together into one community of prayer, advocacy and service." CWU "is unified by a common faith in Christ; is committed to the empowerment of women; works for global justice and peace."

ORGANIZATION AND FUNDING

CWU has approximately 500,000 supporters (this number is based on the numbers who participate in the three days of celebration that are the most visible and popular activities of the organization: World Day of Prayer, May Fellowship Day, and World Community Day). Members are divided administratively into fifty state organizations, a group for the District of Columbia, and 1,600 local units. CWU had a 1993 budget of about $1.6 million, of which 70 percent was raised from the Days of Celebration. The remainder came from individual donations, subscriptions, and the sale of materials and investments. The Washington office has a budget of $80,000.

POLICY CONCERNS AND TACTICS

CWU has had a long-term interest in promoting racial harmony and equal opportunity for women of color. In addition, priorities for 1992–96 are counteracting the povertization of women and children, especially supporting economic alternatives, and support for health care reform. In addition to its own lobbying, Church Women United supports a variety of coalitions and works to stimulate grass-roots backing for its policy objectives.

AFFILIATION

Ecumenical Christian.

PUBLICATIONS

Churchwoman (bimonthly magazine); *Act* (bimonthly legislative update); *Inform* (special action alerts).

CHURCH WORLD SERVICES (CWS)

475 Riverside Drive
New York, NY 10115-0050

110 Maryland Avenue, NE, Suite 108
Washington, DC 20002

Phone: (212) 870-2061   (202) 543-6336
Fax: (212) 870-2055   (202) 543-1297
Executive Director: Lani J. Havens (New York office), Carol Capps (Washington office)

ORIGINS AND DEVELOPMENT

Church World Services was organized by the National Council of the Churches of Christ in the U.S.A. (NCC)* in 1944 as an ecumenical war relief, refugee assistance, and economic development agency. In 1946 its Immigration and Refugee Program was organized separately due to the large number of persons it was assisting. Since that time it has assisted over 350,000 refugees from twenty-five countries. The overseas operations of CWS are handled by a staff of forty-five persons. Whenever possible, assistance is channeled through local relief agencies. In addition, there are twenty-seven regional offices around the United States. The Education and Fundraising Program is located in Elkhart, Indiana; the Office of Global Education in Baltimore, Maryland; and the Office of Development Policy in Washington, DC. CWS remains a division of the NCC but is governed by its own committee, composed of persons nominated by affiliated churches and organizations.

MISSION STATEMENT

In response to changing world conditions, the mission of CWS has moved from simple relief to "enhancement of the quality of life." From a theological perspective, "quality of life requires more than providing basic physical necessities. It depends upon the interplay of the spiritual, intellectual and social aspects of human existence. A life of quality results when fundamental moral and ethical values are manifested in and promoted by the social, political, economic and personal dimensions of life."

From a political perspective CWS has categorized the essential elements of "quality of life" under the principles of justice, participation, and sustainability. Justice refers to each person and group's equitable access to the elements that allow for full human life. Participation requires that each person be able to contribute to, and act on behalf of, their own well-being and the well-being of society as a whole, that is, to be involved in the social, economic, and political processes that shape their lives. Sustainability is the need to act upon the natural environment in ways that preserve the resources required by a life of quality for this and future generations. This includes the elimination of nuclear armaments and working for world peace.

ORGANIZATION AND FUNDING

Church World Services remains a semiautonomous division of the NCC and is divided into programs, as just noted. Funding for programs amounts to nearly $40 million a year and comes from a variety of sources. Approximately 20 percent comes from member churches. The U.S. government provides grants for refugee resettlement, overseas shipment of relief materials, and other in-kind support. The remainder comes from fund-raising efforts, foundation grants, and some investment income.

POLICY CONCERNS AND TACTICS

Activities of Church World Services are divided into six major areas: (1) financial, material, personal, and spiritual assistance to people afflicted by natural or humanly caused disasters; (2) assisting refugees and displaced persons find permanent homes and employment; (3) immediate economic assistance for refugees; (4) enhancing ecumenical links with the Christian community throughout the world and other minority religions; (5) pursuing a domestic public awareness campaign concerning the causes of poverty, oppression, and so on; and (6) advocating public policy measures before Congress and other federal agencies on behalf of refugees and displaced, oppressed, and unemployed people throughout the world.

AFFILIATION

Ecumenical Protestant.

PUBLICATIONS

Monday (weekly newsletter) and a wide variety of topical and issue pamphlets and brochures.

CLERGY AND LAITY CONCERNED (CALC)

340 Mead Road
Decatur, GA 30030
Phone: (404) 377-1983
Fax: (404) 377-5367
Executive Director: Emory R. Searcy, Jr.

ORIGINS AND DEVELOPMENT

CALC was founded in 1965 by a group of Roman Catholic clergy opposed to U.S. involvement in the Vietnam War. It was quickly broadened to include Protestant and Jewish clergy and eventually, laypeople. When the war ended, the group shifted its focus to broader concerns.

MISSION STATEMENT

"CALC is a multi-religious, multi-racial network of more than 25,000 people throughout the country. We believe that true religious commitment *demands* social action. We believe that working through the religious community is the surest way to achieve peace and justice. The men and women in CALC come from many different groups—Protestant, Catholic, Jewish, Muslim, Buddhist— and from many different racial groups. . . . But whatever our differences, all members of CALC are united in a common struggle against those forces— whether giant corporations or repressive governments—that oppress and torture people, take away their rights and their lives, or deny them the opportunity to feed themselves and their families.''

ORGANIZATION AND FUNDING

CALC operates on a budget of $400,000 raised from membership dues, a mass mailing solicitation, and other contributions. It functions with a staff of seven, and its 25,000 members are organized into thirty-five local groups, which work to influence legislators, recruit new members, and educate their communities about specific issues.

POLICY CONCERNS AND TACTICS

In its early years CALC was highly visible in antiwar demonstrations, sit-ins, and so on. After the Vietnam War ended, the group expanded its focus to include the Campaign for a Nuclear Moratorium; reconstruction of, and reconciliation with, Vietnam; the World Hunger Action Campaign; and International Human Rights in general, with a particular interest in countries receiving foreign aid from the United States. Most recently CALC focused on providing an alternative voice in the Columbian celebrations. It is working to develop in schools what it calls ''Racism Free Zones'' and has a ''Covenant Against Apartheid'' program to work against racism in South Africa. Issues are selected by a National Advisory Committee and submitted to the membership for approval. At the present time CALC tactics include joining larger coalitions addressing specific policy areas, educational campaigns, and urging members to contact their representatives.

AFFILIATION

Independent Ecumenical.

PUBLICATIONS

CALC Report (a monthly newsletter).

COMMENTS

CALC is a good example of an organization that was formed for one purpose, and when that purpose was accomplished—end of the Vietnam War—instead of disbanding, it turned its focus to other issues consistent with its liberal perspective. A line at the bottom of its 1991 stationery reads, ''26 Years and **Still** concerned about the giant triplets: Racism, Materialism and Militarism.''

COALITION TO STOP GUN VIOLENCE (CSGV)

100 Maryland Avenue, NE
Washington, DC 20002
Phone: (202) 544-7190
Fax: (202) 544-7213
Executive Director: Michael K. Beard

ORIGINS AND DEVELOPMENT

The Coalition to Stop Gun Violence was organized in 1974. It has thirty-four organizational members and a staff of five.

MISSION STATEMENT

"The goal of the CSGV is the orderly elimination of most handguns from the US society. CSGV seeks to ban handguns and assault weapons from importation, manufacture, sale, transfer, ownership, possession and use by the general American public. There would be reasonable exceptions: the police, military, security officers, and gun clubs where the guns are secured on the club's premises. Gun dealers would also be permitted to trade in antique and collectable weapons kept and sold in unfirable condition.

"While working to ban these weapons, the coalition supports intermediate steps to reduce gun violence. These steps include, but are not limited to, applying strict liability on handguns and assault weapons; waiting periods and background checks on *all* firearms purchases; restricting dealers' licenses to actual gun stores that comply with local laws; reenabling the Consumer Product Safety Commission to examine the safety of firearms and ammunition; and increasing the tax on handguns to compensate victims."

ORGANIZATION AND FUNDING

Of the coalition's thirty-four institutional members, eighteen are identified as religiously affiliated, including American Ethical Union,* American Jewish Committee,* American Jewish Congress,* General Board of Church and Society of the United Methodist Church,* Presbyterian Church USA,* and Jesuit Social Ministries.* The 1992 budget was $507,000, raised primarily from direct mail solicitation.

POLICY CONCERNS AND TACTICS

The CSGV pursues the following policies: (1) waiting periods and background checks before any individual can purchase any firearm; (2) banning assault weapons; (3) strict liability for makers and sellers of handguns; (4) limits on the number of weapons an individual may purchase within a specific time period; (5) more strict licensing of gun dealers; (6) lifetime prohibition against convicted felons' regaining the right to own or carry arms; and (7) establishing a gun victims fund through a tax on firearm sales. In addition to lobbying and drafting model legislation, coalition staff gather statistics and write numerous editorials aimed at educating citizens about the reality of gun violence.

AFFILIATION

Independent Ecumenical.

PUBLICATIONS

Reprints of editorials, statistical information.

COMMITTEE IN SOLIDARITY WITH THE PEOPLE OF EL SALVADOR (CISPES)

P.O. Box 12156
Washington, DC 20005
Phone: (202) 265-0890
Fax: (202) 265-7843
Executive Director: Diane Greene

ORIGINS AND DEVELOPMENT

CISPES was begun in 1980 to protest U.S. support of the repressive government in El Salvador and to inform public opinion about the atrocities of the U.S.-backed forces. CISPES organized a number of demonstrations in U.S. cities and led delegations of citizens to El Salvador. Apparently feared by the U.S. government, CISPES was several times infiltrated by Federal Bureau of Investigation (FBI) agents, possibly illegally, and accused of a number of illegal actions, which it denied. When the Peace Agreement was signed in El Salvador, the group became a watchdog operation.

MISSION STATEMENT

CISPES favors self-determination for the people of El Salvador, an end to human rights violations, and U.S. aid to the poor of El Salvador.

ORGANIZATION AND FUNDING

CISPES is a grass-roots organization with about 7,000 supporters divided roughly into four regional and seventy local groups. It has a national staff of eighteen, plus interns and volunteers and an annual budget of $500,000.

POLICY CONCERNS AND TACTICS

CISPES remains focused on Central America in general and El Salvador in particular, believing that continued publicity and a regular flow of information are the best assurance that the Peace Accords will be followed and peace maintained in El Salvador. In addition to providing regular information to Congress and the media, CISPES sponsors U.S. tours by El Salvadorian labor, religious, and human rights activists. It also leads tours to El Salvador by interested U.S. citizens. It is currently working on voter registration and preparing the upcoming elections in El Salvador.

AFFILIATION

Independent Christian.

PUBLICATIONS

Peace Accords Watch (monthly newsletter).

CONCERNED WOMEN FOR AMERICA (CWA)

370 L'Enfant Promenade, SW
Suite 800

Washington, DC 20024
Phone: (202) 488-7000
Fax: (202) 488-0806
President: Beverly LaHaye

ORIGINS AND DEVELOPMENT

CWA was founded in 1979 by Beverly LaHaye as an alternative to the feminist movement in general and to oppose the Equal Rights Amendment in particular. Started with nine women in San Diego, CWA has grown to 600,000 members with chapters in every state. After its successful opposition to the ERA, Concerned Women for America turned to a variety of conservative causes.

MISSION STATEMENT

"To preserve, protect and promote traditional and Judeo-Christian values through education, legal defense, legislative programs, and related activities that represent the concerns of men and women who believe in these values."

ORGANIZATION AND FUNDING

The 1992 budget of $10 million was raised almost entirely from membership dues and donations. Staff at the national office is thirty-three, and membership is listed at 600,000 individuals. These are organized into somewhat more than 1,000 grass-roots chapters.

POLICY CONCERNS AND TACTICS

Concerned Women for America has been an active opponent of abortion rights, euthanasia, mandated family and medical leave, and sex education in schools. It has promoted abstinence education and parental involvement laws. More recently it has included the issue of gays in the military.

CWA engages in coalition formation, lobbying at all levels, congressional testimony, and litigation. It also has developed an extensive educational outreach and a "caring for life" network of crisis pregnancy centers, adoption agencies, and national women's services. It is probably most known for "Beverly LaHaye Live," a daily radio call-in talk show hosted by the CWA president.

AFFILIATION

Independent Christian. Politically conservative.

PUBLICATIONS

Family Voice Magazine (eleven times a year) and *Issues at a Glance* (monthly).

COMMENTS

"Mrs. LaHaye's CWA is not the only political haven for conservative women, of course. Phyllis Schlafly's Eagle Forum claims some 80,000 members. But though their politics may agree, their styles couldn't be more different. 'Phyllis is the aggressive, confrontational type—that's her comfort zone' says Mrs. LaHaye. 'I couldn't be that way. We network together, but some people are attracted to her style, and some people are attracted to mine' '' (*Dallas Morning News,* 18 November 1992).

"Concerned Women for America claims to have more members than the National Organization for Women (250,000), the League of Women Voters (110,000) and the National Women's Political Caucus (75,000) combined. CWA's 600,000 claim is repeatedly challenged because it counts as members women who have contributed money or lent their voices or signatures to the cause. The group says it updates its mailing lists every 18 months, purging those who are not active, just like NOW'' (*Detroit Free Press,* n.d.).

COUNCIL OF JEWISH FEDERATIONS (CJF)

730 Broadway
New York, NY 10006

Phone: (212) 475-5000
Fax: (212) 888-7538
Executive Director: Martin S. Kraar

227 Massachusetts Avenue, NW
Suite 220
Washington, DC 20002
(202) 785-5900
(202) 785-4937

ORIGINS AND DEVELOPMENT

The Council of Jewish Federations was established in 1952 as the central coordinating unit for some 2,000 local Jewish federations scattered throughout the United States and Canada. Local federations serve as coordinators or umbrella groups for a wide variety of educational and charitable efforts.

MISSION STATEMENT

CJF endeavors ''to strengthen the work and impact of Jewish Federations by developing programs to meet changing needs, providing an exchange of successful community experiences, establishing guidelines for fundraising and operations, and engaging in joint planning and action on common purposes dealing with local, regional and international needs.''

ORGANIZATION AND FUNDING

CJF is directed by the council officers, a group of twenty people, and a Board of Directors, elected at the annual business meeting of its General Assembly. The assembly consists of some 700 local leaders elected annually by their own Federations. This group, drawn from a rigorously decentralized constituency, sets the council's policies, approves its programs, and arranges its budget. The annual budget is approximately $23 million, raised primarily from membership dues and grants from government agencies to carry out specific social service activities.

POLICY CONCERNS AND TACTICS

CJF is primarily a social welfare organization that supports programs for women, the elderly, education, and Jewish refugees. The Washington ''Action Office'' has a staff of ten to monitor legislation and agency rulings, solicit government funding, and testify before congressional committees and government agencies about CJF policy positions.

AFFILIATION

Jewish.

PUBLICATIONS

Annual Report plus brochures and newsletters focused on specific topics and projects of the council.

E

/

EAGLE FORUM (EAGLE)

P.O. Box 618
Alton, IL 62002
Phone: (618) 462-5415
Fax: (618) 462-8909
President: Phyllis Schlafly

316 Pennsylvania Avenue, SE
Washington, DC 20003
(202) 544-0353
(202) 547-6996

ORIGINS AND DEVELOPMENT

Eagle Forum was begun in 1975 by conservative writer and activist Phyllis Schlafly (author of *A Choice, Not an Echo* plus a dozen other books) to represent the values and aspirations of traditional, conservative women and men in American politics. While the Supreme Court's decision in *Roe v. Wade* was not the only factor in Mrs. Schlafly's decision to form a new organization, it was a major impetus. Since its inception Eagle Forum has developed chapters in every state as well as the Eagle Forum Education and Legal Defense Fund and Eagle Forum PAC. The political agenda has broadened considerably to include opposition to the Equal Rights Amendment, opposition to sex education in public schools, and support for the Strategic Defense Initiative.

MISSION STATEMENT

''To participate effectively in the process of self-government for conservative and pro-family goals.''

ORGANIZATION AND FUNDING

The Eagle Forum has its headquarters in Alton, Illinois, but maintains a Washington office. In addition it has independently funded chapters in each state. The national organization has a staff of fourteen and a 1993 budget of about

$800,000. Funds are raised 75 percent from individual donations, 10 percent from membership dues, 10 percent from publications, and 5 percent from foundation grants.

POLICY CONCERNS AND TACTICS

The Eagle Forum currently is working on child care alternatives, parental rights in education, tax relief for families, and support for military preparedness. It has proven to be an experienced, effective lobbying force at both the national and state levels and engages in grass-roots organizing, coalition formation, and media outreach.

AFFILIATION

Independent Christian.

PUBLICATIONS

Education Reporter (monthly); *The Phyllis Schlafly Report* (monthly). Books: *Bibliography on Contemporary Issues; Child Abuse in the Classroom; Equal Pay for Unequal Work; Meddlesome Mandate: Rethinking Family Leave; Pornography's Victims; Stronger Families or Bigger Government?; Who Will Rock the Cradle?;* as well as several videotapes, such as ''We the People.''

COMMENTS

In many respects Phyllis Schlafly remains the heart and soul of the Eagle Forum. Her prominence at the Republican National Convention in 1992 highlights her and Eagle Forum's importance among conservatives in American politics.

ECUMENICAL PROGRAM ON CENTRAL AMERICA AND THE CARIBBEAN (EPICA)

1470 Irving Street, NW
Washington, DC 20010
Phone: (202) 332-0292
Fax: (202) 332-1184
Executive Director: Minor Sinclair

ORIGINS AND DEVELOPMENT

The Ecumenical Program on Central America and the Caribbean was founded in 1969 by Rev. Philip Weaton, a former Episcopal missionary in the Dominican Republic. The name was originally the Ecumenical Program for Interamerican Communication and Action, but this was changed in 1988. Although the group had the help of the National Council of the Churches of Christ in the U.S.A.* to get started, it is now an independent, nonprofit entity in its own right.

MISSION STATEMENT

EPICA has "sought to educate and mobilize North Americans on issues of social justice, liberation and self determination in the Americas. . . . As a specialized press on the Caribbean and Central America, we reach out to diverse U.S. constituencies to inform, encourage dialogue and change public opinion about a region of 40 million people in 35 countries, territories or colonies in a hemisphere of the Americas. . . . In working for social change we understand that providing information to the public is not enough. People need to participate in an experiential process of analysis and reflection which leads to specific actions.''

ORGANIZATION AND FUNDING

EPICA is not a membership organization, but a small group of dedicated activists who are funded by donations from churches; workshop, seminar, and tour fees; and the sale of publications. It functions with a three-person staff and has an operating budget of under $100,000.

POLICY CONCERNS AND TACTICS

The organization considers itself primarily educational, providing resource materials to both Congress and other governmental agencies and to diverse North American constituencies working for a new U.S. foreign policy for Central America and the Caribbean. As part of the broader peace and justice movement, EPICA publicizes human rights violations by U.S.-backed regimes, promotes nonintervention in military conflicts, and promotes an "integrated, solidaristic perspective" to solve the region's problems. The staff organizes study tours of Central America and presents workshops, seminars, and so on. It has been heavily involved with the sanctuary movement and the broader issue of refugees from Latin America.

AFFILIATION

Independent Ecumenical.

PUBLICATIONS

In English, it has published such titles as *Guatemalan Women Speak; Death and Life in Morazan; Condoning the Killing;* and *Indian Guatemala.* It distributes a number of Spanish-language titles published by the Jesuit-run University of Central America in San Salvador.

EPISCOPAL CHURCH ÆWASHINGTON OFFICE (EPISC)

110 Maryland Avenue, NE
Suite 309
Washington, DC 20002
Phone: (202) 547-7300 or 1 (800) 228-0515

Fax: (202) 547-4457

Executive Directors: Rev. Robert J. Brooks and Dr. Betty A. Coats

ORIGINS AND DEVELOPMENT

The Washington office of the Episcopal Church was established by the General Convention of the Episcopal Church in 1979 and was reorganized in 1988. The national church is headquartered in New York City.

MISSION STATEMENT

"As directed by the General Convention, one purpose of the Washington Office is to bring the Resolutions of the Episcopal Church to the attention of our national policy makers. The Washington Office serves to open the line of communication between our elected officials and the Episcopal community. . . . Serving as a source for information, the Washington Office works to provide Episcopalians across the country with current legislative reports on key issues . . . to encourage church members to initiate their own advocacy efforts in response to the General Council and Executive Council Resolutions.''

ORGANIZATION AND FUNDING

The Washington office follows the policy guidance of the triennial meetings of the General Convention, composed of a House of Bishops and a House of Deputies. In the interim, policy guidance comes from the Executive Council, which is led by the presiding bishop. There are a staff of four and an annual budget of less than $100,000 (actual figures were not provided).

POLICY CONCERNS AND TACTICS

The Washington office does not limit itself to Episcopalians in Congress but works actively in major coalitions with other liberal religious interest groups and public policy advocates, such as Interfaith Impact for Justice and Peace* and Washington Interreligious Staff Council.* Current issues are increased public and private housing for low- and middle-income persons; advocacy of moderate welfare reform with particular concern for Aid to Dependent Children; voluntary service opportunities; humane immigration policies for refugees fleeing civil strife in Central America; greater assistance for treatment of drug and alcohol problems; providing cost-effective health care for AIDS victims; restoration of civil rights; condemnation of hate crimes; confrontation of global environment concerns; more care for Native Americans in health and education; and diplomatic and economic leverage on South Africa. In each of these areas the staff monitors and lobbies for specific pieces of legislation that would promote the social policy goals of the church. The policy goals are many and wideranging and parallel those of other liberal church groups.

AFFILIATION

The Episcopal church.

PUBLICATIONS

Legislative Update (monthly).

COMMENTS

The Washington office emphasizes the legislative branch, and it is not clear that it lobbies executive agencies as well as Congress or whether it is able to convince and influence the leaders who are communicants.

ETHICS AND PUBLIC POLICY CENTER (EPPC)

1015 Fifteenth Street, NW
Washington, DC 20005
Phone: (202) 682-1200
Fax: (202) 408-0632
President: Mr. George Weigel

ORIGINS AND DEVELOPMENT

The Ethics and Public Policy Center was established in 1976 under the auspices of Georgetown University, with Ernest Lefever as director. In 1980 it became an independent organization incorporated in the District of Columbia. In 1989 the James Madison Foundation, of which George Weigel was president, was absorbed by the EPPC, and Weigel became director.

MISSION STATEMENT

''To clarify the bond between the Judeo-Christian moral tradition and domestic policy through a program of research, writing, publications and conferences; to encourage debate on domestic and foreign policy issues among religious, academic, political, business and other leaders. . . . The Center affirms the moral validity and political wisdom of the great Western ethical imperatives: respect for the human person, individual freedom, justice, the rule of law, and limited government.''

ORGANIZATION AND FUNDING

The Ethics and Public Policy Center is an independent, nonpartisan but conservative think tank. The center is a 501(c)(3) organization supported by contributions from foundations, corporations, and individuals. Its 1993 budget is about $1.2 million, of which 85 percent comes from foundation contributions, 5 percent from corporations, 4 percent from individuals, 5 percent from sale of publications, and 1 percent from other sources.

POLICY CONCERNS AND TACTICS

The EPPC strives to utilize the Christian scriptures and worldview to interpret domestic and foreign policy needs and problems and provide public policy proposals based upon evangelical values and insights. ''The Center's work falls mainly into four categories: the Church and Society Project, the School and Society Project, the Business and Society Project, and the Pacific Project.'' Historically a number of areas have been addressed: the abortion debate, modern Catholic thought, politics and art/culture, poverty and welfare, race relations, just war theory, the future of Hong Kong, the cold war in high school textbooks, U.S. foreign policy, religion in the former Soviet Union and Eastern Europe, Strategic Defense Initiative (SDI), and the church in the Third World.

The primary tactic is broadly educational, through books, conferences, press releases, editorials, and seminars. It often brings public officials to the center for discussions and exchange of ideas. Center staff occasionally visit Capitol Hill but do not rely on public lobbying to any great extent.

AFFILIATION

Independent Protestant.

PUBLICATIONS

Ethics and Public Policy Newsletter (quarterly); *American Purpose* (ten times per year commentary on foreign policy); *The American Character* (three times per year commentary on domestic policy); *American Orthodoxy* (newsletter). In addition center fellows regularly publish books, including Terry Eastland, *Energy in the Executive: The Case for the Strong Presidency* (New York: Free Press, 1992); Robert Royal, *1492 and All That: Political Manipulation of History;* George Weigel, *A New Worldly Order: John Paul II and Human Freedom;* and James Johnson, *Just War and the Gulf War.*

COMMENTS

The EPPC has been in the forefront of forging an Evangelical–Roman Catholic alliance to find common conservative ground for public policy proposals.

EVANGELICALS FOR SOCIAL ACTION (ESA)

10 Lancaster Avenue
Philadelphia, PA 19151
Phone: (215) 645-9390
Fax: (215) 649-3834
President: Ronald J. Sider

ORIGINS AND DEVELOPMENT

ESA traces its roots to a 1973 statement on social justice issued in Chicago by a group of some forty Evangelical leaders but was formally organized in 1978. Emphases have been on developing biblically based public policy recommendations and encouraging Christians and churches to be active in reaching out into their communities to change the structures of society to be more responsive to the needs of justice and peace. The (1993) Chicago Declaration on Evangelism and Social Transformation signaled ESA's move to a broader concern for holistic mission.

MISSION STATEMENT

''ESA's overall mission is to integrate prayer, evangelism and social transformation. Public policy education continues to be a major concern for ESA. In its public policy work ESA seeks to combine biblical principles and careful, sophisticated social analysis.''

ORGANIZATION AND FUNDING

Evangelicals for Social Action is an individual membership organization with some 2,000 members. The 1993 budget is $350,000, which supports a staff of five. Funding comes from individual member dues, grants from churches, individual donors, and foundation grants.

POLICY CONCERNS AND TACTICS

The ESA defies categorization as liberal or conservative (preferring instead to be labeled biblical). It promotes a ''consistent life ethic.'' In pursuit of that ethic ESA favors arms control, nuclear disarmament, empowerment of the poor, strengthening the family, supporting democracy and freedom, and environmental protection and opposes abortion on demand. ESA staffers maintain regular contact with Congress and the White House, join coalitions, and act as a clearinghouse for Evangelicals.

AFFILIATION

Independent Protestant Evangelical.

PUBLICATIONS

PRISM (monthly); Crossroads, ESA's public policy program, publishes ten major monographs each year on various topics. Brief, popular versions of these are disseminated free.

F

/

FAMILY RESEARCH COUNCIL (FRC)

700 13th Street, NW
Suite 500
Washington, DC 20005
Phone: (202) 393-2100
Fax: (202) 393-2134
Executive Director: Gary L. Bauer

ORIGINS AND DEVELOPMENT

Begun in 1981 as a conservative, Evangelical, profamily think tank and advocacy organization, FRC was taken over in 1988 by Focus on the Family.* In 1992, however, the council again became independent. Since that time it has expanded its focus to include welfare reform, inner-city concerns, educational reform, and cultural studies.

MISSION STATEMENT

"The Family Research Council is . . . dedicated to ensuring that the interests of the family are considered and respected in the formation of public policy. The Council works to create in Legislative, Executive and Judicial branches of the federal government an understanding of the overall pro-family agenda."

ORGANIZATION AND FUNDING

The 1993 budget was $7.0 million, of which publications produced 33 percent, foundation grants 23 percent, general donations 19 percent, fund-raising events 13 percent, and direct mail solicitation 12 percent. FRC currently has a staff of twenty-six, plus interns and volunteers.

POLICY CONCERNS AND TACTICS

FRC concerns itself with abortion, adoption and foster care, definition of the family, divorce reform, educational choice (including home schooling), homosexuality, parental rights, and tax relief for families with children. More recently it has addressed the issue of welfare reform, inner-city problems, and cultural studies. Its primary means of pursuing its goals are coalition formation, congressional testimony, lobbying at all levels, grass-roots organizing, functioning as an information resource center and clearinghouse, and litigation.

AFFILIATION

Independent Christian.

PUBLICATIONS

Family Policy (bimonthly); *Washington Watch* (monthly newsletter); plus books and pamphlets such as *Children at Risk* and *When Families Fail: The Social Costs.*

COMMENTS

'' 'If Pat Robertson and Jerry Falwell and whoever else you wanted to name all announced tomorrow that they were leaving American politics, it would not in one iota lessen this reaction I think is happening all across America,' says Gary Bauer, whose Family Research Council is singled out by liberal foes as one of the strongest Christian right opponents of gay rights'' (*Courier-Journal,* 2 May 1993, p. D-1).

FELLOWSHIP OF RECONCILIATION (FOR)

Box 271
Nyack, NY 10960
Phone: (914) 358-4601
Fax: (914) 358-4924
Executive Director: Douglas Hostetter

ORIGINS AND DEVELOPMENT

The Fellowship of Reconciliation was founded in 1915 when pressures to enter World War I were rising. Among the earliest of the pacifist groups, it has struggled to maintain and develop a credible message of nonviolence and reconciliation among potential enemies. Several of its affiliates are organized along denominational lines. These are Catholic Peace Fellowship, Jewish Peace Fellowship, Lutheran Peace Fellowship, Presbyterian Peace Fellowship, and Episcopal Peace Fellowship.

MISSION STATEMENT

"The Fellowship attempts through education and social action to substitute nonviolence and reconciliation for violence in international relations, racial and ethnic conflicts and other areas where the potential for violence is greatest."

ORGANIZATION AND FUNDING

FOR has a membership list of 18,000, roughly affiliated with seventy-five local groups around the country. There is a national staff of twenty, supported almost entirely from membership dues and donations.

POLICY CONCERNS AND TACTICS

FOR focuses its energies entirely on efforts to solve problems in a nonviolent manner. The specific areas of concern, however, change as crises rise and recede around the world. Efforts may be made in Latin America, the Middle East, South Africa, and certainly in the United States. Tactics vary from joining in peaceful demonstrations to letter-writing campaigns to joining coalitions to grass-roots educational efforts. FOR maintains a speakers' bureau, a library, and archives on nonviolence and war.

AFFILIATION

Ecumenical.

PUBLICATIONS

Fellowship (a quarterly newsletter); also pamphlets, books, and occasional papers.

COMMENTS

A 16 October 1990 article in the *New York Times* reported that a group from FOR went on a nine-day peace mission to the Middle East, carrying 1,000 pounds of antibiotics and vitamins worth $67,000 to Iraq, and tried unsuccessfully to meet with Saddam Hussein. A 1 May 1991 article in *Christian Century* reported that FOR, along with the Mennonite Central Committee, received a license to ship medical supplies to Iraq.

FOCUS ON THE FAMILY

420 North Cascade Avenue
Colorado Springs, CO 80903
Phone: (719) 531-3400
Fax: (719) 531-3385
President: James C. Dobson

ORIGINS AND DEVELOPMENT

Focus on the Family began in 1977 with a fifteen-minute broadcast on forty stations by Rev. James Dobson. Since that time it has expanded exponentially. Currently a daily thirty-minute program is aired on over 1,800 stations worldwide. In addition programs are taped for sale, and various shortened versions provide inspirational moments at other times of the day. Spanish and Russian translations are also broadcast, as are short radio "docudramas" based on biblical stories.

A book division was established in 1986 to publish family-oriented books and popular magazines—currently eight separate titles. One, entitled *Citizen,* specifically focuses on government regulations, legislation, and policies that affect families.

In 1988 the Family Research Council in Washington, D.C., merged with Focus on the Family to provide a united base for public policy research and influence. In 1991 the two entities split. In 1992 Focus on the Family moved from southern California to Colorado Springs, where its 1,100 employees now work on a new 47-acre campus.

MISSION STATEMENT

"Focus on the Family is a non-profit Christian organization. Our only reason for existing is to contribute to the stability of the families in our society. That purpose is based on a foundation of four guiding philosophies: (1) We believe that the ultimate purpose in living is to glorify God and to attain eternal life through Jesus Christ, our Lord. This begins within our own families. From there we are committed to reaching out to a suffering humanity that does not know of His love and His sacrifice. (2) We believe that the institution of marriage is a permanent, lifelong relationship between a man and a woman. . . . (3) We believe children are a gift of God; a heritage from the Lord. Therefore we are accountable to God for molding, shaping and preparing them for a life of service to Him and to their fellow man. (4) We believe that human life is of inestimable worth and significance in all its dimensions. This includes the unborn, the aged, the widowed, the mentally retarded, the unattractive, the physically challenged and every other condition in which humanness is expressed from conception to the grave.''

ORGANIZATION AND FUNDING

Focus now encompasses some fifty different ministries. A staff of 1,100 was supported by a 1992 budget of nearly $78 million, of which $68,894,000 was raised from individual donations, $4 million from a grant, and $5 million from film sales and rentals.

POLICY CONCERNS AND TACTICS

Focus is primarily a service and resource center for families, including inspirational materials, counseling services, practical "how to" tips on rearing a family, and Christian-centered family education and entertainment resources. In its public policy positions Focus is pro-life, supports school choice plans, and opposes the gay rights agenda, media violence, and pornography. It is also active in taxation and housing policies as these affect families.

AFFILIATION

Independent Christian.

PUBLICATIONS

Focus on the Family (monthly); *Clubhouse, Clubhouse Jr., Brio,* and *Breakaway* (all childrens' magazines); *Physician, Parental Guidance,* and *Teachers in Focus* (adult support magazines); and *Citizen* (political action guide).

FRIENDS COMMITTEE ON NATIONAL LEGISLATION (FCNL)

245 2nd Street, NE
Washington, DC 20002-5795
Phone: (202) 547-6000
24-hour Legislative Update: (202) 547-4343
Fax: (202) 547-6019
Executive Secretary: Joseph Volk

ORIGINS AND DEVELOPMENT

FCNL was founded in 1943 as an appointed committee of members of the Religious Society of Friends (Quakers). Initially FCNL sought support for the rights of conscientious objectors during World War II and spoke out with a deep concern over the pervasive role of military policy in American life. FCNL has since broadened its agenda to include a wide variety of peace, economic, environmental, and social justice issues related to these original concerns. An articulated goal is "to work toward a nonmilitary world order based so firmly on justice, spiritual unity, and voluntary cooperation that there would be no place for war." FCNL's legislative staff and constituency inform members of Congress, their staffs, and colleague organizations about peace and social justice issues. FCNL also works with grass-roots activists across the nation to educate and organize for peace and social justice.

MISSION STATEMENT

"We seek a world free of war and the threat of war. We seek a society with equality and justice for all. We seek a community where every person's potential may be fulfilled. We seek an earth restored. . . . The Friends committee on National Legislation is composed of Friends who attempt to bring spiritual values to bear on public policy decisions. We believe that God's love endows every person and all creation with worth and dignity. Through individual and corporate worship we try to be open to the will of God and to express the spirit of Christ in all areas of life: personal, community, national, and worldwide. As Christians and seekers after Truth, Friends strive to ensure that the social, economic, political and environmental aspects of our lives are consistent with spiritual values and work together to secure justice and freedom for all people, at peace with one another and the earth. . . . Above all we depend on God's guidance to help us chart our way." "Our legislative policy grows out of our basic belief that there is that of God in every human being. Undergirding all of the legislative actions advocated . . . are moral convictions that ultimately cannot be legislated. They live in the conscience of every person, forged and nurtured through ties to family and community, growing out of a continual search for truth. Government action must always respect and protect the moral freedom of individual conscience. It cannot compel private morality, but integrity and honesty on the part of government agencies and officials can help to create a climate conducive to high ethical standards. In turn, the public integrity will be strengthened by widespread adherence to high standards of morality in the personal lives of individual citizens.''

ORGANIZATION AND FUNDING

The FCNL has a General Committee of some 250 Friends, appointed by twenty-six yearly meetings, eight Friends' organizations, or chosen at large. An Executive Committee, drawn from the General Committee, oversees the programs and administration of FCNL. There are specialized working committees, a staff of eighteen, and hundreds of volunteers who assist the work through grass-roots activism. There are also some 8,000 members/contributors of many different religious and ethical traditions who financially support the work of FCNL. The 1993 budget is about $1 million.

POLICY CONCERNS AND TACTICS

Although FCNL functions autonomously, it seeks to remain responsive to the concerns of Quakers generally. Current areas of concern include human rights, basic human needs, health care, refugees, militarism and disarmament, U.S. foreign policy, United Nations (UN) affairs, and Native American issues such as treaty rights, self-determination, and U.S. trust responsibilities.

As a long-term lobbying group in Washington and the first to refuse a tax-exempt status, the FCNL engages in monitoring government actions, lobbying members of Congress and federal agencies, forming and cooperating with coalitions, and managing an extensive public relations program. It provides internship programs for volunteers and a series of how-to pamphlets on influencing Congress.

AFFILIATION

Religious Society of Friends.

PUBLICATIONS

Action Bulletin (periodic); *Indian Report* (three to four times a year); *Washington Newsletter* (monthly); *Visions of a Warless World* (book); *Congressional Directory* (biannual); in addition, how-to pamphlets and position papers to educate its members.

COMMENTS

The Friends Committee on National Legislation is one of the oldest well-respected religious lobby groups in Washington. While its policy positions are generally to the left of the mainstream, it has provided well researched and articulated policy statements and such experienced leadership that its influence is far greater than its budget or staff size would indicate.

G

/ ———

GENERAL BOARD OF CHURCH AND SOCIETY OF THE UNITED METHODIST CHURCH (GBUMC)

110 Maryland Avenue, NE
Washington, DC 20002
Phone: (202) 488-5600
Fax: (202) 488-5619
General Secretary: Rev. Thom White Wolf Fassett

ORIGINS AND DEVELOPMENT

The General Board of Church and Society (GBUMC) was formed in 1960 under the title of General Board of Christian Social Concerns. It was created by uniting three existing Methodist boards: the General Board of Social and Economic Relations, established in 1952; the General Board of World Peace, established in 1924; and the General Board of Temperance, established in 1888. In 1972 the United Methodist Church adopted a sweeping restructuring plan for its many boards and agencies. At this time the General Board of Christian Social Concerns took its present name.

MISSION STATEMENT

The board follows a formal statement of purpose adopted by the church in 1980 and made part of *The Book of Discipline of the United Methodist Church:* "To relate the gospel of Jesus Christ to the members of the Church and to the persons and structures of the communities and world in which they live. It shall seek to bring the whole life of man and woman, their activities, possessions, and community and world relationships, into conformity with the Will of God. It shall show the members of the church and society that the reconciliation which God effected through Christ involves personal, social and civil righteousness.''

More specifically, the GBUMC follows a set of guidelines called the Social Principles, which are updated every four years by the General Conference. These principles are then specified even more into *The Book of Resolutions,* which provides the priorities for action for the GBUMC.

ORGANIZATION AND FUNDING

The GBUMC had a 1992 budget of $2,420,000 and a professional staff of forty people. Day-to-day work of the board is done through three ministry units: Ministry of God's Creation—environmental justice, peace with justice; Ministry of God's Human Community—human welfare, drugs, and alcohol; Ministry of Resourcing Congregational Life—Communications, congregational life. Funding comes primarily from the United Methodist Church's Benevolence fund, with some additional money coming from donations, sale of publications, and investments. The General Board has eighty-four members who meet twice a year to formulate specific policies and direct the activities of the professional staff.

POLICY CONCERNS AND TACTICS

The GBUMC can fairly be characterized as a liberal, general-purpose religious interest group. A listing of the departments within the Issue Development and Advocacy Division illustrates the thrust and range of issues pursued: Human Welfare, Political and Human Rights, Social and Economic Justice, Peace and World Order, Environmental Justice and Survival, and Ethnic and Local Church Concerns.

The GBUMC is very sensitive to charges of ''lobbying'' and prefers to say that it ''exerts a positive influence on national legislative and executive policies.'' Indeed, the group not only does research and develops issues, provides expert testimony before committees, and stimulates grass-roots lobbying but has been a major participant and leader in coalitions, working consistently with some twenty other groups.

AFFILIATION

United Methodist Church.

PUBLICATIONS

Christian Social Action (monthly magazine); *Word from Washington* (newsletter); and a series of pamphlets such as ''Faithful Witness for Today's World,'' ''Hunger and Poverty,'' and several special reports.

COMMENTS

Over the years the United Methodist Church has been a major player among liberal religious interest groups. Indeed, many such groups find Washington office space in the United Methodist Building, which sits adjacent to both the Capitol and the Supreme Court building. About a decade ago it was publicly accused of pursuing policy objectives more liberal than the views of ordinary church members and of not informing members of their efforts. Since that time the board has taken great pains to focus on policies explicitly endorsed by the General Conference, not only to inform church members but to actively solicit their support. The 1990 reorganization of the board has focused more effort on organizing and educating constituents through the annual conferences (state-level offices) of the church.

H

/

HADASSAH (HAD)

50 West 56th Street
New York, NY 10019
Phone: (212) 355-7900
Fax: (212) 303-8282
Executive Director: Beth Wohgelernter

ORIGINS AND DEVELOPMENT

Acting on the advice of Theodore Herzl, a noted Zionist leader, who advocated organizing American women to support the cause of Zionism, Emma Gottheil formed the Daughters of Zion, a series of study groups in Harlem. This became the nucleus of Hadassah. On 12 February 1912 these groups met to develop a large organization of women Zionists to promote Jewish institutions in Palestine and to foster Jewish ideals. Henrietta Szold was elected president by the thirty-eight founding members. At a national convention in June 1914, the name Hadassah was adopted. The group continued to expand and became a force for health and education welfare for all human beings, but particularly for the Jewish community. It was an important contributor to the development of the State of Israel and the enhancement of the Jewish community in the United States.

MISSION STATEMENT

"As a community of women, Hadassah understands the dramatic changes and challenges for women in the world today. Recognizing that women are confronting the demands of multiple roles and responsibilities—in the family, in the workplace, and in society at large—Hadassah offers each member, within her own time-frame, an opportunity to realize fully her potential as a powerful and positive force within the Jewish community and in the United States.''

ORGANIZATION AND FUNDING

Hadassah has about 385,000 members divided into 1,500 local chapters and 36 regions. It has a full-time staff of 150. In 1993 Hadassah raised over $50 million for its charitable causes, primarily from membership dues and a variety of fund-raising events staffed by volunteers. For local charitable causes, local groups are autonomous, but national and international causes are handled by the New York office.

POLICY CONCERNS AND TACTICS

Hadassah must be seen primarily as a service, not a political activist, organization. In its service capacity it focuses heavily on religious education of young Jews, leadership development, meeting social and recreational needs in their communities, and supporting medical services. Hadassah has been very successful in expanding connections between American and Israeli Jews and supporting specific projects such as land acquisition, hospital construction, and educational projects in Israel.

When the security or economic well-being of Israel is at issue, Hadassah members become very involved in developing political support and exercising political influence over legislators. Its primary tactic is training individual members in the techniques of political influence.

AFFILIATION

Jewish.

PUBLICATIONS

The American Scene; Hadassah Magazine; Hadassah Associates Medbriefs; and *Hadassah National Studies Bulletin.*

COMMENTS

"Of all the Zionist organizations in the United States, Hadassah has been perhaps the most opposed to negating the Diaspora. It has placed particular emphasis on affirming Jewish existence in the United States, so it is thus reasonable to expect a special appreciation for the history of the Diaspora experience" (Allon Gal, *Studies in Zionism* [New York: Schocken Books, 1973]).

HOME SCHOOL LEGAL DEFENSE ASSOCIATION (HSLDA)

P.O. Box 159
Paeonian Springs, VA 22129
Phone: (703) 882-3838
Fax: (703) 338-2733
President: Michael P. Farris

ORIGINS AND DEVELOPMENT

The Home School Legal Defense Association was founded in 1983 to provide legal and educational support for families who wish to educate their children at home rather than in a public or private school. In 1991 the National Home Education Research Institute was added to provide information to parents and HSLDA staff and to provide a mechanism for parents to test their children's educational progress.

MISSION STATEMENT

The Home School Legal Defense Association seeks to ''bring together a large number of home schooling families so that each can have a low-cost method of obtaining quality legal defense. We give the families the freedom to home school without the fear of facing legal threats alone.''

ORGANIZATION AND FUNDING

The HSLDA is an independent organization funded through membership fees of $100 per family per year and the sale of literature. The association has a membership of 20,000, 4 attorneys, a support staff of 15, and a 1993 budget of about $2 million. Only parents home schooling their children are eligible for membership.

POLICY CONCERNS AND TACTICS

While the Home School Legal Defense Association began its operation primarily as a defensive, reactive organization whose main weapon was the lawsuit, it has since branched out considerably, initiating a number of civil rights actions on behalf of members, assisting several state home schooling organizations with legislative battles in their legislatures and providing a lobbying effort in Washington, DC, on behalf of home schoolers. In addition it has become an information resource for people interested in home schooling.

AFFILIATION

Independent Protestant.

PUBLICATIONS

The Home School Court Report (bimonthly newsletter). Pamphlets: *Should Home Schoolers Obey the Law?; The Case for Home Schooling; A Nationwide Study of Home Education: Family Characteristics, Legal Matters and Student Achievement;* and *Home School Statute Chart of the 50 States.* Books: *Constitutional Law for Christian Students; Home Schooling and the Law;* and *Home Schooling in the United States: A Legal Analysis.*

HUMAN RIGHTS CAMPAIGN FUND (HRCF)

P.O. Box 1396
Washington, DC 20013
Phone: (202) 628-4160

Fax: (202) 347-5323
Executive Director: Timothy I. McFeeley

ORIGINS AND DEVELOPMENT

In 1980 the Gay Rights National Lobby initiated the Human Rights Campaign Fund as a political action committee to provide financial support for political candidates supportive of gay rights. In 1982 the two organizations merged. While the HRCF is not itself religious, like the American Civil Liberties Union* it works in an area of major concern to religious organizations, works closely with such groups as the Religious Action Center of Reform Judaism* and the Religious Coalition for Abortion Rights,* is itself supported by a number of gay religious groups, and is a major player in the struggle over gay rights. For that reason we include the fund in this study.

MISSION STATEMENT

"To exert the power of lesbian and gay Americans on national politics and legislation."

ORGANIZATION AND FUNDING

In 1992–93 the Human Rights Campaign Fund had a budget of $5.3 million. Fund-raising dinners and special events generated 40 percent of this, several major donors 31 percent, direct mail solicitation 14 percent, and a "Speak Out" program and other field activities 13 percent, with 2 percent coming from other sources.

HRCF has a staff of thirty full-time people, plus several interns. It depends heavily on volunteers nationwide. HRCF currently has 70,000 members organized into "cores" in different cities.

POLICY CONCERNS AND TACTICS

HRCF was heavily involved in organizing the 1993 March on Washington. Current concerns are funding for AIDS research and support for AIDS victims, lesbian and gay civil rights, discrimination in the military, and domestic partnership and family issues.

HRCF focuses its efforts on electoral politics, including PAC contributions, grass-roots organizing, letters to the editor, providing staff members to work on campaigns, and so on. It also engages in coalition formation and lobbying at all levels. It maintains a national lesbian and gay family registry and a computer bulletin board to provide updates on political developments in Washington and discussion on issues of interest to gays and lesbians.

AFFILIATION

Independent secular.

PUBLICATIONS

Capitol Hill Update (bimonthly); *Federal Club Letter* (monthly); and *Momentum* (quarterly).

COMMENTS

''The Human Rights Campaign Fund, a gay lobbying group, was the ninth largest independent PAC during the last presidential election, and 25th on the Federal Election Commission's list of fund raisers. Politicians have come to recognize the implications of the rise of an openly gay middle class—vast numbers of educated, articulate gays who can and do vote'' (*Newsweek,* 12 March 1990, as reported in *Public Interest Profiles 1992–93* [Washington, DC: Foundation for Public Affairs, 1993]).

''The nation's largest political organization for homosexuals'' (*Seattle Post-Intelligence,* 3 March 1990).

I

INSTITUTE ON RELIGION AND DEMOCRACY (IRD)

1331 H Street, NW
Suite 900
Washington, DC 20005-4706
Phone: (202) 393-3200
Fax: (202) 638-4948
Executive Director: Kent R. Hill

ORIGINS AND DEVELOPMENT

In 1981 a group of Protestant and Roman Catholic clergy and laity, concerned that the churches were abandoning their spiritual mission to support nondemocratic political regimes, formed the Institute on Religion and Democracy as a project of the Foundation for Democratic Education. A year later it became a separate entity.

MISSION STATEMENT

"IRD consists of churches, ministers and church members dedicated to restoring democratic values to churches. We examine the connection between religion and the promotion of democratic institutions worldwide. We oppose efforts by some American churches to provide international financial and ideological support to movements the institute believes are neglectful of democratic values, promote leftist views in the U.S., and are wrongfully silent about violations of religious freedoms abroad. We demand accountability of church groups for aid rendered for political purposes.''

ORGANIZATION AND FUNDING

The Institute on Religion and Democracy had a 1993 budget of $533,000, a staff of 11, and a membership of 1,200. Funding comes primarily from grants and endowments.

POLICY CONCERNS AND TACTICS

The first concern of IRD is to call churches back from a primary focus on their political agendas to an overarching spiritual purpose that can unite within a congregation people with very different political viewpoints. The second concern is to push for the support of democratic values in churches that do make political pronouncements. In addition to a media outreach program, IRD holds seminars, often on Capitol Hill, maintains a speakers' bureau, and sponsors research and publication.

AFFILIATION

Independent, Christian.

PUBLICATIONS

Religion and Democracy (monthly newsletter) and *Anglican Opinion* (quarterly). Books: *The Barren Fig Tree; Peace and Freedom: Christian Faith, Democracy and the Problem of War; Sanctuary: Challenge to the Churches;* and *South Africa: Revolution or Reconciliation?*

COMMENTS

Over the years IRD has been very successful in forcing churches to be more accountable to their membership and more reflective of member views and values. Its efforts gained extraordinary publicity in *Readers Digest, Time, The Wall Street Journal,* and *Christian Century* and on "60 Minutes."

INTERFAITH CENTER ON CORPORATE RESPONSIBILITY (ICCR)

475 Riverside Drive
Room 566
New York, NY 10115
Phone: (212) 870-2295
Fax: (212) 870-2023
Executive Director: Timothy Smith

ORIGINS AND DEVELOPMENT

Begun in 1974 as a project of the National Council of the Churches of Christ in the USA* to utilize the power of religious institutional investments to influence American corporations to act with social and environmental sensitivity in their business dealings.

MISSION STATEMENT

"To address issues of corporate social responsibility with our resources, particularly our investments . . . [and] to work ecumenically for justice in and

through economic structures and for stewardship of the earth and its resources.''

ORGANIZATION AND FUNDING

The ICCR had a budget of $601,000 in 1991. Of this, 75 percent came from
membership dues, 15 percent from foundation and individual contributions, and
10 percent from sale of publications. The ICCR has a staff of ten, seven professional and three support. Its membership consists of 225 Roman Catholic religious
orders and dioceses and twenty-five Protestant agencies and denominations. It is a
''sponsor-related movement of the National Council of Churches.''

POLICY CONCERNS AND TACTICS

Current concerns are investments of American corporations and financial and
religious institutions in a socially responsible manner. In particular ICCR re-
searches alternative investment opportunities, conservation and environmental
issues, equal employment opportunities, food irradiation, infant formula, toxic
waste disposal, and nuclear energy.

ICCR uses a variety of methods to influence both public and business policy,
including boycotts, coalition formation, congressional testimony, litigation, prep-
aration of briefs to submit before the Securities and Exchange Commission,
development of shareholder resolutions, and solicitation of votes by institutional
investors. It provides a research, monitoring, and mediation service for its member institutions. The ICCR does not itself own any stock.

AFFILIATION

Christian Ecumenical.

PUBLICATIONS

Alternative Investment Newspackets (quarterly); *Corporate Examiner* (ten
times yearly); and a number of brochures: *Church Proxy Resolution 1992; The
Conscientious Investors Guide to Socially-Responsible Mutual and Money Market Funds and Investment Services; Corporate Responsibility Challenges, Spring
1990; Directory of Alternative Investments;* and *Guide to Church Alternative
Investment Funds.*

INTERFAITH IMPACT FOR JUSTICE AND PEACE (IIJP)

110 Maryland Avenue, NE
Washington, DC 20077-0620
Phone: (202) 543-2800
Fax: (202) 547-8107
Administrator: Ms. Jozianne Bazile

ORIGINS AND DEVELOPMENT

Interfaith Impact is a new group combining two earlier groups, National Impact
and Interfaith Action for Economic Justice. The parent groups date back to 1975.
It has approximately forty member organizations, which include a wide range of

Christian groups as well as one Islamic and one Jewish group. IIJP also solicits individual memberships. It has a nonlobbying branch, the Interfaith Impact Foundation, to accept tax-deductible contributions. There are state units in half the states.

MISSION STATEMENT

"The purposes for which Interfaith Impact is organized and operated are to advance the jointly shared religious purposes of the organizations represented by this membership, namely, to carry out their theological imperative to increase the possibilities for peace, economic and social justice and human rights by (1) promoting a public policy that reflects prophetic Jewish-Christian values, (2) advocating to the United States government the enactment of public policies that are just, promote peace and protect the environment, (3) developing and nurturing people of faith at congressional district, state and national levels to be effective advocates of public policies that are just, promote peace and protect the environment, (4) maximizing the voice, visibility and ability of member agencies and denominations or faith groups to advocate for public policies that are just, promote peace, and protect the environment, (5) educating and broadening the base of knowledgeable and concerned people among congregations and the general public on the public policy issues of major concern to the interreligious community."

ORGANIZATION AND FUNDING

Interfaith Impact has five classes of membership. The first two are voting levels composed of the religious groups that support it and local, state, and regional affiliates. The at-large members have no vote. Policies are determined by a Board of Directors, primarily from the national religious organizations, with numbers of seats dependent upon size of financial contribution. In 1991 they had expenditures of $737,453.

POLICY CONCERNS AND TACTICS

The agenda for Interfaith Impact is broad and typical of the mainline "liberal" religious groups. It concentrates on winning rights for women and families, promoting international peace, working for a more just economic policy, assuring health care for everyone, improving civil, human and voting rights, fighting poverty, and protecting and preserving the environment. Task forces exist on all of these major topics as they relate to specific legislation in the Congress, and background reports are sent to members.

AFFILIATION

Interfaith.

PUBLICATIONS

Interfaith Impact Magazine is published quarterly. *Interfaith Impact Voting Record* is an annual update of House and Senate members' scores on a set of issues thought to be vital. They also issue action alerts, *Action* and *Networker,* periodically for the different issue networks, as well as reports from the working groups of Interfaith Impact.

COMMENTS

Interfaith Impact is formally organized and is a coordinating and functioning group. It overlaps with Washington Interreligious Staff Council,* which is an important but informal coordinating process for staff of many of the same groups that belong to IIJP.

INTERRELIGIOUS HEALTH CARE ACCESS CAMPAIGN (IHCAC)

110 Maryland Avenue, NE
Box 26, Suite 504
Washington, DC 20002
Phone: (202) 543-5878
Fax: (202) 546-5103
Facilitator: Kevin L. Ogle

ORIGIN AND DEVELOPMENT

A cooperative project with Interfaith Impact for Justice and Peace* and the National Council of the Churches of Christ in the USA,* the campaign is supported by over eighty faith-based member organizations. It arose out of five interreligious consultations on health care reform. It will continue to exist until its legislative objectives in Congress are met. On 7 January 1992 the affiliated religious groups set up the Interreligious Health Care Access Campaign and released its "Working Principles" document.

MISSION STATEMENT

"We seek a national health care plan which grants universal access to health care benefits, including access to primary and acute health care, immunization services, early diagnostic and treatment programs, provider and consumer education, programs of extended care and rehabilitation, mental health, and health and wellness promotion. Such a program should provide for education, training and retraining of health care workers as well as just compensation and affirmative action in hiring. An effective plan will provide for cost containment, equitable financing, and will assure quality of services."

ORGANIZATION AND FUNDING

Campaign president Leontine T. C. Kelly, a Methodist bishop, points out that "the religious community provided health care services long before the advent of modern medicine," and most of the early hospitals were religiously based. "Everyone living in the United States has a right to health care." The endorsing organizations range from the African Methodist Episcopal Church to the Union of American Hebrew Congregations to the Unitarian Universalist Service Committee. The IHCAC emphasizes a high level of cooperation rather than a top-down control structure and has a staff of two persons. The 1993 budget was about $100,000.

POLICY CONCERNS AND TACTICS

The campaign is dedicated to universal access to health care and systemic health care reform. Members support the "American Health Security Act" submitted by Senator Paul Wellstone (D-MN) and Representatives Jim McDermott (D-WA) and John Conyers (D-MI) as the best example of publicly financed health reform. They encourage cosigners in the Congress, promote support through the constituent groups, and urge letter writing to Congress. Most important, they coordinate the work of a host of religious interest groups on this topic.

AFFILIATION

Interreligious.

PUBLICATIONS

Pamphlets and fliers, such as *Visiting Members of Congress to Advocate for Health Care Reform* and *Working Principles for Assessing National Health Care Legislation.*

J

J / ——

JESUIT SOCIAL MINISTRIES (JSM)

1424 16th Street, NW
Suite 300
Washington, DC 20036-2286
Phone: (202) 462-7008
Fax: (202) 328-9212
Executive Director: Rev. Peter Klink, S.J.

ORIGINS AND DEVELOPMENT

Begun in 1972 to provide a Jesuit presence among interest groups in Washington, DC, Jesuit Social Ministries joins various coalitions to achieve a faith-based positive impact upon national legislation and government policy.

MISSION STATEMENT

The national office of Jesuit Social Ministries is ''to provide service to Jesuits in the field of social ministries and to provide a Washington, DC, Jesuit presence working at influencing public policy and public opinion in the areas of vital interest to social justice, peace, and human rights, especially on behalf of the poor and oppressed.''

ORGANIZATION AND FUNDING

The office is supported by the ten Jesuit provinces in the United States through the structure of the U.S. Jesuit Conference. The operating budget is about $150,000, including salaries and wages for three full-time and one part-time staff members.

POLICY CONCERNS AND TACTICS

Jesuit Social Ministries monitors the areas of peace/disarmament, economic justice, racial equality, and ecology. Its current particular focus is in the areas of children's issues, national health care system reform, national economic priorities, and the plight of U.S. cities. Its major tactic is joining coalitions to influence the formation of public policy and public opinion.

AFFILIATION

The Society of Jesus (Jesuits) is a religious order of the Roman Catholic Church.

PUBLICATIONS

A newsletter, informational updates, and legislative updates are provided as needed.

COMMENTS

JSM can be characterized as a low-budget operation that generally supports social justice causes.

JEWISH WAR VETERANS OF THE UNITED STATES OF AMERICA (JWV)

1811 R Street, NW
Washington, DC 20009
Phone: (202) 234-5662
National Executive Director: Col. Herb Rosenblath, U.S.A. (Ret.)

ORIGIN AND DEVELOPMENT

The Jewish War Veterans of the United States of America proclaims itself to be the nation's oldest veterans' organization. It was founded in 1896 by seventy-eight Jewish veterans of the Civil War. The group organized in direct response to the anti-Semitic slander that had unjustly and undeservedly criticized the lack of Jewish participation in the Civil War. Originally known as the Hebrew Union Veterans, the organization experienced early growth and took on its present name more recently.

MISSION STATEMENT

In addition to pointing out Jewish contributions in the Civil War, the JWV began to take stands on human rights and other issues. The JWV has evolved into an organization that not only tries to point out the Jewish contribution to American military history but also ''combats anti-semitism in all its forms, carries on an extensive program committed to upholding America's democratic traditions, and fights bigotry, prejudice, injustice, and discrimination of all kinds.'' Its status as a veterans' organization gives JWV the capacity to lobby in the Congress, without restrictions, on all issues of concern to the entire Jewish community.

ORGANIZATION AND FUNDING

There are a little over 100,000 members of the JWV, some on active duty. Many members belong to other veterans' groups as well. Policies and initiatives are generally determined by the National Executive Committee. There is an annual national convention, which votes on issues. These decisions are conveyed to the membership through local meetings, newsletters, and action alerts. The annual budget is approximately $1 million.

POLICY CONCERNS AND TACTICS

The JWV actively supports a strong national defense and the maintenance of U.S. security interests throughout the world. The group lobbies on behalf of Israeli causes and is an advocate for oppressed Jews worldwide and worked on behalf of emigration of refugees from Russia. JWV works for veterans' benefits, civil rights, the needs of the disabled, and separation of church and state. It can lobby on behalf of the entire Jewish community as well. The members volunteer in veterans' hospitals throughout the country and work with Jewish Boy Scouts and Eagle Scouts.

AFFILIATION

Jewish.

PUBLICATIONS

Various brochures and information bulletins and a newsmagazine, *The Jewish Veteran.*

JUSTLIFE AND JUSTLIFE ACTION (JUST)

P.O. Box 7165
Grand Rapids, MI 49510
Phone: (616) 247-1155
Executive Director: Jill Mann
President: Michael Kruse

ORIGINS AND DEVELOPMENT

JustLife was formed in 1986 as a political action committee, now called "JustLife Action," to elect persons to Congress "who uphold a consistent life ethic—who will work to protect the lives of the unborn, reverse the arms race, and bring justice to the poor." Their nonprofit tax-exempt arm, JustLife Education Fund, was established in 1987 and now carries the name JustLife. Both are characterized by emphasizing a "consistent life ethic," not just antiabortion but promoting other aspects of protecting or enhancing the life of those born. It has both Catholic and Protestant participants. Originally quartered in Washington and Philadelphia, it now has its office in Grand Rapids.

MISSION STATEMENT

"JustLife is an ecumenical gathering of Christians who press for a just political order in American society. JustLife is grounded in the belief that every member of the human family has been created in God's image and is of immeasurable moral worth. . . . Each human being is loved by God and possesses certain God-given rights, the most basic of which is the right to life itself.'' They believe that God wants governments to protect human rights and foster ''human flourishing.'' They work for those who are made vulnerable because of poverty as well as those in danger of being aborted and those who might be killed in war. Regional chapters are being organized in six states.

ORGANIZATION AND FUNDING

The JustLife Education Fund had total predicted revenue for 1993 of $94,000, more than half of that coming from direct-mail solicitation. The JustLife Action PAC had revenues in 1992 of $24,466, expenses of $32,495, and gave direct contributions to candidates for Congress of $4,979. They recently cut their full-time staff from two to one.

POLICY CONCERNS AND TACTICS

In addition to its PAC contributions, which are modest in size, the bipartisan endorsements by JustLife are reinforced by a wide variety of publications. They published six issues of ''JustLife News'' in 1993 and publish before elections an election study guide, such as *JustLife/92*. In 1988, thirty-five of its forty endorsees for congressional seats were winners. They send out legislative alerts in regard to specific pieces of legislation.

AFFILIATION

Roman Catholic and Protestant.

PUBLICATIONS

A variety of publications, including ''JustLife News'' and *JustLife/92*, an election study guide.

L

/

LATTER-DAY SAINTS PUBLIC AFFAIRS DEPARTMENT (LDS)

National Press Building
529 14th Street, NW
Suite 902
Washington, DC 20045
Phone: (202) 662-7550
Fax: (202) 662-7558

Twenty-Fifth Floor
50 East North Temple Street
Salt Lake City, UT 84150

(801) 340-4395

North American Northeast Area Director: T. LaMar Sleight

ORIGINS AND DEVELOPMENT

The Public Affairs Department of The Church of Jesus Christ of Latter-day Saints was organized in 1972 for channeling and coordinating information about the growing Church throughout the world. The department handles news media relations, hosts visiting dignitaries, and maintains liaison with volunteer public communications representatives called to serve in stakes and missions. In 1983 the department's name was expanded to Public Communications/Special Affairs after the original department merged with Special Affairs, the Church's government and community relations office.

MISSION STATEMENT

"The mission of the Church Public Affairs Department is to support the mission of The Church of Jesus Christ of Latter-day Saints to 'invite all to come unto Christ and be perfected in him.' The department assists in increasing the positive awareness of the Church and its Christ-centered doctrine, reaffirms the

Church's role as a vital source of answers to life's challenges and build bridges of friendship and understanding. The goals of the department are to: (1) assist in increasing positive worldwide public awareness of the Church and its divine restoration and Christ-centered doctrine, (2) help people better understand the Church, its members, and its beliefs, and (3) provide a positive influence on key public and social issues, as approved by the First Presidency and Quorum of the Twelve Apostles, and join with others to build bridges of friendship and understanding.''

ORGANIZATION AND FUNDING

Divisions in the department include Media Relations, Area Relations, Public Relations, and Administrative Services. Area offices with full-time directors are located in Washington, DC; Los Angeles, California; London, England; Frankfurt, Germany; Sao Paulo, Brazil; and Sydney, Australia. The headquarters staff in Salt Lake City coordinates the efforts of local public affairs directors, designated to serve in the stakes, regions, and areas. The department is funded by, responsible to, and counsels with the Church's Public Affairs Committee, comprised of members of the Council of the Twelve Apostles. Budget figures are not available.

POLICY CONCERNS AND TACTICS

The Public Affairs Department coordinates the volunteer service of 3,500 local public affairs directors in the stakes and missions of the Church. These individuals, many of them business and professional leaders, interact with local media and arrange coverage of Church events of local interest. The Washington, DC, office monitors legislative issues affecting the Church, its operations, and its members. In addition, designated members of the staff join with representatives of other Churches and national organizations committed to combat such things as pornography, alcohol abuse, gambling, and various other social problems.

AFFILIATION

The Church of Jesus Christ of Latter-day Saints.

PUBLICATIONS

None.

LUTHERAN CHURCH MISSOURI SYNOD OFFICE OF GOVERNMENT INFORMATION (LCMS)

5 Thomas Circle, NW
Washington, DC 20005
Phone: (202) 387-8001
Fax: (202) 387-8027
Interim Director: Elizabeth Foegel

ORIGINS AND DEVELOPMENT

In the mid-1970s the Lutheran Church–Missouri Synod withdrew from the Office of Governmental Affairs of the Lutheran Council in the USA because its activism and views were often contrary to LCMS theological principles and policies. Yet many in the LCMS felt the synod needed to reestablish a liaison with those who make and influence public policy. Begun in 1985 on an experimental basis with a part-time director, the Office of Government Information was expanded in 1987. The office is not incorporated independently from the Lutheran Church–Missouri Synod.

MISSION STATEMENT

The OGI was created to (1) establish a Lutheran Church–Missouri Synod presence in Washington, DC, and provide a mechanism to present Lutheran views to policymakers when requested to do so, (2) to gather information on government activities and legislation in order to keep church leaders informed about things that affect church doctrine and policies, and (3) to increase LCMS visibility with the media and the general public.

ORGANIZATION AND FUNDING

The Office of Government Affairs has a two-person staff and an annual budget of $250,000, furnished by the Missouri Synod. It functions as an administrative unit of the Office of the LCMS president. There is a Washington Advisory Council appointed by the president from among clergy and laity familiar with government to advise both the president and director of the Washington office.

POLICY CONCERNS AND TACTICS

The office has been very reluctant to take positions on issues of public policy and takes no positions except when requested by the synod president. Most recently it has opposed the Religious Restoration Act, believing that the language could be used to imply a right to abortion. In general it has been supportive of pro-life policies, Christian education, inclusion of religious organizations in any child care legislation, and religious liberty issues.

AFFILIATION

Lutheran Church–Missouri Synod.

PUBLICATIONS

A bimonthly column in *Lutheran Witness* and periodic articles for *Reporter* and *Reporter/Alive,* a church monthly.

COMMENTS

The Lutheran Church–Missouri Synod has been reluctant to participate in the political process, based on Luther's two kingdoms doctrine. When it does participate, it tends to represent a politically conservative position.

LUTHERAN OFFICE ON GOVERNMENTAL AFFAIRS
(LOGA)

122 C Street, NW
Suite 300
Washington, DC 20001-2172
Phone: (202) 783-7507
Fax: (202) 783-7502
Executive Director: Kay Dowhower

ORIGINS AND DEVELOPMENT

The Legislative Office on Governmental Affairs (LOGA) represents the Evangelical Lutheran Church in America as an arm of the Commission for Church and Society. LOGA has a Washington staff of ten.

MISSION STATEMENT

''In the Evangelical Lutheran Church in America we unite in service to One Triune God. We are called, as part of our missionary task to serve in response to God's love to meet human needs, caring for the sick and the aged, advocating dignity and justice for all people, working for peace and reconciliation among nations, and standing with the poor and powerless and committing ourselves to their needs.''

ORGANIZATION AND FUNDING

As a denominational liaison office the Lutheran Office on Governmental Affairs is funded directly by the Evangelical Lutheran Church in America and reflects the church's views on political matters.

POLICY CONCERNS AND TACTICS

''The issues LOGA addresses include the rights of women, children and the poor, the federal budget, arms control, U.S. foreign policy, human rights at home and abroad, immigration and refugee concerns, healthcare policy, housing, job training and employment policy, education, the environment and racial justice.''

AFFILIATION

Evangelical Lutheran.

PUBLICATIONS

Legislative Backgrounder (periodic) and *Legislative Update* (monthly).

M

/

MARCH FOR LIFE (MFL)

Box 90300
Washington, DC 20090
Phone: (202) 543-3377
Fax: (202) 543-8202
President: Nellie J. Gray

ORIGINS AND DEVELOPMENT

Began in 1974 as a protest of the majority opinion of the Supreme Court in *Roe v. Wade*. The first of its organized marches took place on 22 January 1974, exactly one year after the decision was handed down, and representatives from state and local pro-life groups incorporated March for Life later that year as a nonprofit, nonpartisan, nonsectarian organization. In addition to organizing the annual protest, which is reported as having 50,000 to 60,000 people, the organization is no longer a registered lobby but testifies before congressional committees.

MISSION STATEMENT

The "Life Principles" are the basic motivating guideline for March for Life. These include the belief that life begins "when the Father's sperm fertilizes the Mother's ovum." The life of the unborn is to be as protected in law as "an infant, teenager, or senile aged." They believe that it should not be predetermined in the law which life can be sacrificed to save another life. They profess that "each human being's life shall be preserved and protected, using all available ordinary means and reasonable efforts, without regard to whose life it is 'better' to preserve and protect." Since their primary goal is to preserve as many lives as possible, an important goal for the organization is the adoption of a "Mandatory Human Life Amendment" to the U.S. Constitution, which would require state laws to conform and provide the same protection.

ORGANIZATION AND FUNDING

The March for Life is not a membership group but works for and with all of the pro-life groups. It is governed by a Board of Directors composed of thirteen experienced pro-life activists. It has only a president and volunteers at its Washington office. The finances of the organization come primarily from individual donations, but it did not provide the size of its budget.

POLICY CONCERNS AND TACTICS

The main policy concern is to promote legislation and an amendment to prevent abortions for any reason. They have lobbied to shut off all federal funds from abortions, successfully in the Reagan and Bush administrations. The major activity is the 22 January march in Washington every year. At the time of the march, they distribute a dozen live red roses to each member of the Congress, along with a note thanking them for support or petitioning their future support.

AFFILIATION

Nondenominational.

PUBLICATIONS

Information sheets sent to members of Congress and *The March for Life Program Journal,* published in conjunction with the annual march.

MENNONITE CENTRAL COMMITTEE/ÆWASHINGTON OFFICE (MCC)

110 Maryland Avenue, NE   Main: 21 South 12th Street
Washington, DC 20002   Akron, PA 17501
Phone: (202) 544-6564   (717) 859-1151
Fax: (202) 544-2820   (717) 859-2171
Executive Director: Delton Franz

ORIGINS AND DEVELOPMENT

The Mennonites grew out of the German pietist tradition, which in turn had roots in the Anabaptists. While Mennonites have been in the United States since 1683, the Mennonite Central Committee was not formed until 1920. The Washington office was established in 1968 to support the church's Peace and Justice Ministry.

MISSION STATEMENT

"The Mennonite Central Committee is built on the conviction that meeting human needs and giving service to others is an integral part of the Christian life and that God intended all people to share the earth's resources. Volunteers work to remove barriers that separate people from each other and from God in a ministry of reconciliation. MCC joins with those who are seeking less costly, nonviolent ways to settle disputes and to secure greater equality and justice.''

ORGANIZATION AND FUNDING

The major work of the MCC is in Third World countries, administering agricultural, educational, medical, and disaster relief and peace programs. The focus of the Washington office is to make MCC policy positions known to Congress and government agencies, seek funding and coordination for relief efforts, and serve as an advocacy group. The Washington office has a full-time staff of four and had a 1993 budget of $220,000, which was provided by the MCC.

POLICY CONCERNS AND TACTICS

The MCC has a long tradition as a nonviolent, peace church and continues this effort through its Washington office. Therefore it works to influence government in areas of the arms race, nuclear arms control, defense spending, and the criminal justice system. It is also a major player in relief and development efforts and exerts its influence here as well. In addition to providing information to Congress, the MCC joins numerous coalitions to make its voice heard.

AFFILIATION

Mennonite (Protestant).

PUBLICATIONS

Conciliation Quarterly; Crime and Justice Network Newsletter (quarterly); *Dialogue on Disabilities* (quarterly); *Food and Hunger Notes* (bimonthly); *Peace Office Newsletter* (bimonthly); and *Washington Memo* (bimonthly). The MCC also publishes *Women's Concerns Report* and various monographs and occasional papers.

MORALITY IN MEDIA (MIM)

475 Riverside Drive
New York, NY 10115
Phone: (212) 870-3222
Fax: (212) 870-2765
President: Robert W. Peters

ORIGINS AND DEVELOPMENT

Morality in Media got its start on the Upper East Side of Manhattan in 1962 after a mother discovered sixth grade boys circulating sadomasochistic magazines. MIM's founder, the late Father Hill, S.J., researched the problem, then recruited a rabbi and a Lutheran minister to start a community organization. Morality in Media rapidly became nationwide in scope after requests for assistance came from many people. In 1968 Fr. Hill was appointed to the Presidential Commission on Obscenity and Pornography and coauthored the Hill-Link Minority Report of the commission, which rejected the majority recommendation that obscenity laws should be repealed.

MISSION STATEMENT

"Morality in Media is a non-profit national organization working by constitutional means to curb the explosive growth of hardcore pornography and related ills, and to turn back the tide of grossly offensive, indecent media."

ORGANIZATION AND FUNDING

In addition to its national office MIM has state offices in Massachusetts and Wisconsin. There are 16,500 dues-paying members and a full-time staff of 16. The annual budget is about $725,000 and comes from corporations, foundations, and individual donations.

POLICY CONCERNS AND TACTICS

MIM focuses its efforts on ridding the nation of pornography whether it be in book form, on the networks, or on cable television. It works primarily through a public awareness campaign to inform, organize, and activate citizens, then by encouraging members to support stores that do not traffic in pornographic books, films, or videos. Members are also urged to speak to store owners who do carry pornographic products and dissuade them if possible. Members are encouraged to contact their district attorneys concerning specific problems and urge action against illegal publications and activities. In 1988 the organization began a "White Ribbon Against Pornography" campaign, which proved highly successful in raising community consciousness of the problems associated with pornography. In 1991 MIM introduced "Real Men Don't Use Porn," a billboard campaign that has now reached over forty states. In addition MIM maintains a National Obscenity Law Center, which functions as a clearinghouse and resource center for prosecutors developing and pursuing cases.

AFFILIATION

Independent Ecumenical.

PUBLICATIONS

Morality in Media publishes two bimonthlies, *MIM Newsletter* and *The Obscenity Law Bulletin,* as well as pamphlets such as *Pornography Has Consequences* and *Cliches—Debunking Misinformation About Pornography and Obscenity Law.* It also publishes a 123-page book for lawyers and prosecutors, entitled *Handbook on the Prosecution of Obscenity Cases.*

N

---- / ----

NATIONAL ABORTION RIGHTS ACTION LEAGUE (NARAL)

1101 14th Street, NW
5th Floor
Washington, DC 20005
Phone: (202) 973-3000
Fax: (202) 973-3096
Executive Director: Kate Michelman

ORIGINS AND DEVELOPMENT

Begun in 1969 to promote women's right to choose abortions, NARAL remains the "leading national abortion-rights lobby group" (*Wall Street Journal,* 29 March 1990, as reported in *Public Interest Profiles, 1992–93* [Washington, DC: Foundation for Public Affairs, 1993]).

MISSION STATEMENT

"To defend and protect a woman's right to choose abortion."

ORGANIZATION AND FUNDING

With a 1991 budget of $6.3 million, NARAL supports a staff of forty-five, twenty-nine professional and sixteen support. In addition it works with interns and more than fifty volunteers. NARAL has 450,000 members with forty-one state affiliate chapters. Contributions and grants account for 88 percent of the budget, investment income for 9 percent, and endowment, bequests, and other sources for 3 percent. NARAL is a 501(c)(4) organization and is affiliated with NARAL Foundation, a 501(c)(3) organization.

POLICY CONCERNS AND TACTICS

Under the umbrella concern of protecting the right to choose abortions, NARAL currently focuses on congressional funding restrictions on abortion, parental consent/notification laws and other state limitations on access to abortion, the appointment of federal judges, and harassment and violence against abortion clinics.

AFFILIATION

Independent secular.

PUBLICATIONS

NARAL News (quarterly); *NARAL Campus Newsletter* (quarterly); and a series of books and pamphlets, such as *Choice—Legal Abortion: Arguments Pro & Con; Congressional Votes on Abortion* (annual report); *The Voices of Women; Who Decides? A Reproductive Rights Issues Manual;* and *Who Decides? A State By State Review of Abortion Rights in America.* In addition NARAL has produced a videotape, ''Voices.''

NATIONAL CATHOLIC EDUCATIONAL ASSOCIATION (NCEA)

1077 30th Street, NW
Suite 100
Washington, DC 20007
Phone: (202) 337-6232
Fax: (202) 333-6706
Executive Director: Sr. Katherine McNamee, CSJ

ORIGINS AND DEVELOPMENT

The NCEA was founded in 1904, when three groups representing the major thrusts of Catholic education—parish schools, colleges and universities, and seminaries—decided to form an umbrella organization to work cooperatively on issues of Catholic education. Currently it has eight departments, five service bureaus, and two commissions.

MISSION STATEMENT

''The goal of the NCEA has been to vitalize and improve Catholic education and, through the witness of its educational programs, to demonstrate the deep concern of the Catholic Church for this nation and for the family of man.''

ORGANIZATION AND FUNDING

Membership in NCEA is made up primarily of Catholic school administrators on college, secondary, and primary grade levels, although parent organizations and individual teachers and parents may also join. School dues are the primary source of funding, followed by income from the annual convention, sale of publications, and services to member schools. The 1992–93 budget was about $4,588,000. NCEA employs a staff of forty.

POLICY CONCERNS AND TACTICS

While a majority of the NCEA's time and resources is dedicated to the internal task of improving Catholic education, it is a significant player in Washington, D.C., on any political issues that affect private religious schools. It supports financial aid for religious schools in the form of vouchers, government grants, scholarships, technical assistance, and so on and serves as a watchdog to limit or defeat government regulation of private schools that it considers excessive or intrusive. On the other hand, it cooperates closely with the Department of Education and other government agencies, providing data about Catholic school enrollments, Catholic positions on policy issues, and potential rules and legislation.

AFFILIATION

Roman Catholic.

PUBLICATIONS

The NCEA publishes a quarterly journal, *Momentum;* a general newsletter, *Alive;* a journal for parents, *Parentcator;* and numerous specialized pamphlets, newsletters, and training tapes for Catholic educators.

COMMENTS

The NCEA is primarily a professional organization that spends a preponderance of its time and resources on strengthening Catholic education. It works on curriculum development, especially in the area of peace and justice education, teacher and administrator formation, special education, parental involvement, and financing Catholic schools. It sees itself as "nonpolitical" but plays a key role in alerting Catholic school personnel about political trends that might affect them, educating members about legal issues in private education, and educating government officials about the Catholic system. If a voucher system of financing education becomes a major political issue, the NCEA may take a higher profile role.

NATIONAL COALITION AGAINST PORNOGRAPHY (N-CAP)

800 Compton Road
Suite 9224
Cincinnati, OH 45231
Phone: (513) 521-6227
Fax: (513) 521-6337
Executive Director: Jerry Kirk

ORIGINS AND DEVELOPMENT

Begun in 1983 by Rev. Jerry Kirk to respond to the expanding presence of, and tolerance for, pornography in the United States, N-CAP has expanded its programs to include citizen education, training for prosecutors, and initiating legal actions. The coalition is an alliance of businesses, foundations, citizen action groups, religious denominations, and faith groups.

MISSION STATEMENT

"The mission of the National Coalition Against Pornography is to significantly reduce sexual violence and victimization of children, women, men and families by eliminating child pornography and removing illegal pornography from the open market." N-CAP's purpose is to help concerned citizens eliminate illegal obscenity and child pornography—materials that are not protected by the Constitution and have been shown to promote sexual violence, degradation, and abuse of both children and adults. N-CAP opposes censorship (prior restraint by the government).

ORGANIZATION AND FUNDING

N-CAP has its national headquarters in Cincinnati but has several other locations for its major subsidiary projects. The "California Care Coalition" is located in Santa Ana, and the "Enough Is Enough" campaign and the National Law Center for Children and Families are located in Fairfax, Virginia. Funding comes primarily from donations from individuals and foundations. The 1992 budget was slightly over $1,157,183.

POLICY CONCERNS AND TACTICS

N-CAP concerns itself with illegal, hard-core pornography, although it cooperates with such groups as Morality in Media,* which are more concerned with legal, soft-core pornography. The coalition attempts to educate the public about the prevalence and severity of illegal obscenity and child pornography in America today, to mobilize and assist citizen groups that support enforcement of existing laws against the production, distribution, and sale of illegal obscenity and child pornography, and to assist government agencies by drafting and supporting legislation that strengthens or initiates such laws. It does initiate lawsuits and provides legal resources and assistance.

AFFILIATION

Independent, Ecumenical.

PUBLICATIONS

Standing Together (bimonthly), plus videos, pamphlets, and fact sheets.

COMMENTS

N-CAP appears to be a true grass-roots movement; it provides subscribers with very practical materials such as "Six Steps to Beat Mail Order Porn"; "Ten Things You Can Do to Combat Pornography"; "Cliche Arguments"; and "Resources for Concerned Citizens."

NATIONAL COALITION TO ABOLISH THE DEATH PENALTY (NCADP)

1325 G Street, NW
Lower Level B
Washington, DC 20005
Phone: (202) 347-2411
Fax: (202) 347-2510
Executive Director: Leigh Dingerson

ORIGINS AND DEVELOPMENT

The National Coalition to Abolish the Death Penalty was established in 1976 under the name National Coalition Against the Death Penalty in direct response to the resumption of executions in the United States. The NCADP was originally based in New York as a project of the American Civil Liberties Union.* In 1982 the group was moved to Philadelphia and separately incorporated. In 1987 the name was changed, and headquarters moved to Washington, DC. Among the more than fifty coalition members are the American Baptist Churches,* the American Civil Liberties Union, Amnesty International,* Church of the Brethren,* Episcopal Church,* Fellowship of Reconciliation,* National Association for the Advancement of Colored People (NAACP), National Bar Association, the National Council on Islamic Affairs, Pax Christi USA,* Presbyterian Church USA,* Synagogue Council of America, Union of American Hebrew Congregations, United Methodist Church,* and the United States Catholic Conference.*

MISSION STATEMENT

The National Coalition to Abolish the Death Penalty works to abolish the death penalty in the United States and to avert all executions. It believes the death penalty to be ineffective as a deterrent to crime.

ORGANIZATION AND FUNDING

''The NCADP is a coalition of over 120 national, state and local organizations. Each affiliate holds one seat on the NCADP Board of Directors, which meets yearly to approve an annual budget, elect officers, and determine general direction for the organization. The annual budget is $200,000 raised primarily from affiliate support dues, individual contributions and fund-raising events. Some funding also comes from foundations, subscriptions and the sale of resource materials.''

POLICY CONCERNS AND TACTICS

The coalition is a single-issue group dedicated to abolishing the death penalty. In addition to efforts to publicize its concerns, persuade lawmakers to pass legislation abolishing the death penalty, and inform public opinion, the coalition supports a litigation committee to pursue its agenda through the courts.

AFFILIATION

Independent Ecumenical.

PUBLICATIONS

The Abolitionist Directory (annual); *The Death Penalty Exchange* (periodic); *Execution Alert* (periodic); *Lifelines* (bimonthly newsletter); *The Death Penalty: The Religious Community Calls for Abolition* (pamphlet); and *Legislative Action to Abolish the Death Penalty* (book).

NATIONAL COUNCIL OF THE CHURCHES OF CHRIST IN THE U.S.A. (NCC)

475 Riverside Drive   110 Maryland Avenue, NE
New York, NY 10115   Washington, DC 20002
Phone: (212) 870-2227   (202) 544-2350
Fax: (212) 870-2030   (202) 543-1297
Executive Director: Rev. Joan B. Campbell

ORIGINS AND DEVELOPMENT

The National Council of Churches was reorganized and renamed in 1950, replacing the older Federal Council of Churches. It is affiliated with the World Council of Churches, although fiscally and organizationally independent. The NCC is "comprised of 32 Protestant, Orthodox, and Anglican member denominations whose combined membership is more than 42 million. The council is a community of national religious bodies, not a church and not an association of individuals."

MISSION STATEMENT

"To be a community through which churches can make visible their unity given in Christ and can live responsibly in witness and service."

ORGANIZATION AND FUNDING

The 1991 budget of $48.2 million was raised from the following sources: 43 percent from public appeals and foundation grants, 27 percent from congregational membership dues, 17 percent from refugee settlement contracts with the U.S. government and federal disaster relief funds, and 13 percent from sale of materials, service fees, and investment income. In addition to the national and Washington offices, the NCC has twenty-five World Service offices across the United States and several overseas representatives. Programs are carried out by four subunits: Church World Service and Witness; Education, Communication and Discipleship; Prophetic Justice; and Unity and Relationships.

POLICY CONCERNS AND TACTICS

Current concerns are apartheid in South Africa, peace in Central America, peace in the Middle East, poverty, racial justice, refugee settlement and disaster relief, world hunger, women's issues, AIDS, and religious liberty.

AFFILIATION

Independent Protestant and Orthodox.

PUBLICATIONS

CORLETTER (bimonthly); *Ecu-Link* (five times yearly); *Intermedia* (occasional); *Lights* (occasional); *Yearbook of American and Canadian Churches* (annual); and a number of reports, including *Apostolic Faith in America, The Church with AIDS: Renewal in the Midst of Crisis,* and *Women and Church.*

COMMENTS

With a staff of 333, the National Council of Churches is by far the largest mainline Protestant interest group. As the successor to the Federal Council of Churches, it has a long and distinguished history. It has rarely been far from controversy, almost always as a voice for theological liberalism and the social gospel. In the 1950s and 1960s, at the height of its power and prestige, it was a very influential voice in government. However, it was considered far too liberal by many fundamentalist and Evangelical churches and became the focus of attacks in the 1980s by conservative groups. Faced with loss of membership and a declining budget, the NCC has placed far greater emphasis in the 1990s on developing working relationships with Roman Catholics and conservative Evangelical groups on issues of common concern. The council has also had to deal with internal conflicts and a large, unwieldy bureaucracy.

NATIONAL INTERRELIGIOUS SERVICE BOARD FOR CONSCIENTIOUS OBJECTION (NISBCO)

1601 Connecticut Avenue, NW
Suite 750
Washington, DC 20009
Phone: (202) 483-4510
Fax: (202) 265-8022
Executive Director: L. William Yolton

ORIGINS AND DEVELOPMENT

Begun in 1940 as a cooperative effort of several peace churches, NISBCO has maintained an office and staff to provide information to individuals, religious groups, and government agencies seeking information about the draft, conscription, and draft registration.

MISSION STATEMENT

A service agency for individual conscientious objectors, churches, and religious groups interested in conscientious objection.

ORGANIZATION AND FUNDING

NISBCO has a national staff of five. Its 1993 budget was $180,000, provided by its thirty coalition members.

POLICY CONCERNS AND TACTICS

Conscientious objection (CO), draft registration, and the process of applying for CO status remain the core issues for NISBCO. It will aid members of the military who refuse to serve in a war effort or who become conscientious objectors after joining the military.

AFFILIATION

Independent Ecumenical.

PUBLICATIONS

Draft Counselor's Manual (annual) and *Reporter for Conscience' Sake* (monthly).

NATIONAL INTERRELIGIOUS TASKFORCE ON CRIMINAL JUSTICE (NITFCJ)

100 Witherspoon Street
Louisville, KY 40202
Phone: (502) 569-5810
Fax: (502) 569-8116
Director: David W. Rogers

ORIGINS AND DEVELOPMENT

During the late 1960s, in the midst of urban unrest, rising crime, and enormous societal changes, several liberal religious leaders began to give violence and police work a priority status. In 1966 representatives of the Episcopal Church, the United Presbyterian Church, and the United Church of Christ (UCC) formed the Joint Urban Executive Committee to explore possible church involvement in solving these problems. When the Methodist, American Baptist, and Reformed churches decided to join, the name was changed to the Joint Strategy and Action Committee (JSAC). Initial funding was provided by the National Council of the Churches of Christ in the U.S.A.*

A Police Power Work Group (PPWG) became the first issue focus of JSAC, and it continued to work on police brutality, particularly as it intersected with racism. In 1973 the group decided that the issues in criminal justice were far broader and required a more integrated approach. The National Interreligious Taskforce on Criminal Justice was formed. JSAC and PPWG have since been discontinued.

MISSION STATEMENT

"NITFCJ is an interfaith association of national religious bodies and other affiliated organizations committed to equal justice, the creation of safe and just communities, and the protection of human rights for offenders and victims alike. It supports a national religious agenda for criminal justice and conflict resolution, collaborates with other national coalitions, and forms linkages with the efforts of local and regional organizations.''

ORGANIZATION AND FUNDING

The NITFCJ serves as an interdenominational reflection, resource, planning, and advocacy group. The National Council of Churches provided startup funds, but the group has always consisted of denominational staff experts committed to the taskforce. NITFCJ functions with a budget below $25,000. Membership consists of some forty to forty-five cooperating denominations and churches and a small number of individuals.

POLICY CONCERNS AND TACTICS

The taskforce concerns itself with a full range of criminal justice issues, including the death penalty; prisoners' rights; alternatives to prison, crime, and racism; drug enforcement; gun control; law enforcement; and illegal immigration policy. The group works through advocacy (which members understand to include not only lobbying and providing information to government officials and agencies, but demonstrations and prayer vigils as well), education of the religious community, and networking with other interest groups.

AFFILIATION

Interfaith.

PUBLICATIONS

Over the years the taskforce has sponsored a number of newsletters, including *Criminal Justice Update, JUSTnews,* and *ICC Link.* The latter was discontinued in 1991, and a new publication is still in the planning stage. In addition, the group has a series of pamphlets, reports, and working papers on criminal justice issues.

NATIONAL LEGAL FOUNDATION (NLF)

6477 College Park Square
Suite 306
Virginia Beach, VA 23464
Phone: (804) 424-4242
Fax: (804) 420-0855
Executive Director: Robert Skolrood

ORIGINS AND DEVELOPMENT

The National Legal Foundation was incorporated in 1985 by Pat Robertson as a public interest law firm and financed by the Christian Broadcasting Network (CBN). By 1988 the NLF had developed a sufficient donor base to becomep an independent organization under its current director, Robert Skolrood. The National Legal Foundation is a 501(c)(3) organization and provides free legal services in defense of civil rights and constitutional liberties, particularly religious liberty, freedom of speech, the freedom of association, and rights of the unborn.

MISSION STATEMENT

"The goal of the National Legal Foundation is to secure religious liberty through effective advocacy." They believe that "the Constitution, through the First Amendment, has provided a hedge of safety for the flourishing of religion in this nation which has blessed the entire world." "Today, legal terrorists attempt to sabotage the Constitution in their effort to transform America into a spiritual wasteland, intolerant of the Faith of our fathers." "The Constitution, despite repeated assaults, remains a strong bulwark for freedom. Upon this heritage we mount our defense of liberty. As lawyers, we are honored to wage this battle in the country's courts and wherever else it must be joined."

ORGANIZATION AND FUNDING

Initial funding was provided by the Christian Broadcasting Network. In 1988, the foundation became entirely independent. The foundation has a 30,000-member donor base to support its operations. The NLF has a staff of ten. Its 1993 budget was approximately $400,000.

POLICY CONCERNS AND TACTICS

The NLF pursues its goals through litigation and education. When cases are referred, the first attempt is to resolve conflicts between the parties before going to court. If a court case appears to be the only or best alternative, cases are chosen that hold promise for establishing more general precedents with national significance. Their attorneys litigate directly and with regional cocounsel. It has a network of 250 affiliate attorneys across America. Examples of litigation in which they were involved include *Westside Community Schools v. Mergens,* which resulted in the Supreme Court's ruling that students seeking to organize a campus Bible club had been denied rights under the 1984 Equal Access Act; and *Doe v. Small,* in which the U.S. Court of Appeals for the Seventh Circuit ruled that free speech rights of private citizens to express religious ideas in public places could not be censored.

AFFILIATION

Independent, conservative, Evangelical.

PUBLICATIONS

"Minuteman Alert!" (a national daily radio broadcast); *The NLF Minuteman* (quarterly newsletter); *Foundations of Freedom: The Constitution & Bill of Rights;* and occasional papers: "In God We Trust"; "Invocations and Benedictions at Public School Graduation Ceremonies"; "Bible Clubs and Student Religious Meetings in Public Schools"; and "Graduation Prayers: Clearing up the Confusion."

NATIONAL RELIGIOUS PARTNERSHIP FOR THE ENVIRONMENT (NRPE)

1047 Amsterdam Avenue
New York, NY 10025
Phone: (212) 932-7441
Fax: (212) 932-7348
Executive Director: Paul T. Gorman

ORIGINS AND DEVELOPMENT

The National Religious Partnership for the Environment (NRPE) is comprised of four major faith groups and denominations. In July 1993 these groups—the United States Catholic Conference,* the National Council of the Churches of Christ in the U.S.A.,* the Consultation on the Environment and Jewish Life, and the Evangelical Environment Network—initiated a three-year, $5 million mobilization on behalf of environmental integrity and justice.

Establishment of NRPE marked the convergence of two streams of effort: accelerated activity by individual American faith groups and a catalytic process of interreligious consultation with scientists organized by the Joint Appeal by Religion and Science for the Environment. The partnership began to take form in response to an Open Letter to the Religious Community issued in January 1990 by thirty-four internationally prominent scientists. In the letter they wrote that ''[environmental] problems of such magnitude and solutions demanding so broad a perspective must be recognized from the outset as having a religious as well as a scientific dimension. . . . Efforts to safeguard and cherish the environment need to be infused with a vision of the sacred.''

Several hundred religious leaders of all major faiths from five continents responded. On 2 June 1991 a small group of religious leaders convened for scientific briefings, conversations with members of Congress, and consideration of future initiatives. At the end of the gathering they concluded that such consensus existed across a significant spectrum of religious traditions that environmental integrity and justice could become a priority of people of faith. In May 1992, fifty religious leaders and fifty Nobel laureate and other scientists convened in Washington, D.C., to hear scientific updates on global environmental conditions and reports on activities within their respective communities. This Mission to Washington was a unique, perhaps unprecedented, gathering of eminent representatives from a diverse world of religion, science, and government in close consultation. At the meeting's conclusion the senior religious leaders formally established the National Religious Partnership for the Environment.

MISSION STATEMENT

''The task before us in this Partnership is both quantitative and qualitative: to build a base of commitment to individual and institutional action which is exponentially broader, more deeply motivated, and in service to a more comprehensive environmental vision integrating ecology and equity.''

ORGANIZATION AND FUNDING

The NRPE's funding of $5 million for a three-year startup was raised from several private foundations. As of this writing it is just getting off the ground, so its ultimate organizational structure is not yet firm. It will have a central communications office that seeks to document the activities of the religious community and facilitate congregations working with each other.

POLICY CONCERNS AND TACTICS

In addition to mounting a major public policy campaign, the partnership plans annually to distribute environmental kits to 53,000 congregations, provide major consultations on issues of environmental justice and international development, hold conferences for leaders of historically black churches and Orthodox Christian churches, develop seminary and religious education curriculum, and support theological scholarship.

AFFILIATION

Ecumenical.

PUBLICATIONS

None.

NATIONAL RIGHT TO LIFE COMMITTEE, INC. (NRL)

419 Seventh Street, NW
Suite 500
Washington, DC 20004
Phone: (202) 626-8800
Fax: (202) 737-9189
Executive Director: David N. O'Steen

ORIGINS AND DEVELOPMENT

Begun in 1973 as a direct response to the Supreme Court's *Roe v. Wade* decision, National Right to Life Committee is the nation's largest pro-life organization. It has branches in each of the fifty states as well as some 3,000 local chapters. Its longtime director, Dr. Jack Wilke, molded the group into a powerful lobby before retiring in 1991. Among antiabortion groups it is considered somewhat moderate, opposing civil disobedience and willing to compromise to get legislation passed.

MISSION STATEMENT

''Works for the protection of all innocent human life threatened by abortion, infanticide and euthanasia.''

ORGANIZATION AND FUNDING

The 1993 budget was approximately $12 million raised from membership dues, direct mail solicitation, and other private donations. State branches work with the national office but often initiate activities on their own.

POLICY CONCERNS AND TACTICS

Current concerns are abortion, euthanasia, and federal funding of abortion and fetal tissue research. National Right to Life engages in a full panoply of legal tactics, from coalition formation to bill writing to testifying before congressional committees. It sponsors a National Right to Life PAC and engages in electoral politics. It also supports litigation, provides a speakers' bureau, and so on. State and local affiliates often sponsor legislation to limit access to permissive abortion.

AFFILIATION

Independent, nondenominational.

PUBLICATIONS

National Right to Life Chapter Newsletter (biweekly); *National Right to Life News* (biweekly); plus numerous books, pamphlets, and videotapes, including *Aborted Women, Silent No More, Abortion: Death Before Life?, Abortion: The Dreaded Complication, Abortion: The Hard Cases, Abortion: Questions and Answers, Abortion: Some Medical Facts, Life Before Birth, Factsheet: Planned Parenthood, The Challenge to Be Pro-Life, When Does Human Life Begin?* and "The Silent Scream" (videotape).

COMMENTS

"The National Right to Life Committee is often at the center of controversy over abortion. Attacked from the left as insensitive to women's rights, it is also attacked from the right as too willing to accommodate and compromise in order to get legislation passed. Its most recent controversy was over the release of 'Silent Scream' a very graphic video of an abortion from the fetal perspective. Nat Hentoff, a columnist for *The Village Voice* who is basically sympathetic with the pro-life movement, has criticized the NRLC because it maintains a 'no position' on contraception, thus undermining its credibility with many people troubled by abortion but not absolutists on the subject" (*Public Interest Profiles, 1992–93* [Washington, DC: Foundation for Public Affairs, 1993]).

NETWORK (NET)

806 Rhode Island Avenue, NE
Washington, DC 20018
Phone: (202) 526-4070
Fax: (202) 832-4635
National Coordinator: Kathy Thornton

ORIGIN AND DEVELOPMENT

Network was founded in 1971 by 47 Roman Catholic nuns. Since that time it has grown to some 10,000 individual members, about 60 percent of them nuns, priests, and brothers and 40 percent laypersons. It is a registered lobby and therefore does not maintain a tax-exempt status, although it does have a tax-exempt educational foundation attached to it.

MISSION STATEMENT

Network calls itself "a national Catholic Social Justice Lobby" and has had several statements, the most important of which is *Toward an Integrated Spirituality*. Among other things it asserts: "Our faith and the commitment to social justice that faith demands of us permeate our total experience. . . . religious people have become more aware of the need for political activity in actualizing a more just world order. . . . Network is involved legislatively because that is where crucial power resides. . . . We believe that consistently throughout Scripture the sign of God's presence is concern for the poor, the afflicted, the marginalized."

ORGANIZATION AND FUNDING

Network's 1992–93 budget was $700,000, derived from member dues, donations, grants from various religious orders and foundations, and the sale of services and publications. Network functions precisely as its name implies: it relies on a telephone tree and newsletter network to alert members to call or write their congresspeople.

POLICY CONCERNS AND TACTICS

Network maintains its overall interest in serving the "poor and underrepresented" in politics. Each year its priorities are set by a vote of the membership. In 1993 these priorities were health care, housing, community economic development, and sustainable development in the Third World. While its agenda is definitely liberal, Network avoids issues that are divisive within the Catholic community, so it has taken no position on the abortion debate, gay rights, and so on.

In addition to its use of a telephone alert tree, Network has developed a widely distributed "Scorecard" for all senators and representatives, recording how each elected official voted each session on issues of concern to Network. Staff and members directly lobby individual congresspeople and their aides. Network also offers summer workshops on issue research and lobbying for interns from around the country. This has proven to be an effective teaching and recruiting tool for the organization. Finally, Network belongs to numerous coalitions and often takes a leadership role in organizing coalitions to address specific issues. For example, it worked as part of the leadership of Citizens Budget Campaign (CBC) during 1992, an effort to change national budget priorities.

AFFILIATION

Independent Roman Catholic.

PUBLICATIONS

The Network *Connection* appears bimonthly; in addition, Action-Alerts are published on an as-needed basis.

COMMENT

Network was one of the many groups begun in the early 1970s as a liberal social action lobby. It considers its work a "political ministry," that is, "a ministry devoted to direct, detailed, day-by-day involvement in political decisions of the federal government." Representing a well-educated, politically active clientele, Network is considered to be a well-prepared, effective lobby, especially considering its small size and limited staff.

NEW CALL TO PEACEMAKING (NCP)

P.O. Box 500
21 South 12th Street
Akron, PA 17501-0500
Phone: (717) 859-1958
Fax: (717) 859-1958
Executive Director: John K. Stoner

ORIGINS AND DEVELOPMENT

On 28 June 1976, representatives from the Society of Friends, Mennonites, and Church of the Brethren* met to consider a proposal from Norval Hadley and other Quakers that there be a new cooperative effort of the Historic Peace churches (HPC). They agreed to the name, New Call to Peacemaking, a statement of purpose, and a plan of action. Following the 1982 conference a decision was made to shift the direction of NCP from revitalizing the peace testimony of the Historic Peace churches to more contact and relationship with other Christian groups open to a more faithful peace witness.

However, in 1989 a decision was made at the HPC meeting that the NCP should "shift into a different format." NCP was essentially scaled back and became part of the larger Historic Peace Church Cooperation. It was agreed that the name should be retained, "recognizing that future developments may suggest another designation for the Historic Peace Cooperation." In 1991 the group reorganized and developed·a new program in which it seeks broad ecumenical participation.

MISSION STATEMENT

"Believing that we are called by Our Lord to be peacemakers in our contemporary world, we seek a positive, creative and practical approach to peace that is biblically based and spiritually sound, which would be a strong witness and which would invite the widest possible participation."

ORGANIZATION AND FUNDING

From 1989 to 1991 the NCP was a file drawer organization kept alive by Mr. Stoner. It was revitalized in 1991 and currently has a $16,000 budget and a 2,200 name mailing list upon which it hopes to build.

POLICY CONCERNS AND TACTICS

The NCP's main policy concerns focus on efforts to make war impossible, including total disarmament, especially a ban on nuclear weapons. The NCP also supports more generalized human rights legislation, including putting an end to apartheid and world hunger. Traditionally Peace Churches focus on evangelism rather than lobbying, but NCP's current efforts, while mostly educational, do include support for Peace Tax Fund legislation.

AFFILIATION

Protestant.

PUBLICATIONS

Call to Peacemaking (sporadic newsletter) and books: *A New Call to Peacemaking* and *Politics of Conscience.*

NEW JEWISH AGENDA (NJA)

87 North 5th Street
San Jose, CA 95112
Phone: (408) 287-2037
Contact Person: Warner Bloomberg

ORIGINS AND DEVELOPMENT

The agenda's founding conference was held in 1980. It was a leading advocate of achieving "a just and secure Israel" through negotiations. In the last few years its finances have been in disarray, and it is currently undergoing reorganization nationally while local chapters remain active. NJA supporters expect that it will survive as a progressive voice in spite of its difficulties and expect the implementation of some of its agenda by the Israeli government.

MISSION STATEMENT

"We are Jews from a variety of backgrounds and affiliations committed to progressive human values and the building of a shared vision of Jewish life. . . . We are dedicated to insuring the survival and flourishing of the Jewish people. Jews must have the rights to which all people are entitled. But survival is only the precondition of Jewish life, not its purpose. Our agenda must be determined by our ethics, not our enemies. . . . Society can be changed and human cooperation can be achieved. Working for social progress not only reflects Jewish ideals, but enhances Jewish security. New Jewish Agenda's national platform upholds progressive Jewish values and affirms that the goals of peace and justice are attainable.''

ORGANIZATION AND FUNDING

The New Jewish Agenda has disbanded its national office in New York and is trying to obtain a secure financial base. At earlier points, it may have had an annual budget of over $1 million.

POLICY CONCERNS AND TACTICS

New Jewish Agenda has a broad spectrum of interests: nuclear disarmament, anti-Semitism, political prisoners in Argentina, women's issues such as reproductive rights and women as rabbis, gay and lesbian rights, and, most significant, peace and coexistence between Israel and the Arabs calling for compromise through negotiations with the Palestinian people and Israel's Arab neighbors. NJA sponsored a disarmament rally in Washington, DC, in 1983. It frequently joins coalitions to advocate progressive solutions to social and political questions.

AFFILIATION

Jewish.

PUBLICATIONS

Agenda in Brief (bimonthly).

O
_____ / _____

OPERATION RESCUE (OR)

P.O. Box 127
Summerville, SC 29484
Phone: (803) 821-8441
Fax: Not publicized
Executive Director: Keith Tucci

ORIGINS AND DEVELOPMENT

Operation Rescue began in 1984 as Project Life when Randall Terry, a seminary student, and his wife began standing outside an abortion clinic to dissuade potential clients from going through with their abortions. They also opened a Crisis Pregnancy Counseling Center and a home for unwed mothers. Such efforts were only modestly successful, and in 1986 the idea of doing dramatic "rescues" developed into Operation Rescue. A trial operation before a Cherry Hill, Pennsylvania, abortion clinic brought nationwide pubicity and revitalized much of the pro-life movement. Other major rescues, notably in Wichita, brought a flood of volunteers to the organization. In 1990 a national association was formed, known officially as Operation Rescue National, and Keith Tucci took over day-to-day administration as executive director.

MISSION STATEMENT

"The pro-abortion secular media would like to portray people who risk arrest to save preborn children as fringe fanatic activists. The truth is that Operation Rescue is made up of Christians who are tired of the rights of preborn children being trampled in the path of the multi-million dollar abortion industry that sells abortions in the same way that the corner drugstore sells aspirin. The Rescue movement is calling Christians to repentance and action. Together we can end the senseless slaughter, and make this world once again safe for the most innocent and helpless of its citizens—the preborn.''

ORGANIZATION AND FUNDING

Operation Rescue is most charitably described as "loosely organized." There are 115 local groups, which carry on the educational and recruitment mission of OR and which provide much of the $400,000 budget. The national staff is comprised of all volunteers.

POLICY CONCERNS AND TACTICS

To date Operation Rescue has focused its efforts on stopping abortions by the dramatic actions of blocking abortion clinics and/or demonstrating outside such clinics with large numbers of people. Such "rescues" are highly organized, nonviolent affairs, and when police order demonstrators to move, they refuse, allowing police to arrest and carry them away. Other tactics include publicizing the names of doctors who perform abortions, following them into public places, alerting their neighbors to the doctors' careers, and so on. The objective is to discourage the medical profession from performing abortions, thus making it a less available option. More recently the organization has begun to branch out, initiating an adoption project and training what are called "impact teams" to continue and develop the confrontational politics that leaders believe is the only effective means to end legalized abortion in the United States.

AFFILIATION

Independent Christian.

PUBLICATIONS

Pro-Life Newsbrief (monthly); *To Rescue the Children: A Manual for Christ-Centered Pro-Life Activism; The Right and Responsibility to Rescue* (booklet); *Higher Laws, Rescue Tract* (tracts); plus videos, audiocassettes, and brochures.

P

/

PAX CHRISTI USA (PCUSA)

348 East Tenth Street
Erie, PA 16503-1110
Phone: (814) 453-4955
Fax: (814) 452-4784
Executive Director: Anne McCarthy, OSB

ORIGINS AND DEVELOPMENT

Although organized in the United States in 1972, Pax Christi is part of Pax Christi International, whose headquarters are in The Hague, Netherlands. The International was founded after World War II by German and French bishops at the prompting of a French woman, Madame Dortel-Claudot. Originally more of a prayer movement than a political action group, Pax Christi International currently has affiliates in 20 countries. The U.S. affiliate was begun by Eileen Egan and Gordon Zahn, longtime peace advocates. While an independent Catholic organization, Pax Christi works closely with the hierarchy and always has a bishop as president. From a simple beginning the organization has grown in 20 years to have over 12,000 members in 272 local groups.

MISSION STATEMENT

"Pax Christi has as its objective to work with people for peace for all humankind, always witnessing to the peace of Christ. The movement springs from a gospel vision of peace. It asks its members to ground their peacemaking in prayer, study and action on the message of Jesus. Pax Christi keeps as its priorities the Christian vision of disarmament, a just world order, primacy of conscience, education for peace and alternatives to violence.''

ORGANIZATION AND FUNDING

Like much of the peace movement, Pax Christi is highly decentralized. Local groups form when local people decide to create one, and there is remarkable autonomy to do whatever action seems appropriate, although groups have a national convention and share experiences, education materials, and so on. The 1993 budget was slightly in excess of $800,000, raised from donation from some 415 communities of sisters, brothers, and priests, as well as 124 Catholic parishes and several thousand individuals.

POLICY CONCERNS AND TACTICS

Pax Christi USA actively opposes violence in all its manifestations, including war, the death penalty, and racial and ethnic conflict. It also opposes creating the instruments of violence such as nuclear arms and arms sales and trading, as well as the more traditional opposition to a military draft. More recently the group has begun to address ''the sacred relationship that binds humankind to the earth,'' that is, environmental concerns, and to focus on particular problem areas such as the Philippines, Haiti, El Salvador, and Brazil.

Pax Christi volunteers expend a great deal of energy on ''peace education.'' It is their belief that listening to each side, especially hearing the pain and injustice, will lead to forgiveness, healing, and mutually acceptable solutions. In addition to press releases, letter writing, phone calling, visiting members of Congress, sending telegrams to the president, and so on, members often engage in public nonviolent demonstrations and vigils at military installations and offices of military suppliers.

AFFILIATION

Roman Catholic.

PUBLICATIONS

Pax Christi USA (quarterly) and a series of reports, such as *Pieces of the Mideast Puzzle: Israelis and Palestinians; The Philippines: Agony and Hope; El Salvador: Testimonies from the Land of the Savior; Human Rights in Central America; Land Conflicts in Brazil;* and *A Dream Deferred: Human Rights in Haiti.* In addition there are videos, postcards, prayer books, and textbooks on conscientious objection.

COMMENTS

Pacifist groups may not be taken seriously by policymakers because their visions (policy positions) are seen as utopian, naive, and hopelessly unrealistic. Pax Christi leadership has, in its training workshops, taken these criticisms seriously and attempts to base its analysis and recommendations on solid factual grounds, as well as develop realistic, workable alternatives to violence in both private relationships and public policy.

PEARL (NATIONAL COALITION FOR PUBLIC EDUCATION AND RELIGIOUS LIBERTY)

9 East 69th Street
New York, NY 10021
Phone: (212) 535-5565
Executive Director: Lisa Thurau

ORIGINS AND DEVELOPMENT

PEARL grew out of a March 1973 conference in Washington, DC, on religious liberty and education organized by people who saw a major threat in proposals to provide public funds for sectarian schools. The organization was officially formed in 1974 as a coalition of other groups and was provided offices in the National Education Association building in Washington, DC, for a time.

MISSION STATEMENT

"The National Committee for Public Education and Religious Liberty is dedicated to preserving religious liberty and the principle of separation of church and state, and to maintaining the integrity and viability of public education. We therefore oppose measures granting government aid generally to nonpublic schools."

ORGANIZATION AND FUNDING

PEARL is an independent, nonprofit organization supported by a coalition of other groups. The 1993 budget was $50,000, which did not include in-kind donations of space and furnishings. Among the supporting groups are the American Civil Liberties Union,* the American Ethical Union,* the American Humanist Association, the American Jewish Congress,* the Americans United for Separation of Church and State,* the Anti-Defamation League of B'nai B'rith,* the Baptist Joint Committee on Public Affairs,* the Central Conference of American Rabbis, the National Association of Laity (Catholic), the National Council of Jewish Women, the National Education Association, the National Women's Conference (American Ethical Union*), the Union of American Hebrew Congregations, the Unitarian Universalist Association,* the United Methodist Church,* and several state and local associations.

POLICY CONCERNS AND TACTICS

PEARL focuses its efforts on two areas: opposing government funding or aid of any kind to nonpublic schools and resisting attempts to promote sectarian influence in public schools. On a day-to-day basis the main purpose of the organization is to collect and disseminate to members any information on proposals to aid nonpublic schools or promote religion within public schools. On several occasions it has successfully litigated to stop what it considers to be unconstitutional practices.

AFFILIATION

Independent, secular.

PUBLICATIONS

Former director Art Must and Lowell Weicker have written *Why We Still Need Public Schools; Church-State Relations and Visions of Democracy* (Buffalo, NY: Prometheus, 1992).

COMMENTS

PEARL is currently a watchdog organization. Despite an enviable record of successful litigation in the 1970s, its normal operation budget is small and it is not as visible as in the 1980s. As educational issues become more prevalent in the 1990s, PEARL may once again expand its influence. PEARL no longer has an office in Washington but hopes to reopen there. Since 1988, it has added to its coalition the National PTA, the General Conference of Seventh Day Adventists, and the National Center for Science Education.

PEOPLE FOR THE AMERICAN WAY (PAW)

2000 M Street, NW
Washington, DC 20036
Phone: (202) 467-4999
Fax: (202) 293-2672
President: Arthur J. Kropp

ORIGINS AND DEVELOPMENT

Founded in 1980 by a group of civil and religious leaders determined to counteract the influence of emerging "religious right" groups, People for the American Way (PAW) is an individual membership organization.

MISSION STATEMENT

"People For The American Way is committed to renewing the spirit of citizenship, community, and democracy. We work to meet the challenges of discord and fragmentation with an affirmation of 'the American Way.' By this we mean pluralism, individuality, freedom of thought, expression and religion, a sense of community, and tolerance and compassion for others" (recruitment brochure).

ORGANIZATION AND FUNDING

As with most such groups, PAW is a nonprofit, tax-exempt research and education group. However, it is affiliated with People for the American Way's Action Fund, which is a lobbying group and not tax-exempt.

POLICY CONCERNS AND TACTICS

PAW maintains an active research agenda to monitor and resist the political activities of the religious Right; it opposes censorship and supports abortion rights activities and other civil rights protections. The group provides research, some financial support, and legal services for individuals and groups it believes to be the victims of censorship or who are supporting the civil rights it supports. It also lobbies extensively and provides national spokespersons to speak to the media. Most recently it has led an effort to oppose prayer at public school graduation ceremonies and to maintain the Lemon test as a rule of law for deciding establishment clause cases.

PAW is somewhat unique in that it has also supported efforts to teach about religion in the public schools and to make certain religion is given its proper significance in history and social science textbooks.

AFFILIATION

Independent Ecumenical.

PUBLICATIONS

Reports on religious Right groups and activities.

COMMENTS

''Groups who oppose the religious right are watching the frenzy [over removal of the ban on gays in the military] with consternation. 'The religious right is deliberately putting a match to this volatile issue and counting on a profit from its explosion,' says John Buchanan, senior vice president of People for the American Way. Mr. Buchanan's group released a study documenting some of the lobbying activities of religious right organizations on the military-ban issue'' (*Wall Street Journal,* 28 January 1993).

PRESBYTERIAN CHURCH USAÆWASHINGTON OFFICE (PRES)

110 Maryland Avenue, NE
Suite 104
Washington, DC 20002
Phone: (202) 543-1126
Fax: (202) 543-7755
Executive Director: Elenora Giddings Ivory

ORIGINS AND DEVELOPMENT

The Presbyterian Church established a Washington office in 1946 with two purposes in mind: (1) to inform U.S. policymakers of the public policy concerns, goals, and recommendations of the General Assembly of the church and (2) to advocate church policy positions by all appropriate methods. The Washington office is part of the Social Justice and Peacemaking unit of the General Assembly of the Presbyterian Church USA, which has its headquarters in Louisville, Kentucky.

MISSION STATEMENT

The church has a Washington office for theological and social reasons. ''Theologically we seek to make faithful and effective political witness because, as the New Brief Statement of Faith puts it: In life and in death we belong to God. . . . In a broken and fearful world the Spirit gives us courage to pray without ceasing, to witness among all peoples to Christ as Lord and Savior, to unmask idolatries in church and culture, to hear voices of peoples long silenced, and to work with others for justice, freedom, and peace.''

ORGANIZATION AND FUNDING

The Washington office has a staff of nine and had a 1993 budget of $500,000, which was allocated by the General Assembly. As a denominational office it has no independent membership or status outside the church.

POLICY CONCERNS AND TACTICS

Following its General Assembly, the Washington office supports a wide variety of policy positions, including arms control, establishing federal budget priorities, civil rights, religious liberty, economic justice, and issues affecting women. The church almost invariably takes liberal political positions. In addition to monitoring government activity and informing Congress and federal officials of church positions, the Washington office works actively in coalitions with other religious and social groups.

AFFILIATION

Presbyterian Church USA.

PUBLICATIONS

Church & Society (six per year); *Presbyterian Survey* (ten per year); *Monday Morning* (ten per year, primarily for ministers); *Horizons* (ten per year, primarily for Presbyterian women); and *The News* (monthly newspaper). All publications are by the national church.

PRESBYTERIANS FOR DEMOCRACY AND RELIGIOUS LIBERTY (PDRL)

1331 H Street, NW
Suite 900
Washington, DC 20006
Phone: (202) 393-3200
Fax: (202) 638-4948
Executive Director: Rev. Alan Wisdom

ORIGINS AND DEVELOPMENT

Presbyterians for Democracy and Religious Liberty is an offshoot of the Institute on Religion and Democracy (IRD),* and was founded in 1985 by that group. It shares office space, phone, and fax facilities with IRD.

MISSION STATEMENT

''Promotes a balance of political discussion in papers and positions presented by the Presbyterian church. Encourages dialogue within the church on its role in national and international politics, especially pertaining to nuclear disarmament and socio-political problems. Believes democracy 'places a value on religious freedom which is consistent with the Gospel' and is the 'form of government best suited to preserve that freedom.' ''

ORGANIZATION AND FUNDING

PDRL has a membership of 6,000, a staff of one, and had a 1993 budget of under $100,000. Funds are raised primarily from membership dues. While membership is Presbyterian, the organization itself is autonomous and not sponsored or endorsed by the Presbyterian Church USA.

POLICY CONCERNS AND TACTICS

PDRL functions something like a watchdog over Presbyterian political statements and positions, advocating ''balanced'' presentations. It sponsors Sanctuary Project, a critical review of Presbyterian support of the Sanctuary movement, bestows the Faith and Freedom Award, and presents an alternative, more conservative Presbyterian voice in national affairs.

AFFILIATION

Independent Protestant.

PUBLICATIONS

Mainstream (quarterly); *PDRL Statement of Purpose* (pamphlet); and *Peacemaking? or Resistance? Presbyterian Perspectives* (booklet).

R

—————————— / ——————————

RELIGIOUS ACTION CENTER OF REFORM JUDAISM (RACRJ)

2027 Massachusetts Avenue, NW
Washington, DC 20036
Phone: (202) 387-2800
Fax: (202) 667-9070
Executive Director: David Saperstein

ORIGINS AND DEVELOPMENT

Begun in 1961 as the Religious Action Center of the Union of American Hebrew Congregations, the name was changed in 1986 when the center also began to represent the Central Conference of American Rabbis.

MISSION STATEMENT

RACRJ is the official liaison between the Union of American Hebrew Congregations, the Central Conference of American Rabbis, and the government.

ORGANIZATION AND FUNDING

Supporting the Religious Action Center are 850 participating synagogues. A staff of ten works to inform constituents of government action that may affect Jewish interests and inform Congress and government officials of the Reform Judaism position on various public policies.

POLICY CONCERNS AND TACTICS

Focuses on social justice issues.

AFFILIATION

Jewish.

PUBLICATIONS

Chai/Impact Newsletter (thirty per year) and *Social Action Briefings* (five per year) plus a variety of books and pamphlets.

RELIGIOUS ALLIANCE AGAINST PORNOGRAPHY (RAAP)

800 Compton Road
Suite 9224
Cincinnati, OH 45231
Phone: (513) 521-6227
Fax: (513) 521-6337
Executive Director: Jerry Kirk

ORIGINS AND DEVELOPMENT

The Religious Alliance Against Pornography (RAAP) was organized in 1986 by Dr. Kirk of the National Coalition Against Pornography* as a means of pulling together religious leaders from a wide variety of faith and political perspectives to present a united front on the issue of pornography, raise public consciousness, and impress law enforcement officials with the unanimity of the religious community on this issue, thereby encouraging them to act aggressively against purveyors of illegal pornography.

MISSION STATEMENT

"The purpose of RAAP is to bring into clear focus a major factor in the assault on human dignity and the consequent dehumanization that it promotes: hard-core and child pornography. RAAP brings together entities that can't agree on even the basics of religious faith, yet they are working closely together in a firm stance on this one disturbing issue."

ORGANIZATION AND FUNDING

RAAP is closely associated with the National Coalition Against Pornography, sharing office space, staff, and the executive director. However, it is separately incorporated, with a separate budget of $62,000, and focuses its efforts on educating and representing the leaders of religious denominations, while N-CAP focuses its efforts on more general citizen education and representation.

POLICY CONCERNS AND TACTICS

The effort is to strengthen obscenity and child protection laws and to encourage more strict enforcement of existing laws. Religious leaders hope to utilize their status and visibility in meetings with political and judicial leaders to impress them with the importance of this issue.

AFFILIATION

Independent Ecumenical.

PUBLICATIONS

None.

COMMENTS

RAAP is an effort to engage as broad a spectrum of the religious community as possible in the battle against pornography. The coalition includes several Roman Catholic cardinals and bishops, leaders from the Church of Jesus Christ of Latter Day Saints, Greek Orthodox, Jewish, and both liberal and conservative Protestant groups, including the National Council of the Churches of Christ in the U.S.A.,* the Southern Baptist Convention, the Episcopal Church,* the Advent Christian General Conference, the United Methodist Church, the Salvation Army, and the National Association of Evangelicals.

RELIGIOUS COALITION FOR ABORTION RIGHTS (RCAR)

100 Maryland Avenue, NE
Suite 307
Washington, DC 20002
Phone: (202) 543-7032
Fax: (202) 543-7820
Executive Director: Ann Thompson-Cook

ORIGINS AND DEVELOPMENT

"RCAR was formed in 1973 as a response by ten denominations and faith groups to the Catholic effort that year to overturn the landmark court decisions, *Roe v Wade* and *Doe v Bolton.* By late 1980 RCAR was incorporated, and the founding denominations and faith groups were joined by additional ones which had adopted a pro-choice position." These groups include the American Ethical Union,* American Jewish Committee,* Women's Caucus—Church of the Brethren,* Episcopal Women's Caucus, Office for Church and Society—United Church of Christ,* General Board of Church and Society of the United Methodist Church,* and YWCA National Board.

MISSION STATEMENT

"RCAR is composed of 34 national Protestant, Jewish and other faith groups. The coalition is committed to the Constitutional guarantees of religious liberty and reproductive rights and affirms women as moral decision makers.

"We hold in high respect the value of potential human life; we do not take the question of abortion lightly. Each denomination represented among us approaches the issue of abortion from the unique perspective of its theology. Therefore, members hold widely varying viewpoints as to when abortion is morally justified. We do not advocate abortion; we advocate choices for women's lives."

ORGANIZATION AND FUNDING

RCAR has six full-time and three part-time national staff members, with affiliates and active groups in twenty-five states. The annual budget is $1.3 million.

POLICY CONCERNS AND TACTICS

RCAR works to maintain and expand the rights of women to choose abortions. Its tactics include coalition formation, demonstrations, grass-roots education, and action alerts. Within the pro-choice movement it focuses its efforts on religious questions and issues around the abortion debate.

AFFILIATION

Ecumenical.

PUBLICATIONS

RCAR Options (quarterly).

RELIGIOUS NETWORK FOR EQUALITY FOR WOMEN (RNEW)

475 Riverside Drive
Room 812-A
New York, NY 10115
Phone: (212) 870-2995
Fax: (212) 870-2338
Coordinator: Zelle W. Andrews

ORIGINS AND DEVELOPMENT

RNEW began in 1976 as the Religious Committee for the ERA, a group of some forty-two religious organizations dedicated to passage of the Equal Rights Amendment. "When the ERA campaign stalled the committee decided to reform and redirect its efforts. While continuing its commitment to legal rights for women, it expanded its agenda to specific economic issues affecting women as workers, poor women and older women."

MISSION STATEMENT

RNEW "is an interreligious coalition of faith groups committed to legal and economic justice for women. It engages in educational and advocacy programs on behalf of women's rights, especially the poor. It lobbies for national legislation on civil rights and economic reform, and participates in the campaign to ratify the U.N. Convention on the Elimination of Discrimination Against Women."

ORGANIZATION AND FUNDING

RNEW has forty-two coalition members from Catholic, Jewish, Mormon, and Protestant denominations, a staff of two, and an annual budget of $98,000. Each coalition partner has a member on the Board of Directors.

POLICY CONCERNS AND TACTICS

Begun to support passage of the ERA, RNEW has focused more in recent years on economic literacy for women and the elderly. It also supports the Family and Medical Leave Act, civil rights actions, and health care legislation. In addition to its advocacy, RNEW has developed basic training materials for economic literacy, which it promotes among its members.

AFFILIATION

Independent Ecumenical.

PUBLICATIONS

RNEW Update (three per year).

RELIGIOUS ROUNDTABLE (RR)

3859 Faxon Avenue
P.O. Box 11467
Memphis, TN 38122
Phone: (901) 458-3795
Fax: (901) 324-0265
President: Edward E. McAteer

ORIGINS AND DEVELOPMENT

The Religious Roundtable was founded in 1979 by Reverend Edward E. McAteer, who brought together a coalition of national leaders, including prominent ministers and laypersons, to provide an authentic Christian voice and influence in the formation of national policy. For several years the roundtable maintained an office in Arlington, Virginia. However, in 1982 headquarters were moved to Memphis, Tennessee.

MISSION STATEMENT

"Primarily [the Religious Roundtable's] objective is to favorably impact federal policy by activating the potential influence of millions of Americans who adhere to traditional, family-based moral principles. Leaders of diverse faiths and denominations are utilized to communicate to their constituents information about public policy and legislation."

ORGANIZATION AND FUNDING

The roundtable has a core coalition group of some 140 members, with chapters in every state and over 30,000 members. Funding comes from several major foundation grants and a mailing list of 175,000. The 1993 budget was approximately $500,000.

POLICY CONCERNS AND TACTICS

The Religious Roundtable focuses on a full range of conservative Christian concerns such as the American family, decency in television programming, gay rights, freedom of worship, pornography, abortion, and child abuse, looking at each issue from a biblical perspective. It has been a major conservative Christian voice in support of Israel. A major effort of the Religious Roundtable is to promote seminars and national affairs briefings for various conservative religious and civic groups. Among its most successful projects has been an annual prayer breakfast in honor of Israel. Speakers invited to its seminars often include major conservative legislative and other political figures.

AFFILIATION

Nondenominational.

PUBLICATIONS

The Roundtable Report.

COMMENTS

The Religious Roundtable is the vehicle for advocating founder Ed McAteer's vision of Christian politics. It has received much credit for forging the Religious Right/New Right bond that helped elect President Ronald Reagan in 1980. During the Reagan-Bush years it worked hard to support the nomination and Senate approval of conservative Supreme Court justices.

RELIGIOUS TASKFORCE ON CENTRAL AMERICA (RTFCA)

1747 Connecticut Avenue, NW
Washington, DC 20009-1108
Phone: (202) 387-7625
Fax: Not published
Cocoordinators: Lee Miller and Margaret Swedish

ORIGINS AND DEVELOPMENT

Begun in 1980 by an ad hoc group of Catholic religious leaders with an interest in El Salvador, the group was designed to gather information from missionaries and other grass-roots sources and monitor U.S. policies to better inform Americans about the effect of U.S. efforts to halt insurgency and support the military in El Salvador. As peace was achieved in El Salvador, the group expanded its interests and changed its name to the Religious Taskforce on Central America (RTFCA).

MISSION STATEMENT

''The RTFCA supports and promotes the witness of people of faith in the US who are working for justice and peace in Central America, and especially in the policies and programs of the US government for the region. We also seek to be a voice for those people of the region who are working to build new societies based on justice and respect for human dignity, and most especially for the poor who invite us to share in their project of life.''

ORGANIZATION AND FUNDING

The group maintains a two-person office advised by a steering committee made up of people from groups such as the Maryknoll Fathers & Brothers Justice and Peace Office, the National Assembly of Religious Women, the Conference of Major Superiors of Men, the Leadership Group of the Sisters of Mercy of the Americas, the United States Catholic Conference,* the U.S. Catholic Mission Association, and the Leadership Conference of Women Religious. It has a budget of under $100,000, raised from direct mail solicitation and sale of its *Central America Report.*

POLICY CONCERNS AND TACTICS

RTFCA focuses on three objectives: (1) to work for U.S. policies that promote human rights, popular participation in new democracies, and social and economic justice; (2) a new relationship between the United States and Central American countries based not on political domination or economic exploitation but on respect for the dignity, freedom, and sovereignty of the region's poor and indigenous peoples; (3) a broader awareness of our growing relationship with the people of Central America for the faith of North Americans; and (4) a greater involvement of the faith community in the United States in the work for justice and peace in Central America. RTFCA works primarily through other coalitions and publicity rather than directly with congressional staffers.

AFFILIATION

Roman Catholic.

PUBLICATIONS

Central America Report (bimonthly).

RUTHERFORD INSTITUTE (RI)

P.O. Box 7482
1445 East Rio Road
Charlottesville, VA 22906-7482
Phone: (804) 978-3888
Fax: (804) 978-1789
President: Mr. John Whitehead

ORIGINS AND DEVELOPMENT

The Rutherford Institute is a classic example of a policy entrepreneur with an idea who develops an interest group with maximum personal effort and minimal resources. Begun out of a basement office in 1982 by Whitehead and his wife, the institute was named after a seventeenth-century Scottish minister, Samuel Rutherford, who argued that all people—even royalty—are subject to law. The institute now employs a staff of thirty in its international office, employs some seventy-five attorneys in several countries, and has over 300 cooperating attorneys. In 1992 it had affiliates in forty states.

MISSION STATEMENT

The Rutherford Institute is a legal organization that vigorously defends persons whom it believes have been denied the right to free exercise of religion. It "seeks to help religious people get a fair shake out of society and also at the same time protect the sanctity of human life. . . . The religious community must understand that the Constitution protects the rights of everybody. If one religious group loses their rights, then everybody loses their rights. If we want to be strategic, we've got to stand up for the rights of everybody."

ORGANIZATION AND FUNDING

The institute currently operates on a budget of $1,250,000, which is raised from contributions by the general public. Membership is individual, although the institute is organized into regional chapters working with volunteer attorneys in their respective states.

POLICY CONCERNS AND TACTICS

The Rutherford Institute positions itself as pro-life, pro-family, and pro-religion, and it protects anyone whom it considers to be illegally prohibited from exercising his or her freedom of religion in relationship to these areas. It focuses particularly on free exercise of religion in the public schools or related issues such as home schooling. More recently it has pursued religious liberty issues in other nations as well. Its primary tool is the lawsuit, and it is known as an aggressive litigator. The mere threat of a lawsuit by the institute has hastened the settlement of many cases.

AFFILIATION

Independent Protestant.

PUBLICATIONS

The institute publishes *Rutherford Journal* (monthly magazine); three white papers entitled *Home Education Reporter, The Religious Liberty Bulletin, Home School Briefs;* and a number of books, primarily by John Whitehead. Titles include *An American Dream; Arresting Abortion; The End of Man; Parents' Rights; The Right to Picket and the Freedom of Public Discourse; The Rights of Religious Persons in Public Education; The Second American Revolution;* and *Home Education: Rights and Reasons.*

T
/

TRADITIONAL VALUES COALITION (TVC)

100 S. Anaheim
Suite 350
Anaheim, CA 92805
Phone: (714) 520-0300
Fax: Not public
Chairman: Louis P. Sheldon
Washington Director: Andrea Sheldon

139 C Street, SE
Washington, DC 20003

(202) 547-8570

ORIGINS AND DEVELOPMENT

Begun in 1982, the Traditional Values Coalition (TVC) was originally the California state chapter of Tim LeHaye's American Coalition for Traditional Values. When that organization was disbanded, the California chapter began its expansion into a national organization.

MISSION STATEMENT

"Recognizing the vast storehouse of influence in America's churches, TVC founder and chairman Rev. Louis P. Sheldon decided many years ago to form an organization capable of helping churches educate their parishioners on the key issues of the day. Americans are slow to anger, but Rev. Sheldon knew the process of church awakening was inevitable. As the anti-God culture continued its radical growth, the sleeping giant of America's churches would eventually take action to set things right, and TVC wanted to be there, ready to help.

"Whether it be educating school officials on the importance of teaching abstinence, addressing the relationship between gangs and America's family crisis, or confronting the radical homosexuals and anti-family crowd with the hard facts, TVC has been there in force. From the state and local levels to the halls of Congress, we know the system, and best of all, we know how to educate and motivate Americans to defend their rights.''

ORGANIZATION AND FUNDING

The TVC is a combination of church groups and individual supporters. It represents approximately 25,000 churches and 50,000 individuals, divided into 17 state organizations. The 1993 budget was in the $1–5 million range, raised primarily from membership contributions.

POLICY CONCERNS AND TACTICS

The coalition supports a full range of conservative Christian issues, including prayer in public schools, family values, and the pro-life position. Members have been particularly vocal concerning sex education in the schools and the issue of gay rights legislation. The group took a leading role in opposition to President Clinton's proposal to allow gays to function openly in the military.

AFFILIATION

Independent Christian.

PUBLICATIONS

A Voter's Guide (monthly); *Traditional Values Report* (monthly); a series of position papers called *Talking Points;* and more broad-ranging position papers entitled *Briefs.*

COMMENTS

''While the Religious Right of the 1980s was almost exclusively a white, middle class movement, an increasing number of black conservative Christians are joining the new battle. Particularly in California, TVC has been successful in forging a network of black churches to help fight gay rights and distribution of condoms in schools. One emerging spokesperson is Star Parker, who heads a Christian publishing company called Not Forsaking the Assembly, and has worked closely with TVC on a number of projects. She has been especially involved in applying conservative principles to inner-city problems'' (*Christianity Today,* 20 July 1992, p. 44).

U

——————————— / ———————————

UNITARIAN UNIVERSALIST ASSOCIATIONÆ
WASHINGTON OFFICE FOR SOCIAL JUSTICE (UUA)

100 Maryland Avenue, NE
Room 106
Washington, DC 20002
Phone: (202) 547-0254
Executive Director: Robert Z. Alpern

ORIGINS AND DEVELOPMENT

"The Unitarian Universalist Association was formed in 1961 by the merger of the American Unitarian Association and the Universalist Church in America. The merger represents a coming together of the two oldest and most conservative segments of the liberal tradition. It is the only body that affirms its base within the Judeo-Christian heritage." The Washington Office for Social Concern was founded in 1975, and its name changed to UUA Washington Office for Social Justice in 1983.

MISSION STATEMENT

"The member congregations of the UUA covenant do affirm and promote: the inherent worth and dignity of every person; justice, equity and compassion in human relations, acceptance of one another and encouragement to spiritual growth in our congregations; a free and responsible search for the truth and meaning; the right of conscience and the use of the democratic process in our congregations and in society at large; the goal of world community with peace, liberty and justice for all; respect for the interdependent web of all existence of which we are a part." The Washington Office for Social Justice "seeks to apply the insights of humanistic ethics and liberal religion to public policy and the formulation of legislation.''

ORGANIZATION AND FUNDING

The Unitarian Universalist Washington Office for Social Justice has a staff of two and had a 1993 budget of $100,000. As an office of the church itself it has no independent membership.

POLICY CONCERNS AND TACTICS

The Washington Office pursues a wide range of liberal political agenda: arms reduction, nuclear disarmament, a test ban treaty, racial justice, religious liberty, public policy affecting women, gay, lesbian and bisexual rights, Middle East issues, reordering of national priorities, economic conversion from military to domestic needs, and so on. The Washington Office joins and supports coalitions advocating its positions. Its staff represents the denomination before Congress and government agencies, conducts training workshops, and leads fact-finding trips to the Middle East. The office runs an annual national workshop on social justice in Washington, DC.

AFFILIATION

Protestant.

PUBLICATIONS

Ethics and Action (quarterly) and *Action Alerts* (periodic).

UNITARIAN UNIVERSALIST SERVICE COMMITTEE (UUSC)

130 Prospect Street
Cambridge, MA 02139
Phone: (617) 868-6600
Fax: (617) 868-7102
Executive Director: Richard S. Scobie

ORIGINS AND DEVELOPMENT

The Unitarian Universalist Service Committee was formed by the merger of the Unitarian Service Committee, founded in 1939, and the Universalist Committee, founded in 1945. The merger happened in 1963.

MISSION STATEMENT

''Grounded in Unitarian Universalist principles that affirm the worth, dignity and human rights of every person, and the interdependence of all life, the Unitarian Universalist Service Committee is a voluntary nonsectarian organization working to advance justice throughout the world.''

ORGANIZATION AND FUNDING

The UUSC has 17,000 members and had a 1993 budget of $3,300,000. It supports a staff of 40 as well as a network of more than 1,500 volunteers. Funds are raised from membership dues, donations from individual Unitarian Universalist congregations, foundations, investments, and major donors. UUSC does not accept funding from the U.S. government, nor does it receive funds from the Unitarian Universalist Association.*

POLICY CONCERNS AND TACTICS

UUSC is an international social action organization that conducts human rights education and promotes citizen action primarily in the areas of children at risk in the United States and self-help development projects in thirteen countries worldwide. UUSC works through coalitions, testifies before congressional committees, and issues news reports on its actions.

AFFILIATION

Nonsectarian: UUSC is an associate member of the Unitarian Universalist Association.

PUBLICATIONS

Service Committee News (quarterly); *Roots and Visions: The First Fifty Years of the Unitarian Universalist Service Committee* (book); study/action guides; *Action Alerts; Advocacy Initiatives;* fact sheets and other periodic publications on international and U.S. children's programs.

UNITED CHURCH OF CHRIST OFFICE OF CHURCH IN SOCIETY (UCC)

700 Prospect Avenue East
Cleveland, OH 44115
Phone: (216) 736-2100
Executive Director: Jay Lintner

110 Maryland Avenue, NE
Washington, DC 20002
(202) 543-1517

ORIGINS AND DEVELOPMENT

In its present form since 1957, the United Church of Christ has 1,600,000 members. It joined the older (1931) merger of the Congregational Church with the General Convention of the Christian Church and the Evangelical and Reformed Church, which had been formed by a merger in 1934. It is regarded as a liberal and progressive denomination, tolerant of diverse theological and political opinions. The Washington office of the UCC was set up in 1944, one of the oldest such offices.

MISSION STATEMENT

''The Office of Church in Society [OCIS] was established by the General Synod 'to assume leadership functions for social action concerns in the United

Church of Christ (UCC) to provide resources to national, Conference and local churches and to strengthen coordination of social action activities within the denomination.' '' The OCIS maintains an office in Washington "to represent and coordinate the denomination's ministry in public policy advocacy.''

ORGANIZATION AND FUNDING

As an arm of the General Synod, headquartered in Cleveland, Ohio, the Washington office is part of the Office of Church and Society, which has "leadership functions for social action concerns in the United Church of Christ. It carries out the objectives of the synod with a total office staff of ten persons. They have not released budget figures.

POLICY CONCERNS AND TACTICS

The United Church of Christ is one of the most active of the religious interest groups, taking part in many coalitions and lobbying on its own to reinforce the policies of the General Synod. Recent issues have included defending a woman's right of choice to terminate her pregnancy, even though some persons in the church disagree; obtaining access to medical care for persons with AIDS; advocacy of divestiture in South Africa since 1965; ending U.S. military aid to rightist regimes in Central America; congressional aid to small and modest-size farms; liberalizing immigration policies and practices; advocating a "just peace" and nuclear disarmament; upholding bans on prayer in schools; and advocating separation of church and state. The legislative agenda for 1993 listed 26 action areas. Their stand supporting gays in the military coincides with the church's position on ordination of homosexuals, and they have testified vigorously on this issue. "Various national agencies of the United Church of Christ have urged members to be involved in government at all levels." Seven of the staff "face" the Hill. They have a 17,000 member network to get alerts out to constituents of the Congresspersons.

AFFILIATION

United Church of Christ Office of Church in Society.

PUBLICATIONS

UCC 1992 Legislative Network Agenda (updated and published for each session); *Courage in the Struggle for Justice and Peace* (monthly newsletter for the Justice and Peace Network); and *Legislative Fact Sheets, United Church of Christ Office for Church in Society.* They also publish a variety of pamphlets such as *How to Write Members of Congress* and *How to Visit Members of Congress,* as well as substantial books and courses on conflict resolution and "peace futuring."

UNITED STATES CATHOLIC CONFERENCE (USCC)

3211 Fourth Street, NE
Washington, DC 20017-1194
Phone: (202) 541-3000

Fax: (202) 541-3322

General Secretary: Msgr. Robert N. Lynch

ORIGINS AND DEVELOPMENT

In the Catholic hierarchical organizational arrangement, each individual bishop reports directly to the papacy; there are no intermediate structures, at least not any with authority over the bishops. Based on its long history in Europe, the Vatican has always looked with suspicion on national organizations of bishops. However, there are support organizations to aid cooperation among bishops, some organized along national lines. In 1917, when the United States entered World War I, the Catholic Bishops organized a National Catholic War Council, with themselves as members, to support the war effort generally and Catholic servicemen in particular. The cooperative effort worked so well that in 1919 the bishops decided to continue cooperating and renamed their group the National Catholic Welfare Council. Three years later the Vatican, nervous that the word "council" in the title might be misinterpreted by some to mean that the organization had some autonomous authority in the church, requested that the group be renamed the National Catholic Welfare Conference. This it remained until 1966, when, following reforms recommended by Vatican Council II, the bishops formed two successor groups, the National Conference of Catholic Bishops (NCCB) and the United States Catholic Conference (USCC). The former is made up of all the bishops in the United States and is theoretically an internal advisory board or "episcopal conference," which focuses on the pastoral needs of the church itself. It engages in no direct political activities and thus is not listed separately in this encyclopedia.

The United States Catholic Conference, on the other hand, is a civil corporation through which the bishops cooperate among themselves, with other groups, and with lay members, who often serve on its various committees. This is the outreach group that works on issues deemed to be of wider societal concern.

There are some 350 bishop members of the NCCB/USCC, representing the Catholic dioceses of the United States. The USCC has three departments (Communications, Education, and International Justice and Peace) and such staff offices as Government Liaison, Public Affairs, Planning and Research, and a General Counsel.

MISSION STATEMENT

The USCC is a nonprofit corporation whose purposes are "to unify, coordinate, promote and carry on all Catholic activities in the United States; to organize and conduct religious, charitable and social welfare work at home and abroad; to aid in education; to care for immigrants and generally to enter into and promote by education, publication and direction the objects of its being."

POLICY CONCERNS AND TACTICS

Foremost among the Catholic Bishops' concerns is supporting the pro-life movement, but in fact they direct a wide variety of efforts from Catholic Relief

Services (an overseas food relief agency of the U.S. Catholic church), to the Campaign for Human Development (its domestic antipoverty agency), to Migration and Refugee Services, to the Military Chaplaincy, to Catholic Education and Hospitals. In addition there is an active effort to educate Catholics and others as well as influence policy in a wide variety of issues such as nuclear weapons, homelessness, food aid, economic structure, capital punishment, immigration, and so on.

ORGANIZATION AND FUNDING

The organization is explained earlier. The annual budget of the NCCB and USCC is about $30,600,000, which supports a staff of 300, plus volunteers. This figure does not include any of the budgets for the affiliated programs mentioned above; these have independent budgets. Funds come from diocesan assessments, calculated at the rate of seven cents per Catholic in the United States. Other income is raised through contributions from religious communities, foundations, and individual donors, as well as from the sale of publications and services.

AFFILIATION

Roman Catholic. The USCC officially represents the Catholic church in the United States.

PUBLICATIONS

USCC publishes numerous pastoral letters and joint statements on both religious and secular topics deemed to be matters of social justice, including race relations, aging, housing, prison reform, capital punishment, the Vietnam War, the Panama Canal, rights of workers, nuclear weapons, education, and, of course, abortion.

COMMENTS

The distinction mentioned above between the NCCB and the USCC is never quite as clear in practice as it is in theory, and the educational or pastoral mission of the bishops very often seems to fall into the social and political realm. This has gotten the organizations into some legal controversy when Abortion Rights Mobilization, Inc. sued them for violating the tax code by their pro-life political activities. While the bishops eventually prevailed, questions remain about what exactly does or does not constitute "political activity." More recently the USCC caused a public furor by contracting with a public relations firm to conduct a pro-life publicity campaign.

Even those opposed to the NCCB/USCC on particular policy issues acknowledge that they are a formidable political force in Washington. With a long history of involvement, a large, highly professional staff, strong financial resources, and an ability to call upon enormous intellectual resources in the Catholic community, the NCCB/USCC is known for the number, variety, and quality of its pastorals and policy papers. Among the most notable recent, not to say controversial, pastorals have been *Pastoral Plan for Pro-life Activities* (1975); *The Challenge of Peace: God's Promise and Our Response* (1983), dealing with nuclear weapons and American defense policy; and *Economic Justice for All: Catholic Social Teaching and the U.S. Economy* (1986).

Catholic bishops, although members of the NCCB/USCC, maintain their independent status and rarely lobby directly on issues. Staff members will testify before congressional committees on occasion. Likewise the USCC rarely enters into coalitions with other groups, preferring to work in a parallel fashion. Nevertheless it must be ranked among the most influential of the religious interest groups.

W

WASHINGTON INTERRELIGIOUS STAFF COUNCIL (WISC)

Phone: (202) 543-1126 or (202) 488-5646
Cochairs: Rev. Bernadine McRipley
        Ms. Jane Hall Harvey

ORIGINS AND DEVELOPMENT

The Washington Interreligious Staff Council, known widely as WISC, is an informal but vital group, "an umbrella interfaith organization for the moderate-to-liberal religious community working on Capitol Hill—for connectedness, problem solving, information sharing and community building." The origin grew out of the need for the National Council of the Churches of Christ in the U.S.A.* and other groups to be able to work with Jewish and Catholic groups. It has been operating at least since the 1970s, and its Statement of Principles and Procedures was approved in 1984. Its membership is composed of Washington offices, and it is open to other members only by application and approval of the constituent members. Its importance is verified by the ubiquitous references to it by persons in the religious advocacy realm. It operates in parallel to the more formal Interfaith Impact for Justice and Peace,* but their memberships do not fully overlap.

MISSION STATEMENT

The purpose set out in the WISC Statement of Principles and Procedures "is to provide a forum for sharing of information and exchange of ideas relating to federal policy issues and for examination of the religious bases for study and action." WISC does not take public policy positions and will not speak to anyone in its own name, nor will it speak for anyone. It assists member groups to set policy positions, devise strategies, and divide up research and advocacy tasks.

ORGANIZATION AND FUNDING

WISC does not have an office address, a staff, a budget or priority issues. It does not lobby directly, has no mailing lists, does no media work, and has no board. It has an Executive Committee consisting of eight members; four are elected each year for two-year terms. Each member group has one vote. A balance of gender and Roman Catholic, Protestant, and Jewish membership on the Executive Committee is deliberately maintained. The officers are cochairs elected from the Executive Committee, which also chooses a treasurer and a recording secretary.

POLICY CONCERNS AND TACTICS

Plenary sessions of WISC are normally held once a month, and an annual retreat is held. It no longer has its own task forces and working groups. WISC is not responsible for setting issue priorities or strategies. The new Interfaith Impact now has a task force structure, but WISC members are not all members of this new group, and the "community" of WISC is perceived to be larger than Interfaith Impact. The plenary sessions are used to distribute information, have speakers, raise common issues, and have communitywide forums. Interfaith Impact and other groups may present plans for a campaign, and new legislative issues are expected to arise in these meetings.

AFFILIATION

Interfaith.

PUBLICATIONS

None.

WASHINGTON OFFICE ON AFRICA (WOA)

110 Maryland Avenue, NE
Washington, DC 20002
Phone: (202) 546-7961
Fax: (202) 546-1545
Executive Director: Imani Countess

ORIGINS AND DEVELOPMENT

The Washington Office on Africa (WOA) was founded in 1972 by a coalition of religious denominations, such as the African Methodist Episcopal Church, the Sacred Heart Fathers and mainline Protestant churches, and labor unions, such as the Amalgamated Textile and Clothing Workers, to lobby on behalf of the movement for freedom from white-minority rule in South Africa. In 1978 a coordinate group, the WOA Educational Fund, was added to do research and provide information. In 1990 WOA expanded its focus to issues affecting grass-roots interests across the continent of Africa. The educational fund has been renamed the Africa Policy Information Center (APIC).

MISSION STATEMENT

"The mission of the Washington Office on Africa is to coordinate, link and promote American and African grassroots agendas that affect public policies in the United States which support peace and political and economic justice in Africa."

ORGANIZATION AND FUNDING

WOA is truly a coalition of other groups and has four full-time employees, an executive director, two legislative assistants, and a part-time associate director for communications, as well as college interns. The primary source of financial support for the lobbying work comes from the nineteen sponsoring churches and three labor unions. Each sponsor holds a seat on the WOA Board of Directors. The 1993 general operating budget totaled $218,480.

POLICY CONCERNS AND TACTICS

Program priorities are (1) supporting a "fair share for Africa" in U.S. government policy on aid and debt; (2) monitoring U.S. aid to South African organizations, to ensure that it benefits grass-roots development and progress toward a democratic nonracial order and does not encourage the government or its allies to persist in violence or in opposition to a truly democratic constitution; (3) supporting Bread for the World and other groups' efforts on the Horn of Africa Recovery and Food Security Act; (4) monitoring the impact of U.S. trade, aid, and debt policies and practices on Africa, concentrating in the first instance on the countries of Southern African Development Community (SADC); (5) opposing any covert or partisan U.S. government involvement in the internal affairs of African countries, lobbying for support for policies that promote democracy and sustainable development; and (6) monitoring other Africa issues, including trade, as they may appear on the congressional agenda. WOA has focused for most of its existence on South Africa and functioned as the "legislative arm" of the antiapartheid efforts in the United States. It has now broadened its attention on Africa and pressured the United States to end its aid to UNITA, the rebel group in Angola; hosted the Nelson Mandela reception after his release; and with the National Council of the Churches of Christ in the U.S.A. (NCC)* sponsored a major conference on Capitol Hill, "U.S. Foreign Policy: An African Agenda."

AFFILIATION

Independent Ecumenical.

PUBLICATIONS

Action Alerts (periodic) and *Washington Notes on Africa* (quarterly). WOA also has a three-minute telephone "hot line," which provides weekly taped messages on legislation and events in Africa.

COMMENTS

WOA is one of the few permanent groups organized by religious and nonreligious interests. Sponsors are the African Methodist Episcopal Church; Amalgamated Clothing and Textile Workers Union; the American Committee on Africa; Christian Church (Disciples of Christ);* Church of the Brethren;* Episcopal Church;* Evangelical Lutheran Church in America; Missionaries of Africa; Presbyterian Church USA;* Progressive National Baptist Convention, Home Mission Board; the Reformed Church in America; Sacred Heart Fathers; Society for African Missions (SMA Fathers); United Automobile, Aerospace and Agricultural Implement Workers of America (United Automobile Workers, UAW); United Church of Christ;* United Methodist Church; and United Steelworkers of America.

WASHINGTON OFFICE ON HAITI (WOH)

110 Maryland Avenue, NE
Suite 310
Washington, DC 20002
Phone: (202) 543-7095
Fax: (202) 547-9382
Executive Director: Claudette Werleigh

ORIGINS AND DEVELOPMENT

The Washington Office on Haiti was created in 1984. Lay and religious leaders in Haiti had requested the creation of ''a voice in Washington for Haiti's poor and oppressed, and to support their movements for justice, empowerment and self-determined development.'' It claims to be the only group addressing the underlying causes of oppression and poverty in Haiti.

MISSION STATEMENT

''The goals of the Washington Office on Haiti are to provide Congress, Government agencies, the media and the general public with expert analysis and accurate information about the true Haitian reality and about Haitian and U.S. policies as they affect this reality, and to network and collaborate with other groups concerned with Haiti's ongoing struggle for Justice and Democracy.''

ORGANIZATION AND FUNDING

WOH is supported primarily by religious organizations, individuals, and smaller foundations.

POLICY CONCERNS AND TACTICS

The goals of WOH are achieved through their Analysis and Information Clearinghouse and its special reports, the Haitian News and Resources Service (HNRS), the Haiti National Network (HNN), the Haiti Information and Media Campaign, the Campaign to Support Democracy and Human Rights, and Delegations to Haiti. They have worked closely with the human rights and democratization groups in Haiti. They work similarly with human rights groups in Canada and the United States. They have gained a reputation for reliable information and expert analysis. They attempt to inform the Congress, government agencies, the media, religious groups, and the American public about the effects of U.S. policies on Haiti. WOH is attempting to increase public and congressional awareness of the Haitian refugee problems, by coordinating and facilitating efforts of the various groups working directly with refugees. They held a major conference in January 1992, which emphasized coordination among private groups. The HNN since that conference has operated an action alert system and a weekly fax update for members.

AFFILIATION

Nondenominational.

PUBLICATIONS

The Haiti Beat (quarterly) and *Haiti News and Resource Service* (monthly).

WASHINGTON OFFICE ON LATIN AMERICA (WOLA)

110 Maryland Avenue, NE
Washington, DC 20002
Phone: (202) 544-8045
Fax: (202) 546-5288
Executive Director: Alexander Wilde

ORIGINS AND DEVELOPMENT

Begun in 1974 by a coalition of religious and civic leaders concerned over the lack of an independent research and advocacy group for Latin America, WOLA functions as an information center/clearinghouse in Washington, DC.

MISSION STATEMENT

''WOLA's task is to bring home to Washington the realities of Latin America. While our role has changed with the times, our purpose remains: to shape a foreign policy that advances human rights, democracy and peace in the hemisphere. To this end, WOLA monitors human rights practices, political developments and U.S. policies in Latin America and the Caribbean; provides U.S. policymakers and the public with information and analysis about the region; and fosters thoughtful interchange among people with diverse perspectives who share our goals.''

ORGANIZATION AND FUNDING

Organized by a coalition, WOLA has a budget of about $500,000, of which 63 percent is provided by foundations, 25 percent by religious communities, 6 percent by individual contributions, and the remainder from subscriptions, sale of publications, and so on. Not a membership group as such, WOLA is supported by grants from some seventeen foundations and trusts as well as grants from some thirty religious organizations, many of them Roman Catholic missionary orders.

POLICY CONCERNS AND TACTICS

WOLA continues its primary focus on human rights, political development, and economic policies in Latin America. Aside from providing highly regarded research on specific issues, its major tactics are to host conferences and seminars (up to 100 a year) that bring together scholars, legislators, and a wide variety of visitors from Latin America. In addition, its staff publishes a number of articles, press releases, and position papers on specific issues they deem to be politically significant.

AFFILIATION

Independent Ecumenical.

PUBLICATIONS

WOLA publishes a bimonthly newsletter, *Latin America Update,* and a series of reports and analyses of specific issues, such as *New Challenges, New Strategies: Human Rights and Elected Civilian Governments in Latin America* and *The Armed Forces and Democratic Accountability: Human Rights and Civil-Military Relations in Argentina, Brazil and Uruguay.*

WITNESS FOR PEACE (WFP)

2201 P Street, NW
Room 109
Washington, DC 20037
Phone: (202) 797-1160; Hot line: (202) 797-1531
Fax: (202) 797-1164
Executive Director: Leigh Carter (interim)

ORIGINS AND DEVELOPMENT

Begun in 1983, Witness for Peace grew from a small ad hoc group opposing U.S. policy in Central America to over 40,000 supporters in all fifty states and took on the broader goal of changing the emphasis of American foreign policy from military support to economic development. After the Gulf War and collapse of the Soviet Union, support slipped to between 30,000 and 35,000. However, to understand the breadth of this group's appeal, we include the names and affiliations of the 1992 Board of Advisors: Bishop John H. Adams (African Methodist Episcopal Church); Oscar Bolioli (National Council of the Churches of Christ in the U.S.A.*); Rabbi Balfour Brickner (Stephen Wise Free Synagogue); Robert McAfee Brown (theologian and author); Stephen G. Cary (American Friends Service Committee*); Joan Chittister, OSB (Benedictine sisters); Bishop Thomas J. Costello (Catholic Archdiocese of Syracuse); Shelly Douglass (Fellowship of Reconciliation*); Rabbi Everett Gendler (Temple Emanuel, Lowell, Massachusetts); Bishop Thomas Gumbleton (Catholic Archdiocese of Detroit); Vincent Harding (Iliff School of Theology); Jorge Lara Braud (Presbyterian Church USA*); Rabbi Eugene Lipman (Temple Sinai, Washington, DC); Joseph E. Lowery (Southern Christian Leadership Conference); Barbara Lundblad (Evangelical Lutheran Church); Alan McCoy, OFM (Franciscan Conference); Bishop Paul Moore, Jr. (Episcopal Diocese of New York); Avery A. Post (United Church of Christ*); Rosemary Radford Ruether (Garrett Evangelical Seminary); Bishop Roy Sano (Denver Area United Methodist Church); Richard Sider (Mennonite Central Committee*); Ronald J. Sider (Evangelicals for Social Action*); Glenn Stassen (Southern Baptist Seminary); Judy Vaughn, OSJ (National Assembly of Religious Women); Jim Walls (Sojourners); George W. Webber (Clergy and Laity Concerned*); Bishop C. Dale White (New York Area United Methodist Church); Loretta Williams (Unitarian Universalist Association*); and Patricia J. Rumer (Church Women United*).

MISSION STATEMENT

"The guiding principles of Witness for Peace as an organization are a prayerful, non-violent search for justice and peace, grounded in religious faith and the belief that we ourselves cannot be free as long as anyone remains oppressed. We believe that U.S. policy is not leading to a new international order, but to the continuation of an old and unjust order that must be changed. We recognize how often our government has intervened unjustly in the affairs of smaller nations. We call upon our government to renounce its policies of military intervention around the world and to commit itself to the peaceful resolution of such crises."

ORGANIZATION AND FUNDING

Witness for Peace is coordinated from the national office, but it does have regional coordinators and local contacts. Funding for 1993 totaled $750,000 and came from the mailing list/membership of 30,000–35,000, grants from foundations, and various religious groups, particularly those represented on the Board of Advisors.

POLICY CONCERNS AND TACTICS

As its major tactic during the war in Nicaragua, Witness for Peace sent volunteers to each "war zone" to witness and report who was doing what to whom. WFP delegations have also been established in Panama, Honduras, Guatemala, Mexico, and El Salvador. While there are a small number of full-time staff observers, most are ordinary American citizens who travel to these countries to spend two to three weeks as observers. During the war in Nicaragua they were often the only sources of information outside government and as such were widely quoted in major news stories. Since the decline of military operations in Central America, WFP has focused on efforts in the Middle East, condemning both the Iraqi invasion of Kuwait and the U.N./U.S. military response.

AFFILIATION

Independent Ecumenical.

PUBLICATIONS

Witness for Peace Newsletter (quarterly).

WOMAN'S CHRISTIAN TEMPERANCE UNION (WCTU)

1730 Chicago Avenue
Evanston, IL 60201
Phone: (708) 864-1396
Fax: None
President: Rachael B. Kelly

ORIGINS AND DEVELOPMENT

The WCTU was founded in 1874 to counter a major threat to the American home: alcoholic beverages. However, from the beginning it has had broader policy objectives, working to strengthen the rights and health of women and children. "The National WCTU believed then, as it does today, that the home/family is the bedrock upon which this nation was built." Supported mainly by mainline Protestant churches, the WCTU expanded rapidly into an international organization. A World WCTU was begun in 1883 and today has chapters in seventy-two countries. From its origins until the early 1900s the WCTU was the single major force behind the prohibition movement. However, despite its name, the group always saw alcohol use as one manifestation of a constellation of problems and prohibition as one part of a wider solution (which included more jobs, higher wages, better treatment of women, better schools for the poor, day-care centers, and so on). Some historians believe that as the WCTU grew in stature, this broader vision was seen as a threat by the economic elite. As a result its preeminence declined as support was thrown to the more aggressive Anti-Saloon League, which focused prohibition efforts on the single objective of getting an amendment to the Constitution. When the amendment was overturned, the Anti-Saloon League disappeared. The WCTU continued its activities but turned more to research to achieve its goals.

MISSION STATEMENT

The National Woman's Christian Temperance Union is a nonprofit, nonpartisan interdenominational organization of Christian women dedicated to the education of our nation's citizens, especially our youth, on the harmful effects of alcoholic beverages, other narcotic drugs, and tobacco on the human body and the society in which we live.

ORGANIZATION AND FUNDING

The WCTU has five national officers who direct a Bureau of Narcotics Education. Programs are divided into Christian Outreach, Education, Home Protection, Projection Methods, Public Relations, Social Service, Publications and Legislative/Citizenship. In addition there are two youth groups, Youth Temperance Council, for teenagers and college students, and Loyal Temperance Legion, for six- to twelve-year-olds.

The WCTU functions with an overall budget of $550,000, raised primarily from dues. However, the organization also receives many gifts, annuities, bequests, and grants for specific projects.

POLICY CONCERNS AND TACTICS

The WCTU maintains its early emphasis on alcohol but has expanded to include other narcotic drugs, including tobacco. While the organization still recognizes that threats to home and family are complex and multifaceted, including gambling, spouse abuse, AIDS, and pornography, its own contribution is in drug and alcohol education. The WCTU's major thrust today is on education of youth, and it creates and distributes hundreds of different leaflets, books, magazines, and videos to public, private, and parochial schools for their use. State and local chapters take responsibility for placement of the materials as broadly as possible.

AFFILIATION

Independent Ecumenical.

PUBLICATIONS

WCTU publishes a monthly magazine, *The Union Signal; The Legislative Update,* a monthly newsletter about current legislation; and *The Young Crusader,* a children's magazine. In addition to its publications the in-house publishing company, Signal Press, provides leaflets, books, films, videos, and so on on the effects of alcohol, drugs, and other threats to the home and family, such as gambling, spouse abuse, AIDS, pornography, steroids, and promiscuity.

COMMENTS

The WCTU is now primarily an educational, rather than a lobbying, group, but it is included in recognition of its remarkable achievements in the history of both religious group activism and the women's movement. For example, WCTU efforts led to laws in every state mandating health classes in the schools (which must include a unit on the effects of alcohol and drugs); the WCTU founded the first day-care centers, pushed state legislators to put women on police forces as matrons and officers, founded the Travelers' Aid Society, and helped found the Parent-Teacher Association (PTA). It founded Legal Aid Societies for Women and the poor who could not afford legal representation, founded the first public kindergartens, promoted equal pay for women doing equal work, lobbied successfully for child labor laws, and founded numerous foster homes and orphanages, as well as homes for "wayward girls" and homes for the elderly. These were in addition to its efforts to promote sobriety and pass the Eighteenth Amendment to the Constitution.

WOMEN'S DIVISION OF THE GENERAL BOARD OF GLOBAL MINISTRIES OF THE UNITED METHODIST CHURCH (WDUMC)

100 Maryland Avenue
Washington, DC 20002
Phone: (202) 488-5661
Fax: (202) 488-5681

475 Riverside Drive, Room 1504
New York, NY 10115
(212) 870-3752
(212) 870-3736

Deputy General Secretary (chief staff officer): Joyce D. Sohl

ORIGINS AND DEVELOPMENT

Methodists have a long history of social activism, rooted in the teachings of John Wesley and dating from opposition to slavery before the Civil War. Methodists were active in the Social Gospel and women's rights movements in the late nineteenth century. A social creed was adopted by the Methodist Episcopal Church in 1908, followed by statements from other Methodist groups. The Women's Division is one of three mission units of the General Board of Global Ministries, formerly the Board of Missions. It is the corporate successor to a host of women's missionary societies of the Methodist and Evangelical United Brethren Churches, the earliest dating to 1869. The primary focus (historically and presently) is ministries to women and to children and youth.

MISSION STATEMENT

"The Women's Division provides spiritual growth, mission education, social action and leadership development opportunities for members of the United Methodist Women in the U.S. and supports ministries with women, children and youth worldwide."

ORGANIZATION AND FUNDING

The organization of the United Methodist Women exists at four denominational levels. Staff is located in New York City and decentralized in eight other cities. The Women's Division is the national policy-making body for United Methodist Women, a 1.2 million membership organization in 25,000+ local churches. It develops programs for the organization and implements the actions of the General Conference. It is an official body of the church with an annual budget of $20 million provided by the giving of individual members.

POLICY CONCERNS AND TACTICS

The Women's Division's areas of concern, divided into portfolios, are (1) racial justice, development education, and global economics; (2) children, youth, and family services; (3) leadership development; (4) constituency education; (5) U.N.–International Affairs; (6) spiritual and theological concerns; (7) public policy; (8) mission education; and (9) women's concerns.

AFFILIATION

United Methodist Church.

PUBLICATIONS

Response (eleven per year).

WORLD PEACEMAKERS (WPEACE)

2925 Massachusetts Avenue, NW
Washington, DC 20036
Phone: (202) 265-7582
Fax: (301) 916-5335
Executive Director: William J. Price

ORIGINS AND DEVELOPMENT

In 1978 several members of the Church of the Saviour founded World Peacemakers. For several years it remained a project of a mission group known as the Eighth Day Faith Community. However, position papers written by the group quickly gained a national readership. When the National Freeze Movement began in 1981, World Peacemakers was a natural leader, "covenanting" with the Fellowship of Reconciliation,* Pax Christi,* Sojourners, and New Call to Peacemaking* to call the religious community to become the "New Abolitionists." This time, of course, the target was slavery to nuclear weapons. As the nuclear threat has declined, efforts are being shifted to influence U.S. policy toward the Middle East.

MISSION STATEMENT

"World Peacemakers is an organization operating on a non-profit, nonpartisan basis for the promotion of an in-depth understanding of what security means and how to achieve it in the closing years of the twentieth century. It pursues its purpose by focusing attention on the ethical, spiritual, economic, and political dimensions and their inter-relationship. It is particularly concerned with increasing public understanding of the unique opportunities and the unprecedented dangers facing mankind. It presents the urgent need and possibilities for the United States to take bold action to stop the arms race, and to move ahead with local and global solutions of problems—e.g. to protect and stabilize its own cities and rural communities, to redirect the global economy toward full employment and to develop new relationships with the world's desperately poor majority."

ORGANIZATION AND FUNDING

In 1990 World Peacemakers operated with a budget of $55,000, which included only one staff salary. Most of the work was done on a volunteer basis. Income was raised from contributions from the Church of the Saviour, other church communities, and individual contributions, plus the sale of materials.

POLICY CONCERNS AND TACTICS

World Peacemakers was the first American religious organization to call for a freeze on nuclear arms buildup and worked from its beginning to develop small grass-roots, reflection-action communities called "inward-outward journey mission groups" within various churches and congregations. As these develop, they undertake various efforts to influence their legislators, public officials, and public opinion to support peace efforts.

AFFILIATION

World Peacemakers began as a project of the nondenominational Christian Church of the Savior in Washington, DC. While independent, it retains close personal ties with the originating church.

PUBLICATIONS

World Peacemakers publishes a number of papers and small books, including *Handbook for World Peacemaker Groups; A Guide for Citizens of Faith: A Journey of Spirituality and Empowered Citizenship; Building Christian Community; Pursuing Peace with Justice; Searching for Real Security: Readings for Reflection; Action Groups in Congregations;* and *National Security and Christian Faith.* In addition they publish a newspaper, *World Peacemaker Quarterly.*

WORLD VISION (WV)

919 West Huntington Drive   220 I Street, N.E.
Monrovia, CA 91016   Washington, DC 20002
Phone: (818) 357-7979   (202) 547-3743
Fax: (818) 358-2896   (202) 547-4834
President: Robert A. Seiple, Andrew Natsios (Washington office)

ORIGINS AND DEVELOPMENT

World Vision was created by Reverend Bob Pierce in Portland, Oregon, in 1950. Reverend Pierce was an evangelist and film maker in Korea before the Korean War began. After the war broke out he returned to the United States to raise funds for orphaned and displaced children of Korea. In 1956 headquarters were moved to California so Reverend Pierce could begin a World Vision radio program. Since that time the organization has expanded into a worldwide service network.

MISSION STATEMENT

"World Vision is an international Christian relief and development agency dedicated to meeting basic human needs throughout the world. Founded . . . to provide care for children in war-torn Korea, World Vision's current focus includes the physical, social and spiritual needs of individuals in more than 80 countries. World Vision projects benefit over 14 million people in these countries through community development, emergency relief, childcare and family assistance, community leadership training and evangelism."

ORGANIZATION AND FUNDING

World Vision had a 1992 budget of $250,092,000. Of this amount $144,691,000 was raised from individuals, churches, and businesses; $86,585,000 was in-kind contributions from government agencies, pharmaceutical companies, and so on; and $16,306,000 came through grants from the U.S. Agency for International Development. Funds are utilized for ministry services (77 percent), for fund-raising (12 percent), and for administrative support (10 percent).

It has been a policy of World Vision to work through existing churches where possible, both in fund-raising and in ministry, in order to avoid competing with local evangelical efforts. World Vision has a national staff (i.e., those working on projects in paid positions) of 24,618. It also utilizes several thousand volunteers.

POLICY CONCERNS AND TACTICS

World Vision is primarily an ecumenical relief and economic development agency. It works for homeless people both in the United States and abroad, healthcare for children, employment initiatives, leadership training, and so forth. More recently World Vision has begun to cooperate with the Evangelicals for Social Action* and the National Religious Partnership for the Environment* to develop awareness of environmental issues in the religious community and to add a religious voice to advocacy efforts in this area.

A primary tactic has been to get individuals, families, and churches involved as sponsors, volunteers, and donors working on specific projects. The Washington office has two functions. The World Vision Relief Development unit works to win government grants, both monetary and in-kind, for worldwide relief. The Government Relations unit monitors government activities and functions as an advocate for the poor and needy around the world.

AFFILIATION

Independent Protestant.

PUBLICATIONS

World Vision (quarterly).

APPENDIXES: INTRODUCTION
———————— / ————————

In the literature on religious interest groups the authors have never seen a listing or breakdown of groups into categories such as the ones that follow—probably for good reason. Such groups are dynamic and only rarely fit neatly into exclusive pigeonholes. However, groups do fit predominantly or "more or less" into certain categories, and we hope it will be useful for readers to so divide them. It should be noted that categories are indicative rather than definitive, not mutually exclusive nor fully inclusive. For example, Protestants and Evangelical/Fundamentalists are certainly overlapping. Nor did we list pro-life and pro-choice groups under civil liberties, although many advocates would claim they should be so listed.

Most of the categories are self-explanatory, although the following may benefit from some explanation.

LITIGATING GROUPS

Normally people think interest groups work to influence Congress and the executive branch. In recent years a number of groups have discovered that working through the courts by filing lawsuits, submitting friend-of-the-court briefs, and providing legal advice and financial support for litigants is also a very effective means of influencing public policy.

TYPOLOGY OF GROUPS

The organizations we have studied have substantially different missions, lines of authority, structures, and funding sources. This typology attempts to highlight those differences. *Denominational groups* are official representatives of specific churches, are funded by these churches, and represent denominational policies. Such policies are usually arrived at by delegate voting in annual meetings or general conventions. The denominational leadership functions as the Board of Directors. Office directors and staff of the interest group are hired by the denomination officers and serve at their pleasure. *Membership groups* represent individuals who have been recruited to support the group and its policies. Financial support comes primarily from members' dues and grants won by the staff. Boards of Directors are chosen from among membership and quite often after a competitive election. Policy positions are chosen after consultation with members and need to change (or remain the same) to reflect membership interests and retain their support. Leaders, sometimes elected by a vote of the membership, are very dependent on meeting members' needs in order to maintain the strength of the organization. *Subscription groups* are similar to membership groups except that policy objectives are set by leaders, often called policy entrepreneurs, who then look for financial support from like-minded citizens. These groups have mailing lists rather than members. People who agree with the objectives of the entrepreneur provide financial support. Much of this will come from foundation and corporation grants, but increasingly as a result of mass mail solicitations. Supporters have no voice in setting policies, selecting leaders, or determining how the organization is run. Boards of Directors are self-selecting. *Coalitions* are groups of groups, often of those already situated in Washington, DC. An individual membership or subscription group is very likely to also be a member of a dozen or more coalitions, some temporary liaisons, some permanent. We have attempted to include only permanent coalitions, not those founded for a single legislative session. *Professional groups* are funded by, and represent, a specific profession or group of businesses, such as the American Association of Christian Schools* and the Christian College Coalition.* Such groups almost always limit their activities to promoting the interests of that profession. Boards of Directors are ordinarily executives of the member schools, hospitals, and so on, and there is no recruitment of members or search for funding sources beyond the profession.

BUDGET CATEGORIES

The budget categories are quite broad and uneven (under $100,000 is a much smaller classification than over $15 million). We utilized such categories for two reasons. For many groups, budgets are considered part of the public record and are available upon request. Others hold such information as confidential but are willing to give very general ranges. We thought these categories are sufficient to indicate the variant sizes of different religious interest groups.

It is important to remember that budgets are very misleading when comparing religious interest groups, since many groups may be subsidized, for example, by donated space and personnel paid for by a denominational headquarters. Other groups do not differentiate between resources used to support charitable works and resources used to monitor and influence public policy. Their budgets will then appear far bigger than would be warranted by their interest group activities. For example, Focus on the Family* has a budget approaching $80 million. While it does indeed engage in attempts to influence public policy, the great majority of its resources go to publication of magazines and producing a regular radio program. As a result, comparing budgets can be done only with great caution and numerous caveats.

We are not satisfied with our division of policy areas, but this seems to be the best we could come up with at this time. Perhaps other scholars can develop more accurate categories. We did want to illustrate that religious interest groups deal with an enormously wide variety of issues and that many different religious groups will be involved in the same areas, often in opposition to each other, but just as often working together.

Granted these explanations, we hope the following listings are of use to our readers.

APPENDIX A: GROUPS BY POLICY AREA

—————————— / ——————————

ABORTION (PRO-LIFE)

American Family Association
American Freedom Coalition
American Life League
Americans United for Life
Catholic League for Religious and Civil Rights
Christian Action Council
Christian Action Network
Christian Coalition
Christian Voice
Concerned Women for America
Eagle Forum
Ethics and Public Policy Center
Evangelicals for Social Action
Family Research Council
Focus on the Family
JustLife
Lutheran Church—Missouri Synod
March for Life
National Legal Foundation
National Right to Life Committee, Inc.
Operation Rescue

Religious Roundtable
Rutherford Institute
Traditional Values Coalition
United States Catholic Conference

ABORTION (PRO-CHOICE)

American Civil Liberties Union
American Jewish Congress
Americans for Religious Liberty
B'nai B'rith Women
Catholics for a Free Choice
Church Women United
General Board of Church and Society of the United Methodist Church
National Abortion Rights Action League
Presbyterian Church USA
Religious Coalition for Abortion Rights
Religious Network for Equality for Women
United Church of Christ Office of Church in Society
Women's Division of the General Board of Global Ministries of the United Methodist
    Church

CHURCH-STATE

American Atheists
American Center for Law and Justice
American Civil Liberties Union
American Coalition of Unregistered Churches
American Jewish Committee
American Jewish Congress
Americans for Religious Liberty
Americans United for Separation of Church and State
Baptist Joint Committee on Public Affairs
Catholic League for Religious and Civil Rights
Christian Legal Society
Church of Christ, Scientist Washington Office
Institute on Religion and Democracy
National Council of the Churches of Christ in the U.S.A.
National Legal Foundation

PEARL

People for the American Way

Rutherford Institute

CIVIL RIGHTS

American-Arab Anti-Discrimination Committee

American Atheists

American Center for Law and Justice

American Civil Liberties Union

American Jewish Committee

American Jewish Congress

Americans for Religious Liberty

Americans United for Separation of Church and State

Amnesty International

Anti-Defamation League of B'nai B'rith

Baptist Joint Committee on Public Affairs

B'nai B'rith Women

Catholic League for Religious and Civil Rights

Christian Advocates Serving Evangelism

Christian Church (Disciples of Christ)

Christian Law Association

Christian Legal Society

Christic Institute

Church of the Brethren—Washington Office

Church Women United

Episcopal Church—Washington Office

Ethics and Public Policy Center

Friends Committee on National Legislation

General Board of Church and Society of the United Methodist Church

Home School Legal Defense Association

Interfaith Impact for Justice and Peace

National Coalition to Abolish the Death Penalty

National Council of the Churches of Christ in the U.S.A.

National Legal Foundation

People for the American Way

Presbyterian Church USA—Washington Office

Religious Action Center of Reform Judaism

Religious Network for Equality for Women

Rutherford Institute

Unitarian Universalist Association for Social Justice—Washington Office

United Church of Christ Office of Church in Society

United States Catholic Conference

Women's Division of the General Board of Global Ministries of the United Methodist Church

EDUCATION

American Association of Christian Schools

American Civil Liberties Union

American Ethical Union

American Family Association

American Freedom Coalition

American Jewish Congress

Americans for Religious Liberty

Americans United for Separation of Church and State

Association of Jesuit Colleges and Universities

Baptist Joint Committee on Public Affairs

Christian Action Network

Christian Coalition

Christian Law Association

Eagle Forum

Ethics and Public Policy Center

Family Research Council

Focus on the Family

Hadassah

Home School Legal Defense Association

Lutheran Church—Missouri Synod Office of Government Information

National Catholic Educational Association

PEARL

People for the American Way

Presbyterian Church USA—Washington Office

Religious Roundtable

Traditional Values Coalition

Unitarian Universalist Association—Washington Office for Social Justice

United States Catholic Conference

Woman's Christian Temperance Union

Women's Division of the General Board of Global Ministries of the United Methodist Church

FOOD, UNEMPLOYMENT, IMMIGRATION, DISASTER RELIEF

American Baptist Church USA—Washington Office

American Friends Service Committee

Association for Public Justice

Bread for the World

Catholic Charities USA

Center for New Creation

Center of Concern

Christian Church (Disciples of Christ)

Christian Life Commission—Southern Baptist

Church World Services

Episcopal Church—Washington Office

Evangelicals for Social Action

Friends Committee on National Legislation

General Board of Church and Society of the United Methodist Church

Interfaith Center on Corporate Responsibility

Interfaith Impact for Justice and Peace

Jesuit Social Ministries

Mennonite Central Committee—Washington Office

National Council of the Churches of Christ in the U.S.A.

Network

Presbyterian Church USA—Washington Office

Religious Taskforce on Central America

Unitarian Universalist Service Committee

United Church of Christ Office of Church in Society

United States Catholic Conference

Washington Interreligious Staff Council

Washington Office on Africa

Washington Office on Haiti

Washington Office on Latin America

Women's Division of the General Board of Global Ministries of the United Methodist Church

World Vision

FOREIGN POLICY

African Faith and Justice Network
American Friends Service Committee
American Israel Public Affairs Committee
American Jewish Committee
American Jewish Congress
Americans for Peace Now
Amnesty International
Church of the Brethren—Washington Office
Church Women United
Church World Services
Clergy and Laity Concerned
Committee in Solidarity with the People of El Salvador
Eagle Forum
Ecumenical Program on Central America and the Caribbean
Ethics and Public Policy Center
Fellowship of Reconciliation
Friends Committee on National Legislation
General Board of Church and Society of the United Methodist Church
Hadassah
Institute on Religion and Democracy
Interfaith Center on Corporate Responsibility
Interfaith Impact for Justice and Peace
Jewish War Veterans of the United States of America
National Council of the Churches of Christ in the U.S.A.
Network
New Jewish Agenda
Pax Christi USA
Presbyterian Church USA—Washington Office
Presbyterians for Democracy and Religious Freedom
Religious Network for Equality for Women
Religious Roundtable
Religious Taskforce on Central America
Unitarian Universalist Association—Washington Office for Social Justice
Unitarian Universalist Service Committee
United States Catholic Conference
Washington Office on Africa

Washington Office on Haiti

Washington Office on Latin America

Witness for Peace

Women's Division of the General Board of Global Ministries of the United Methodist Church

World Peacemakers

PORNOGRAPHY

American Civil Liberties Union

American Family Association

Christian Action Network

Christian Coalition

Focus on the Family

Latter-day Saints Public Affairs Department

Morality in Media

National Coalition Against Pornography

Religious Alliance Against Pornography

Religious Roundtable

WORLD PEACE AND ARMS REDUCTION

American Ethical Union

American Friends Service Committee

Christian Life Commission—Southern Baptist

Church of the Brethren—Washington Office

Church World Services

Clergy and Laity Concerned

Ethics and Public Policy Center

Evangelicals for Social Action

Fellowship of Reconciliation

Friends Committee on National Legislation

General Board of Church and Society of United Methodist Church

Jesuit Social Ministries

Mennonite Central Committee—Washington Office

National Council of the Churches of Christ in the U.S.A.

New Call to Peacemaking

Pax Christi USA

Unitarian Universalist Service Committee

Witness for Peace
World Peacemakers

MISCELLANEOUS

AIDS National Interfaith Network (ANIN)
Christian Action Network (anti–gay rights)
Christian Voice (anti–gay rights)
Coalition to Stop Gun Violence
Family Research Council (anti–gay rights)
Human Rights Campaign Fund (pro–gay rights)
Institute on Religion and Democracy
Interreligious Health Care Access Campaign
National Coalition to Abolish the Death Penalty
National Interreligious Service Board for Conscientious Objection
National Interreligious Taskforce on Criminal Justice (prisoners' rights)
National Religious Partnership for the Environment
Operation Rescue (anti-euthanasia, anti–gay rights)
Pax Christi USA (anti–death penalty)
Traditional Values Coalition (anti–gay rights)
United Church of Christ Office of Church in Society (pro–gay rights)
Washington Interreligious Staff Council (strategy)
Washington Office on Africa (human rights)
Woman's Christian Temperance Union (drugs and alcohol)

APPENDIX B: GROUPS BY RELIGIOUS AFFILIATION

———————— / ————————

CATHOLIC

African Faith and Justice Network
Association of Jesuit Colleges and Universities
Catholic Charities USA
Catholic League for Religious and Civil Rights
Catholics for a Free Choice
Jesuit Social Ministries
National Catholic Educational Association
Network
Pax Christi USA
United States Catholic Conference

MAINLINE PROTESTANT

American Baptist Church USA—Washington Office
American Friends Service Committee
Americans for Religious Liberty
Baptist Joint Committee on Public Affairs
Christian Church (Disciples of Christ)
Christian Legal Society
Christian Life Commission—Southern Baptist
Church of Christ, Scientist—Washington Office

Church of the Brethren—Washington Office

Church World Services

Episcopal Church—Washington Office

Friends Committee on National Legislation

General Board of Church and Society of the United Methodist Church

Lutheran Church—Missouri Synod Office of Government Information

Lutheran Office on Governmental Affairs

Mennonite Central Committee—Washington Office

New Call to Peacemaking

Presbyterian Church USA—Washington Office

Presbyterians for Democracy and Religious Freedom

Unitarian Universalist Service Committee

Unitarian Universalist Association—Washington Office for Social Justice

United Church of Christ—Office of Church in Society

Woman's Christian Temperance Union

Women's Division of the General Board of Global Ministries of the United Methodist
    Church

ECUMENICAL

AIDS National Interfaith Network

Americans United for Life

Americans United for Separation of Church and State

Bread for the World

Center for New Creation

Churches for Middle East Peace

Church Women United

Clergy and Laity Concerned

Coalition to Stop Gun Violence

Committee in Solidarity with the People of El Salvador

Ecumenical Program on Central America and the Caribbean

Fellowship of Reconciliation

Institute on Religion and Democracy

Interfaith Center on Corporate Responsibility

Interfaith Impact for Justice and Peace

Interreligious Health Care Access Campaign

Morality in Media

National Coalition Against Pornography

National Coalition to Abolish the Death Penalty

National Council of the Churches of Christ in the U.S.A.

National Interreligious Service Board for Conscientious Objection

National Interreligious Taskforce on Criminal Justice

National Religious Partnership for the Environment

National Right to Life Committee, Inc.

New Call to Peacemaking

PEARL

Religious Alliance Against Pornography

Religious Coalition for Abortion Rights

Religious Network for Equality for Women

Religious Taskforce on Central America

Washington Interreligious Staff Council

Washington Office on Africa

Washington Office on Haiti

Washington Office on Latin America

Witness for Peace

World Peacemakers

World Vision

EVANGELICAL AND FUNDAMENTALIST CHRISTIAN

American Association of Christian Schools

American Coalition of Unregistered Churches

American Family Association

American Freedom Coalition

American Life League

Association for Public Justice

Christian Action Council

Christian Action Network

Christian Advocates Serving Evangelism

Christian Coalition

Christian Law Association

Christian Voice

Concerned Women for America

Eagle Forum

Ethics and Public Policy Center
Evangelicals for Social Action
Family Research Council
Focus on the Family
Home School Legal Defense Association
JustLife
March for Life
National Legal Foundation
Operation Rescue
Religious Roundtable
Rutherford Institute
Traditional Values Coalition
World Vision

JEWISH

American Israel Public Affairs Committee
American Jewish Committee
American Jewish Congress
Americans for Peace Now
Anti-Defamation League of B'nai B'rith
B'nai B'rith Women
Hadassah
Jewish War Veterans of the United States of America
New Jewish Agenda

MUSLIM

American-Arab Anti-Discrimination Committee

OTHER OR UNSPECIFIED FAITH COMMITMENT

American Atheists
American Civil Liberties Union
American Ethical Union
Amnesty International
Christic Institute
Human Rights Campaign Fund

Latter-day Saints Public Affairs Department
National Abortion Rights Action League
People for the American Way

.

APPENDIX C: GROUPS BY POLITICAL IDENTIFICATION

————————— / —————————

CONSERVATIVE

American Association of Christian Schools

American Coalition of Unregistered Churches

American Family Association

American Freedom Coalition

American Life League

Association for Public Justice

Catholic League for Religious and Civil Rights

Christian Action Council

Christian Action Network

Christian Advocates Serving Evangelism

Christian Coalition

Christian Law Association

Christian Voice

Concerned Women for America

Eagle Forum

Ethics and Public Policy Center

Family Research Council

Focus on the Family

Home School Legal Defense Association

Institute on Religion and Democracy

JustLife

Latter-day Saints Public Affairs Department

Lutheran Church—Missouri Synod Office of Government Information

March for Life

National Legal Foundation

National Right to Life Committee, Inc.

Operation Rescue

Presbyterians for Democracy and Religious Freedom

Religious Roundtable

Rutherford Institute

Traditional Values Coalition

Woman's Christian Temperance Union

LIBERAL

African Faith and Justice Network

AIDS National Interfaith Network

American Baptist Church USA—Washington Office

American Civil Liberties Union

American Ethical Union

American Friends Service Committee

American Jewish Committee

American Jewish Congress

Americans for Peace Now

Americans for Religious Liberty

Amnesty International

Anti-Defamation League of B'nai B'rith

Bread for the World

Catholics for a Free Choice

Center for New Creation

Center of Concern

Christian Church (Disciples of Christ)

Christic Institute

Church of the Brethren—Washington Office

Church Women United

Church World Services

Clergy and Laity Concerned

Coalition to Stop Gun Violence

Committee in Solidarity with the People of El Salvador

Ecumenical Program on Central America and the Caribbean

Episcopal Church—Washington Office

Evangelicals for Social Action

Fellowship of Reconciliation

Friends Committee on National Legislation

General Board of Church and Society of the United Methodist Church

Hadassah

Human Rights Campaign Fund

Interfaith Center on Corporate Responsibility

Interfaith Impact for Justice and Peace

Interreligious Health Care Access Campaign

Jesuit Social Ministries

Mennonite Central Committee—Washington Office

National Abortion Rights Action League

National Coalition to Abolish the Death Penalty

National Council of the Churches of Christ in the U.S.A.

National Interreligious Taskforce on Criminal Justice

National Religious Partnership for the Environment

New Call to Peacemaking

Network

Pax Christi USA

People for the American Way

Presbyterian Church USA—Washington Office

Religious Coalition for Abortion Rights

Religious Network for Equality for Women

Religious Taskforce on Central America

Unitarian Universalist Service Committee

Unitarian Universalist Association—Washington Office for Social Justice

United Church of Christ Office of Church in Society

Washington Office on Africa

Washington Office on Haiti

Washington Office on Latin America

Witness for Peace

Women's Division of the General Board of Global Ministries of the United Methodist
Church

World Peacemakers

APPENDIX D: SINGLE-ISSUE GROUPS

———————— / ————————

AIDS National Interfaith Network

American Association of Christian Schools

American Family Association

American Israel Public Affairs Committee

American Life League

Americans for Peace Now

Americans for Religious Liberty

Americans United for Life

Americans United for Separation of Church and State

Amnesty International

Anti-Defamation League of B'nai B'rith

Association of Jesuit Colleges and Universities

Baptist Joint Committee on Public Affairs

Bread for the World

Catholic Charities USA

Catholic League for Religious and Civil Rights

Catholics for a Free Choice

Christian Action Council

Christian Action Network

Christian Advocates Serving Evangelism

Christian Law Association

Church of Christ, Scientist—Washington Office

Coalition to Stop Gun Violence

Committee in Solidarity with the People of El Salvador

Ecumenical Program on Central America and the Caribbean

Fellowship of Reconciliation

Home School Legal Defense Association

Human Rights Campaign Fund

Interfaith Center on Corporate Responsibility

Interreligious Health Care Access Campaign

JustLife

March for Life

Morality in Media

National Abortion Rights Action League

National Catholic Educational Association

National Coalition Against Pornography

National Coalition to Abolish the Death Penalty

National Interreligious Service Board for Conscientious Objection

National Legal Foundation

National Right to Life Committee, Inc.

New Call to Peacemaking

New Jewish Agenda

Operation Rescue

PEARL

Religion Coalition for Abortion Rights

Religious Alliance Against Pornography

Religious Taskforce on Central America

Washington Office on Africa

Washington Office on Haiti

Washington Office on Latin America

Witness for Peace

Woman's Christian Temperance Union

World Peacemakers

APPENDIX E: GROUPS BY TYPE OF MEMBERSHIP

—————————— / ——————————

COALITION

African Faith and Justice Network
AIDS National Interfaith Network
Churches for Middle East Peace
Church World Services
Coalition to Stop Gun Violence
Interfaith Center on Corporate Responsibility
Interreligious Health Care Access Campaign
National Coalition Against Pornography
National Coalition to Abolish the Death Penalty
National Council of the Churches of Christ in the U.S.A.
National Interreligious Service Board for Conscientious Objection
National Interreligious Taskforce on Criminal Justice
National Religious Partnership for the Environment
PEARL
Religious Action Center of Reform Judaism
Religious Coalition for Abortion Rights
Religious Network for Equality for Women
Traditional Values Coalition
Washington Office on Africa
Washington Office on Haiti
Washington Office on Latin America
Washington Interreligious Staff Council

DENOMINATIONAL

American Baptist Church USA—Washington Office

American Ethical Union

American Friends Service Committee

Baptist Joint Committee on Public Affairs

Catholic Charities USA

Christian Church (Disciples of Christ)

Christian Life Commission—Southern Baptist Convention

Church of Christ Scientist—Washington Office

Episcopal Church—Washington Office

Friends Committee on National Legislation

General Board of Church and Society of the United Methodist Church

Lutheran Church—Missouri Synod Office of Government Information

Lutheran Office on Government Affairs

Mennonite Central Committee—Washington Office

Presbyterian Church USA—Washington Office

Unitarian Universalist Association—Washington Office for Social Justice

Unitarian Universalist Service Committee

United Church of Christ—Office of Church in Society

United States Catholic Conference

Women's Division of the General Board of Global Ministries of the United Methodist
   Church

INDIVIDUAL MEMBERS

American-Arab Anti-Discrimination Committee

American Atheists

American Civil Liberties Union

American Freedom Coalition

American Jewish Committee

American Jewish Congress

American Life League

Americans for Religious Liberty

Americans United for Separation of Church and State

Amnesty International

Anti-Defamation League of B'nai B'rith

B'nai B'rith Women

Bread for the World

Catholic League for Religious and Civil Rights

Catholics for a Free Choice

Center for New Creation

Christian Action Council

Christian Action Network

Christian Coalition

Christian Legal Society

Church Women United

Clergy and Laity Concerned

Concerned Women for America

Eagle Forum

Evangelicals for Social Action

Fellowship of Reconciliation

Hadassah

Home School Legal Defense Association

Human Rights Campaign Fund

Jewish War Veterans of the United States of America

Morality in Media

National Abortion Rights Action League

National Right to Life Committee, Inc.

Network

New Jewish Agenda

Operation Rescue

Pax Christi USA

People for the American Way

Presbyterians for Democracy and Religious Freedom

Traditional Values Coalition

Woman's Christian Temperance Union

Women's Division of the General Board of Global Ministries of the United Methodist Church

SUBSCRIPTION

American Family Association

American Israel Public Affairs Committee

Americans United for Life

Association for Public Justice

Center of Concern

Christian Advocates Serving Evangelism

Christian Law Association

Christian Voice

Christic Institute

Committee in Solidarity with the People of El Salvador

Ecumenical Program on Central America and the Caribbean

Ethics and Public Policy Center

Family Research Council

Focus on the Family

Institute on Religion and Democracy

JustLife

March for Life

Morality in Media

National Coalition Against Pornography

National Legal Foundation

New Call to Peacemaking

Religious Alliance Against Pornography

Religious Taskforce on Central America

Religious Roundtable

Rutherford Institute

Witness for Peace

World Peacemakers

World Vision

PROFESSIONAL

American Association of Christian Schools

Association of Jesuit Colleges and Universities

Christian College Coalition

National Catholic Educational Association

Washington Interreligious Staff Council

APPENDIX F: LITIGATING GROUPS

————————— / —————————

American Atheists
American Civil Liberties Union
American Jewish Committee
American Jewish Congress
Americans for Religious Liberty
Americans United for Life
Americans United for Separation of Church and State
Anti-Defamation League of B'nai B'rith
Baptist Joint Committee on Public Affairs
Catholic League for Religious and Civil Rights
Christian Advocates Serving Evangelism
Christian Law Association
Christian Legal Society
Christic Institute
Home School Legal Defense Association
National Coalition to Oppose the Death Penalty
National Legal Foundation
PEARL
Rutherford Institute

APPENDIX G: GROUPS BY SIZE OF BUDGET

——————— / ———————

UNDER $100,000

African Faith and Justice Network
American Coalition of Unregistered Churches
American Ethical Union
Center for New Creation
Churches for Middle East Peace
Ecumenical Program on Central America and the Caribbean
Episcopal Church—Washington Office
Fellowship of Reconciliation
Interreligious Health Care Access Campaign
JustLife
National Interreligious Taskforce on Criminal Justice
New Call to Peacemaking
PEARL
Presbyterians for Democracy and Religious Freedom
Religious Network for Equality for Women
Unitarian Universalist Association—Washington Office for Social Justice
Washington Interreligious Staff Council
World Peacemakers

$100,000 TO $500,000

AIDS National Interfaith Network
American Association of Christian Schools

American Baptist Church USA—Washington Office

Americans for Religious Liberty

Association for Public Justice

Association of Jesuit Colleges and Universities

Catholics for a Free Choice

Center of Concern

Christian Action Network

Christian Voice

Clergy and Laity Concerned

Committee in Solidarity with the People of El Salvador

Evangelicals for Social Action

Jesuit Social Ministries

Lutheran Church—Missouri Synod Office of Government Affairs

Mennonite Central Committee—Washington Office

National Coalition to Abolish the Death Penalty

National Interreligious Service Board for Conscientious Objection

National Legal Foundation

Network

Operation Rescue

Presbyterian Church USA—Washington Office

Washington Office on Africa

Washington Office on Haiti

Washington Office on Latin America

$500,000 TO $1 MILLION

American Atheists

Americans for Peace Now

Baptist Joint Committee on Public Affairs

Catholic League for Religious and Civil Rights

Christian Action Network

Christian Life Commission of the Southern Baptist Convention

Christic Institute

Coalition to Stop Gun Violence

Eagle Forum

Institute on Religion and Democracy

Interfaith Center on Corporate Responsibility

Interfaith Impact for Justice and Peace

Jewish War Veterans

Morality in Media

Pax Christi USA

Presbyterian Church USA—Washington Office

Religious Roundtable

Witness for Peace

$1 MILLION TO $5 MILLION

American Freedom Coalition

American Life League

Americans for Peace Now

Americans United for Life

Americans United for Separation of Church and State

Bread for the World

Catholic Charities USA

Christian Action Council

Christian Advocates Serving Evangelism

Christian Legal Society

Church Women United

Ethics and Public Policy Center

Friends Committee on National Legislation

General Board of Church and Society of the United Methodist Church

Home School Legal Defense Association

National Catholic Educational Association

National Coalition Against Pornography

Rutherford Institute

Traditional Values Coalition

Unitarian Universalist Service Committee

$5 MILLION TO $15 MILLION

American Center for Law and Justice

American Civil Liberties Union

American Family Association

American Israel Public Affairs Committee

American Jewish Congress

American Life League

B'nai B'rith Women

Christian Coalition

Concerned Women for America

Family Research Council

Hadassah

Human Rights Campaign Fund

National Abortion Rights Action League

National Right to Life Committee, Inc.

OVER $15 MILLION

American Civil Liberties Union

American Friends Service Committee

American Jewish Committee

Amnesty International

Anti-Defamation League of B'nai B'rith

Church World Services

Focus on the Family

National Council of the Churches of Christ in the U.S.A.

United States Catholic Conference

Women's Division of the General Board of Global Ministries of the United Methodist Church

World Vision

UNKNOWN

American-Arab Anti-Discrimination Committee

Christian Action Council

Christian Church (Disciples of Christ)

Christian Law Association

Church of the Brethren—Washington Office

Episcopal Church—Washington Office

Latter-day Saints Public Affairs Department

People for the American Way

Woman's Christian Temperance Union

BIBLIOGRAPHIC ESSAY
———————— / ————————

Once the domain of religious historians, civil libertarians, and eccentric political scientists, the study of relations between religion and government has expanded rapidly in the 1980s and 1990s, accompanied by a veritable explosion of books and articles. The reasons for the renewed interest are varied and complex. One major impetus was conservative reaction to the enormous changes in American culture in the 1960s and 1970s, particularly the political activism of liberal churches and other religious groups in the causes of civil rights and ending the Vietnam War. Reinvigoration of Evangelical and fundamentalist traditions within American Christianity and of Islamic and Jewish fundamentalism in the Middle East led to the collapse of smug secularization theories of earlier writers who assumed that religion would just "go away" with expanding education, economic opportunity, and technological innovation. This collapse left an intellectual vacuum, which scholars are still striving to fill. The study of religion and politics is now very much a mainstream academic pursuit. While it is safe to say that the major focus of such studies is now comparative in nature, this essay looks only at sources dealing with the American experience.

GENERAL

For an overview of the field, A. James Reichley's *Religion in American Public Life* (Washington, DC: Brookings Institution, 1985) remains a valuable resource combining a psychological-historical perspective. Kenneth D. Walds's *Religion and Politics in the United States* (New York: St. Martin's Press, 1987) provides a brief, more quantitative political study quite suitable for classroom use. Robert Wurthnow's *The Restructuring of American Religion* (Princeton, NJ: Princeton University Press, 1988) focuses on new political and religious alignments from a sociological perspective, and Robert Booth Fowler's *Religion and Politics in*

America (Metuchen, NJ: Scarecrow Press, 1985) approaches the topic from a political-philosophy point of view. Probably no body has more influenced or encouraged the rise of conservative Christian political activism than Richard John Neuhaus's *The Naked Public Square* (Grand Rapids, MI: Eerdmans, 1984), a persuasively argued justification for the inclusion of Christian beliefs, symbols, and values in the formation of public policy.

HISTORICAL

There are numerous books on the history of religion in America, but most do not deal extensively with the political activities of religious organizations or even look at religious organizations not directly related to mainline denominations. There are some valuable exceptions. Most useful for our chapter on the history of religious interest group activism is the late Sydney E. Ahlstrom's *A Religious History of the American People, Vols. 1, 2* (Garden City, NY: Doubleday-Image Books, 1975), a highly readable, marvelously detailed description of religious activism through the years. Martin E. Marty's *Pilgrims in Their Own Land: 500 Years of Religion in America* (New York: Penguin Books, 1985) provides a wide sweeping overview that gives a context to more specific period pieces such as his *American Religion, Vol. 1: The Irony of It All 1893–1919* (Chicago: University of Chicago Press, 1986). Equally useful for that critical period of time is Seymour Martin Lipset, ed., *Emerging Coalitions in American Politics* (San Francisco: Institute for Contemporary Studies, 1978). Mark Noll, ed., *Religion and American Politics: From the Colonial Period to the 1980s* (New York: Oxford University Press, 1990) takes a different but insightful approach in a series of essays on religion and ethnicity.

INTEREST GROUP THEORY

While this volume contains no discussion of general interest group theory, interested readers may wish to consult Philip A. Mundo's *Interest Groups: Cases and Characteristics* (Chicago: Nelson-Hall, 1992) for an overview of the field, although Mundo does not discuss religious interest groups at all. A second informative general book is Jeffrey Berry, *The Interest Group Society* (Boston: Little, Brown, 1984). It treats public or nonprofit groups as a distinct category but has little on religious groups as such. A more sophisticated analysis that does include a theoretical discussion of religious interest groups is the late Jack L. Walker, Jr.'s *Mobilizing Interest Groups in America: Patrons, Professions, and Social Movements* (Ann Arbor: University of Michigan Press, 1991).

RELIGIOUS INTEREST GROUPS

The literature on religious interest groups is quite sparse. This is most likely because such groups, while experiencing explosive growth in the past thirty years, are still a very small part of the overall lobbying industry and rarely a threat to the business, financial, and labor interests that dominate the field. Scholars have tended to concentrate on the larger, more visible, and better-financed groups. Adding to the problem is the fact that data on religious groups are extraordinarily difficult to come by, a deficiency we hope to alleviate somewhat with this book. Coming from different religious and ideological traditions, with different agenda and funding sources, being formed and disbanded with remarkable speed and only now developing permanent coalitions, religious groups have never developed a directory or who's who that has gone beyond the thirty or so major denominational groups. Nevertheless, there are some sources. The first book on the topic is Luke Eugene Ebersole, *Church Lobbying in the Nation's Capitol* (New York: Macmillan, 1951). This is not a sympathetic look; Ebersole sees church lobbying as an evil, not to mention an unconstitutional, use of church energy and resources. Somewhat more positive in tone, but still ambivalent, is James L. Adams, *The Growing Church Lobby in Washington* (Grand Rapids, MI: Eerdmans, 1970). Adams sees dangers in the lobbying effort, but he utilizes several case studies, notably civil rights and anti-Vietnam War legislative battles, to illustrate the expanding clout of religious groups in pursuit of moral policy objectives.

The most extensive and theoretically sophisticated coverage to date is Allen D. Hertzke's *Representing God in Washington: The Role of Religious Lobbies in the American Polity* (Knoxville, TN: University of Tennessee Press, 1988). Hertzke takes for granted that religious interest groups are a permanent and significant part of the American policy-making process. He locates them within the larger context of interest group theory, dealing with standard interest group questions such as insider versus outsider strategies, recruitment, mobilization, maintenance, representativeness, and the role of entrepreneurs. One weakness of this and other writings on religious interest groups is that they deal with less than a third of the working groups, representing primarily mainstream denominations.

Aside from these books, the most fruitful source of information continues to be the series of research papers presented at the American Political Science Association (APSA) annual meetings by scholars such as James Guth, John Green, Mary Hanna, Greg Ivers, Lyman Kellstedt, Hugh Morken, Corwin Smidt, Charles Strickwerda, and Robert Zweir. Unfortunately the only way to gain access to such papers is to review APSA Programs for individual years and request copies of the papers from individual authors.

SPECIFIC GROUP INFORMATION

There simply is no one source for information about specific groups. The very best place to begin is the *Encyclopedia of Associations* (Detroit: Gale Research, 1993). This encyclopedia is also available on CD-ROM and very useful for basic information if one knows the name of the organization. The drawbacks are that a number of groups are not listed separately because they are too new or are units of larger organizations, and if one is "prospecting," there are over

84,000 entries to peruse. Nonetheless, this is by far the most exhaustive source of basic information. *Public Interest Profiles 1992–93* (Washington, DC: Foundation for Public Affairs, 1993) is also useful for certain groups and has separate listings for religious and public policy organizations. It provides somewhat more information than the *Encyclopedia of Associations* but has far fewer entries.

Most of the specific information about individual groups came from hundreds of brochures, pamphlets, newsletters, position papers, action alerts, and recruiting letters published by the individual groups. Other information came from newspaper and magazine articles mentioning the various groups, often in the context of one or another policy battle. The authors followed up with office visits, phone conversations, and letters to verify facts and check references. It is our hope that the information provided in this encyclopedia will make it easier for future scholars to uncover the kinds of information needed to more fully understand the range and depth of religious interest group activities.

INDEX

/

About the Authors

PAUL J. WEBER, University Distinguished Teaching Professor and Chair of the Political Science Department at the University of Louisville, is Director of the McConnell Center for Political Leadership. An authority on religion and government, his previous books published by Greenwood are *Private Churches and Public Money* (1988), *Unfound Fears* (1989), and *Equal Separation: Understanding the First Amendment* (1990).

W. LANDIS JONES is Professor of Political Science at the University of Louisville.